Edexcel GCSE
Chinese

Written by
Hua Yan, Linying Liu, Michelle Tate,
Lisa Wang, Yu Bin and Xiaoming Zhu

Reviewed by
Peking University, School of
Chinese as a Second Language

Series editor: Katharine Carruthers
Specialist Schools and Academies Trust

A PEARSON COMPANY

Published by Pearson Education Limited, a company incorporated in England and Wales, having its registered office at Edinburgh Gate, Harlow, Essex, CM20 2JE. Registered company number: 872828

www.pearsonschoolsandfecolleges.co.uk

Edexcel is a registered trade mark of Edexcel Limited

Text © Pearson Education Limited 2009

First published 2009

15

10 9

British Library Cataloguing in Publication Data
A catalogue record for this book is available from the British Library

ISBN 978 1 846905 17 9

Produced for Pearson Education by g-and-w PUBLISHING, Chinnor, Oxfordshire, UK
Edited by Gene Teo-Cooke and Lauren Bourque
Designed by Siu Hang Wong, Doug Hewitt and Krystyna Hewitt
Typeset by Doug Hewitt and Krystyna Hewitt
Original illustrations © Shirley Chiang, Kel Dyson, Clive Goodyer, Doug Hewitt, Shiny Leung 2009
Illustrated by Shirley Chiang, Kel Dyson, Clive Goodyer, Doug Hewitt, Shiny Leung
Picture research by Ingrid Booz Morejon
Cover photo © feilzy/shutterstock
Printed in Malaysia (CTP-PJB)

Acknowledgements
We would like to thank Naomi Li, Ma Yan and Anne Martin for their support in the development of this course.

We would also like to thank the following SSAT Confucius Classrooms which are supported by the Chinese Language Council International, Hanban: Hummersknott School and Language College, Kingsford Community School, Katharine Lady Berkeley's School, Calday Grange Grammar School and Djanogly City Academy.

The author and publisher would like to thank the following individuals and organisations for permission to reproduce photographs:
p. 7 Getty Images/Robert Harding World Imagery/Jochen Schlenker. **p. 9** WAMVD/Shutterstock. **p. 18** Getty Images/Robert Harding World Imagery/Jochen Schlenker. **p. 19 & 115** Travellinglight/ Linda & Colin McKie/iStockphoto. **p. 22** Ingrid Booz Morejohn. **p. 27** Peter Ford/Christian Science Monitor/Getty Images. **p. 31** Gogo Images Corporation/Alamy. **p. 32** Redchopsticks.com LLC / Alamy. **p. 33 L** Pearson Education/Alexandra Caminada. **p. 33 R** Peer Point/ Alamy. **p. 36** GoGo Images Corporation/Alamy. **p. 39** Keystone/ Hulton Archive/Getty Images. **p. 40** Peer Point/Alamy. **p. 47 T** Photo Alto/ Photolibrary.com. **p. 47 B** Zhu difeng/istockphoto. **p. 49** Janet Wishnetsky/CORBIS. **p. 50 & 69** Chris Schmidt/istockphoto. **p. 52** 4x6/istockphoto. **p. 56** Aflo Foto Agency / Alamy. **p. 57 L** Zhang bo/ Istockphoto. **p. 57 R** Joshua Blake/istockphoto. **p. 58** huaxiadragon/ iStockphoto. **p. 60** © Michael Cole/CORBIS. **p. 65** Ingrid Booz Morejohn. **p. 66 T** Fotohunter/shutterstock. **p. 66 B** Shangara Singh/Alamy. **p. 67** Alex Segre / Alamy. **p. 68 L** Matthew Jacques/

Shutterstock. **p. 68 R** Cancan Chu/Getty Images. **p. 73** Jose Gil/ Shutterstock. **p. 74** Robert Vos/AFP/Getty Images. **p. 75** The Kobal Collection/ Columbia/Guangxi Film Studio. **p. 76 L** Wolf/Laif/Camera Press, London. **p. 76 R** Jacom Stephens/iStockphoto. **p. 82** China Daily Information Corp - CDIC/Reuters. **p. 92 TL** Ingrid Booz Morejohn. **p. 92 TM** Jon Arnold Images Ltd/Alamy. **p. 92 TR** Richmatts/Ricardo De Mattos/iStockphoto. **p. 92 BL** Amtman/Mak Tsz Fung/iStockphoto. **p. 92 BM** Ingrid Booz Morejohn. **p. 92 BR** rest/iStockfoto. **p. 100** Ingrid Booz Morejohn. **p. 102** © Jon Arnold Images Ltd / Alamy. **p. 107 L** GoGo Images Corporation/Alamy. **p. 107 R** WizData, Inc./ Shutterstock. **p. 110 T** Ingrid Booz Morejohn. **p. 110 B** Caitlin Cahill/ iStockphoto. **p. 114** Joe Brandt/iStockphoto. **p. 122** Sami Sarkis Travel/ Alamy. **p. 124** Ke Wang/Shutterstock. **p. 130** Ingrid Booz Morejohn. **p. 132 L** Gil Cohen Magen/Reuters. **p. 132 M** Ingrid Booz Morejohn. **p. 132 R** Claro Cortes IV/Reuters. **p. 137** Age fotostock/SuperStock. **p. 139 T, M, B,** Ingrid Booz Morejohn. **p. 148 L** Adrian Dennis/AFP/ Getty Images. **p. 148 ML** Ross Kinnaird/Getty Images. **p. 148 M** Jon Kopaloff/FilmMagic/Getty Images. **p. 148 MR** Mark Mainz/Getty Images. **p. 148 R** China Photos/Getty Images. **p. 149** Mountain landscape with waterfall and pine tree (detail). Drawing with black China ink, c. 1930 (?) by Liu Haisu (1896-1994). Nanjing, Academy of Fine Arts/akg-images/Gilles mermet. **p. 152** Ingrid Booz Morejohn. **p. 154 T** Vittorio Zunino Celotto/Getty Images. **p. 154 B** Dylan Martinez/Reuters. **p. 155** Dan Chung/Reuters. **p. 157** Steven Wynn/ wynnter/iStockphoto. **p. 158 T** Public domain: From the book: Wan hsiao tang-Chu chuang -Hua chuan. **p. 158 B** Public domain: "Confucius as a scholar", Qing Dynasty. **p. 166** Vladimir Wrangel/ Shutterstock. **p. 169** Ingrid Booz Morejohn. **p. 171** Antonio Mo/Stone/ Getty Images. **p. 172** STR/AFP/Getty Images. **p. 174** WizData, inc./ Shutterstock. **p. 176** Nir Elias/Reuters. **p. 194** Dylan Martinez/AFP/ Getty Images.

Every effort has been made to contact copyright holders of material reproduced in this book. Any omissions will be rectified in subsequent printings if notice is given to the publishers.

Disclaimer
This material has been published on behalf of Edexcel and offers high-quality support for the delivery of Edexcel qualifications.

This does not mean that the material is essential to achieve any Edexcel qualification, nor does it mean that it is the only suitable material available to support any Edexcel qualification. Edexcel material will not be used verbatim in setting any Edexcel examination or assessment. Any resource lists produced by Edexcel shall include this and other appropriate resources.

Copies of official specifications for all Edexcel qualifications may be found on the Edexcel website: www.edexcel.com

目录 CONTENTS

1 我的生活 wǒ de shēng huó MY LIFE

复习 fù xí 1	Review 1	Revising basic Chinese	6
复习 fù xí 2	Review 2	Understanding basic introductions	8
1 我喜欢 wǒ xǐ huan	1 I like	Likes and dislikes	10
2 我的父母 wǒ de fù mǔ	2 My parents	Jobs and daily routines	12
3 我的朋友 wǒ de péng you	3 My friends	Describing people	14
4 爱好 ài hào	4 Hobbies	Asking yes/no questions	16
5 国籍 guó jí	5 Nationalities	Talking about places you have visited	18
口语 kǒu yǔ	Speaking assessment	Preparing for a speaking task (open interaction)	20
写作 xiě zuò	Writing assessment	Preparing for an extended writing task about a famous personality	22
重要语言点 zhòng yào yǔ yán diǎn	Key language	Key words and phrases in Chapter 1	24

2 学校 xué xiào SCHOOL

复习 fù xí	Review	Talking about school subjects	26
1 我的学校 wǒ de xué xiào	1 My school	Saying where things are	28
2 学校的一天 xué xiào de yì tiān	2 My school day	Expressing opinions	30
3 学校比较 xué xiào bǐ jiào	3 Comparing schools	Making comparisons	32
4 校服 xiào fú	4 School uniform	Talking about school uniforms	34
5 学校生活 xué xiào shēng huó	5 School life	Talking about school in more depth	36
听力和阅读 tīng lì hé yuè dú	Exam – Listening and Reading	Preparing for the Listening and Reading exam	38
口语 kǒu yǔ	Speaking assessment	Preparing for a speaking task (presentation)	40
写作 xiě zuò	Writing assessment	Preparing for an extended writing task about school	42
重要语言点 zhòng yào yǔ yán diǎn	Key language	Key words and phrases in Chapter 2	44

3 空闲时间 kòng xián shí jiān LEISURE

复习 fù xí	Review	Sports and hobbies	46
1 运动中心 yùn dòng zhōng xīn	1 The sports centre	Talking about sports facilities	48
2 课外活动 kè wài huó dòng	2 Activities outside school	Frequency and duration of activities	50
3 爱好和兴趣 ài hào hé xìng qù	3 Hobbies and interests	Talking about hobbies and interests	52
4 锻炼身体 duàn liàn shēn tǐ	4 Exercise	Talking about keeping fit	54
5 奥运会 ào yùn huì	5 The Olympic Games	Talking about sports in more detail	56
口语 kǒu yǔ	Speaking assessment	Preparing for a speaking task (picture-based discussion)	58
写作 xiě zuò	Writing assessment	Preparing for an extended writing task about hobbies	60
重要语言点 zhòng yào yǔ yán diǎn	Key language	Key words and phrases in Chapter 3	62

4 媒体 měi tǐ MEDIA

复习 fù xí	Review	Understanding basic information about media	64
1 BBC 和 CCTV BBC hé CCTV	1 BBC and CCTV	Giving opinions about the media	66
2 电视 diàn shì	2 Television	Giving opinions about programmes	68
3 上网 shàng wǎng	3 Surfing the net	Talking about preferences	70
4 电影和音乐 diàn yǐng hé yīn yuè	4 Film and music	Talking about films and music	72
5 名人 míng rén	5 Celebrities	Talking about people's lives	74
6 不同的生活 bù tóng de shēng huó	6 Different lives	Making comparisons	76
听力和阅读 tīng lì hé yuè dú	Exam – Listening and Reading	Preparing for the Listening and Reading exam	78
口语 kǒu yǔ	Speaking assessment	Preparing for a speaking task (open interaction)	80
写作 xiě zuò	Writing assessment	Preparing for an extended writing task about films	82
重要语言点 zhòng yào yǔ yán diǎn	Key language	Key words and phrases in Chapter 4	84

5 我住的地方 wǒ zhù de dì fang WHERE I LIVE

复习 fù xí	Review	Talking about the home and where things are	86
1 我的家 wǒ de jiā	1 My house	Describing people's homes	88
2 我的城市 wǒ de chéng shì	2 My town	Talking about where places are	90
3 我住的地方 wǒ zhù de dì fang	3 My local area	Using adjectives to give opinions	92
4 方位 fāng wèi	4 Where things are	Using 在 and place words to describe locations	94
5 问路 wèn lù	5 Finding the way	Asking for directions	96
6 留学体会 liú xué tǐ huì	6 Exchange visits	Making comparisons	98
口语 kǒu yǔ	Speaking assessment	Preparing for a speaking task (presentation)	100
写作 xiě zuò	Writing assessment	Preparing for an extended writing task to advertise your house and area	102
重要语言点 zhòng yào yǔ yán diǎn	Key language	Key words and phrases in Chapter 5	104

6 度假 dù jià HOLIDAYS

复习 fù xí	Review	Revising weather and transport	106
1 天气 tiān qì	1 The weather	Talking about the weather	108
2 交通 jiāo tōng	2 Transport	Talking about different means of transport	110
3 度假经历 dù jià jīng lì	3 Holiday experiences	Talking about a past holiday	112
4 假期计划 jià qī jì huà	4 Holiday plans	Talking about the future	114
5 订旅馆 dìng lǚ guǎn	5 Booking a hotel	Asking and answering questions	116
6 旅行安排 lǚ xíng ān pái	6 Making travel arrangements	Talking about sequences of activities	118
听力和阅读 tīng lì hé yuè dú	Exam – Listening and Reading	Preparing for the Listening and Reading exam	120
口语 kǒu yǔ	Speaking assessment	Preparing for a speaking task (picture-based discussion)	122
写作 xiě zuò	Writing assessment	Preparing for an extended writing task about a past holiday	124
重要语言点 zhòng yào yǔ yán diǎn	Key language	Key words and phrases in Chapter 6	126

7 食品和饮料 shí pǐn hé yǐn liào FOOD AND DRINK

复习 fù xí	Review	Talking about likes and dislikes	128
1 学校的饭菜 xué xiào de fàn cài	1 School meals	Giving opinions	130
2 在餐馆吃饭 zài cān guǎn chī fàn	2 Eating out in a restaurant	Ordering food	132
3 健康饮食 jiàn kāng yǐn shí	3 Healthy eating	Talking about diet and healthy lifestyles	134
4 饮食习惯 yǐn shí xí guàn	4 Eating Habits	Talking about regional food	136
5 节日饮食 jié rì yǐn shí	5 Food and festivals	Talking about celebrations	138
听力和阅读 tīng lì hé yuè dú	Exam – Listening and Reading	Preparing for the Listening and Reading exam	140
口语 kǒu yǔ	Speaking assessment	Preparing for a speaking task (open interaction)	142
写作 xiě zuò	Writing assessment	Preparing for an extended writing task about healthy living	144
重要语言点 zhòng yào yǔ yán diǎn	Key language	Key words and phrases in Chapter 7	146

8 生活方式 shēng huó fāng shì LIFESTYLE

复习 fù xí	Review	Describing clothes	148
1 服饰 fú shì	1 Clothing and accessories	Describing what people wear	150
2 买东西 mǎi dōng xi	2 Shopping	Buying and returning goods	152
3 运动明星 yùn dòng míng xīng	3 Famous sports people	Describing famous people	154
4 采访名人 cǎi fǎng míng rén	4 Interviewing celebrities	Conducting an interview	156
5 历史人物 lì shǐ rén wù	5 Historical figures	Talking about figures from the past	158
口语 kǒu yǔ	Speaking assessment	Preparing for a speaking task (stimulus-based discussion)	160
写作 xiě zuò	Writing assessment	Preparing for an extended writing task about a family makeover	162
重要语言点 zhòng yào yǔ yán diǎn	Key language	Key words and phrases in Chapter 8	164

9 工作 gōng zuò THE WORLD OF WORK

复习 fù xí	Review	Talking about jobs	166
1 工作经验 gōng zuò jīng yàn	1 Work experience	Talking about work experience	168
2 未来计划 wèi lái jì huà	2 Future plans	Talking about future plans	170
3 理想的工作 lǐ xiǎng de gōng zuò	3 Ideal jobs	Talking about your ideal job	172
4 申请工作 shēn qǐng gōng zuò	4 Applying for a job	Writing a CV and letter of application	174
5 博客 bó kè	5 Blogs	Talking about the Internet	176
6 性格 xìng gé	6 Personalities	Describing people	178
听力和阅读 tīng lì hé yuè dú	Exam – Listening and Reading	Preparing for the Listening and Reading exam	180
口语 kǒu yǔ	Speaking assessment	Preparing for a speaking task (presentation)	182
写作 xiě zuò	Writing assessment	Preparing for an extended writing task applying for a holiday job	184
重要语言点 zhòng yào yǔ yán diǎn	Key language	Key words and phrases in Chapter 9	186

EXTRA READING AND WRITING PRACTICE	188
GRAMMAR	206
WRITING CHINESE CHARACTERS	216
GLOSSARY – CHINESE/ENGLISH	220
GLOSSARY – ENGLISH/CHINESE	230

复习 Review 1 – Revising basic Chinese

1
Reading

Match the pictures with the Chinese characters.

1	姐姐	3	弟弟	5	奶奶	7	爸爸
2	爷爷	4	妈妈	6	妹妹	8	哥哥

9.叔叔 father side
10.阿姨
11.舅舅 男天
12.母 男天 mothers side

2
Reading

Match the characters for these verbs with their English equivalents.

1	吃	6	住	a	be	f	want
2	有	7	是	b	live	g	eat
3	要	8	喜欢	c	be called	h	have
4	看	9	喝	d	drink	i	listen
5	听	10	叫	e	like	j	watch/read

listen 听 yīn yuè music

EXAM TIP

Try to learn a list of useful verbs really well, so that you have them at your fingertips when you are asked to write a piece of Chinese. Sentences rely heavily on verbs, so start with the ten in Activity 2 and keep building your list throughout the book. Practise writing them regularly to ensure accuracy.

3
Writing

Use the verbs in Activity 2 to write ten sentences. Try to use any vocabulary you have learnt previously to write varied sentences. Use the examples to help you get started.

妈妈喜欢看书。Mum likes reading books.

哥哥天天喝红酒。My older brother drinks red wine every day.

jiǔ

4 **Speaking**

Take it in turns with a classmate to say the sentences you each wrote in Activity 3. Listen carefully and compare what you have written. Make a note of the vocabulary that is new to you.

5 **Listening**

Listen to the words and find the correct English meanings (a–t) in the box. (1–20)

a	but	f	dog	k	not	p	in
b	TV	g	cat	l	be called	q	he
c	who	h	older sister	m	grandad	r	goldfish
d	have	i	listen	n	like	s	watch
e	music	j	family/home	o	don't have	t	want

6 **Reading**

Match the Chinese characters (1–20) to the English words (a–t) in Activity 5.

1 听 i *Jin*	6 姐姐 h	11 看 s	16 要 t
2 金鱼 r	7 电视 b	12 但是 a	17 他 q
3 喜欢 n	8 在 P	13 狗 f	18 爷爷 m
4 猫 g	9 谁 c *shé*	14 音乐 e	19 家 j
5 不 k	10 叫 l	15 没有 o	20 有 d

19/11 2016

7 **Writing**

Write down the missing words. Only use the characters in Activity 6 to describe the imaginary relative pictured on the right. *Hint!* There may be more than one answer for some gaps.

我 1 叫王海。他住 2 中国。他很 3 狗。
他家有一只狗，4 猫。他天天 5 音乐。
他 6 喜欢 7 电视。

8 **Reading**

Match the questions with the correct answers.

1 你叫什么名字？ a 我喜欢听音乐。
2 你多大了？ b 我没有弟弟，有妹妹。
3 你住在哪儿？ c 我十五岁。
4 你有没有弟弟？ d 我叫李红。
5 你喜欢做什么？ e 我家在上海。

1 我的生活 wǒ de shēng huó MY LIFE

复习 Review 2 – Understanding basic introductions

Reading

Read the texts about Wang Ming, Chen Xiaohong and Mao Wen and answer the questions in Chinese.

www.chineselifeforum.cn	搜索

用户名: 王明

我叫王明。我十六岁。我家在上海。我有一个可爱的妹妹叫王丽。她很喜欢猫, 可是我们家有一只狗, 没有猫。我喜欢听中国音乐。

用户名: 陈小红

我姓陈, 叫陈小红, 我十五岁。我住在中国北京, 北京很大！我有一个哥哥叫陈海, 他十九岁。他很有意思。我也有一个姐姐, 叫陈希, 她爱看电影。我不太喜欢看电影, 但是我喜欢看电视。我们家没有宠物。

interesting

用户名: 毛文

我姓毛, 叫毛文。我住在香港。我的生日是四月二十六号, *biao* 我十八岁。我有一个弟弟叫小明, 他十岁。他有一只大黑狗, 我有很多金鱼。我喜欢看英文书, 也喜欢游泳。

you yong

谁？

1　...十八岁？

2　...十六岁？

3　...有姐姐、也有哥哥？

4　...有弟弟？

5　...住在上海？

6　...喜欢看书？

7　...喜欢听音乐？

8　...没有宠物？

9　...有金鱼？

10　...喜欢猫, 可是家里没有猫？

姓 xìng	be called (surname)
宠物 chǒng wù	pet

CULTURE

When Chinese people introduce themselves, they give their family name first followed by their given name. For example: 我姓张 (my family name is Zhang) 叫张小红 (my name is Zhang Xiaohong).

22/11 2016

GRAMMAR: Verb-adjectives

Adjectives often act as verbs too; there is no need to say 'is' in Chinese in this case. Just state the subject followed by the adjective. Generally speaking 很 (very, quite) is used before the adjective for emphasis. For example:

noun	verb-adjective	English meaning
狗	很大。	The dog is big.
弟弟	很好玩儿。	[My] little brother is fun.
猫	很可爱。	The cat is very cute.

2 Speaking

Ask and answer questions in Chinese.

姓名：刘花　　　　　　　　（你叫什么名字？）

年龄：十六岁　　　　　　　（你多大了？）

出生日期：一九九二年八月十五号

　　　　　　　　　　　　　（你是什么时候出生的？）

出生地点：中国上海　　　　（你是在哪儿出生的？）

地址：中国上海浦东区　　　（你住在哪儿？）

家人：妈妈、爸爸、姐姐　　（你家都有谁？）

宠物：狗　　　　　　　　　（你有宠物吗？）

身份证
IDENTITY CARD
刘花　1234 5678 9101
出生日期：
1992-08-15
出生地点：
中国上海

浦东区 pǔ dōng qū	Pudong, a district in Shanghai

3 Listening

Listen to the passage and answer the questions in English.

1　What is Hai's family name?

2　How old is he?

3　Where does he live?

4　What pet does his brother have?

5　What pet does his sister have?

4 Writing

Write a short paragraph about yourself. Use the framework to help you.

你好，我姓…、叫…。

我…岁。

我的生日是…月…号。

我住在…。

我有…（弟弟、姐姐）。他/她叫…。

我们家有…（猫、狗、鱼）。它…（大、小）。

我喜欢…（看书、听音乐、看电视）。

Likes and dislikes

Reading

Read the text about Liu Dong's likes and dislikes. Answer the questions in Chinese.

我爱看中文书，也爱看英文书。星期六我喜欢去图书馆看书。图书馆有很多书，我很高兴。我也喜欢听音乐。做作业的时候，我常常听中国的新音乐。我不喜欢爸爸听的音乐，很不好听！可是我爸爸说他的音乐很好听！

1　他喜欢看什么样的书？
2　他星期几去图书馆？
3　他什么时候听音乐？
4　他为什么不喜欢听爸爸喜欢的音乐？
5　他爸爸说他听的音乐怎么样？

Listening

Listen to the description of Wang Li. Answer the questions about her in English.

1　What does Wang Li do every day?
2　She really likes English books, but what is her problem with them?
3　What kind of music does she love?
4　Which country's music is she not so fond of?
5　What drinks does she like?

Speaking

Interview your classmates.
Record your results in a chart.

1　你喜欢看什么？
2　你不喜欢看什么？
3　你喜欢喝什么？
4　你不喜欢喝什么？
5　你喜欢吃什么？
6　你不喜欢吃什么？

GRAMMAR: When

Note that in Chinese the use of 的时候 (when) comes at the end of the part of the sentence to which it refers. For example:
吃饭的时候，我常常看电视。
= When I am eating, I often watch television. (literally 'eating-meal-when, I often…')

4
Reading

Read the text about Chen Hua. Copy and complete the sentences.

wú liáo /boring
yīnwèi interesting yì si

我很不喜欢看电视，因为没有意思。我的朋友们每天都看一个多小时的电视，他们说电视上有很多好节目。因为运动对身体好，所以我每个星期二和星期四都跟朋友一起打篮球。我们也一起喝茶，一起说话。我爱打篮球，可是不爱在电视上看篮球比赛。哥哥说因为我不看电视，所以我不酷。他不酷，因为他没有好朋友！

12./1./17

一个多小时 yí ge duō xiǎo shí	more than an hour
节目 jié mù	programme
身体 shēn tǐ	body
跟…一起 gēn... yì qǐ	with...
比赛 bǐ sài	competition, match
酷 kù	cool

1 她很不喜欢 _____。
2 朋友们说电视 _____。
3 她说运动 _____。
4 她爱 _____。
5 可是不喜欢 _____。

19.1.17

GRAMMAR: More than

To say 'more than...' add 多 after the measure word. For example:
她在法国住了一个多月。She stayed in France for more than a month.

Note that time 'how long' (as in 'more than a month') comes after the verb.

5
Writing

Write a short paragraph about your classmates' likes and dislikes. Use vocabulary that you know and try to expand your sentences by adding conjunctions, such as 'and' (和) and 'also' (也).

EXAM TIP

Remember to use 她 / 他 rather than 我 when reporting other people's views!

For example:

我的朋友叫…。他十四岁。他喜欢看足球和篮球。
他不喜欢听中国音乐，也不喜欢听英国音乐。

Jobs and daily routines

a 医生 yī shēng　**b** 老师 lǎo shī　**c** 工程师 gōng chéng shī　**d** 售货员 shòu huò yuán　**e** 服务员 fú wù yuán　**f** 司机 sī jī

1

Listening and Reading

Read and listen to the texts about what jobs Mao Xi, Dahong and Xiaoming's parents do. Match the jobs in the pictures to their parents.

毛希

> **1**　我爸爸在学校工作, 他教英语和地理。我妈妈每天从天安门广场开车到长城。在公共汽车上, 她喜欢给大家讲长城的历史。

大红

> **2**　我爸爸在大饭店工作, 他很忙。他常常问客人："您吃点儿什么？"。妈妈在工厂工作。

小明

> **3**　我爸爸在医院工作, 他每天都给病人看病。他工作的时候穿白色的衣服。我妈妈在商店工作。

Now copy and fill in the grid below in Chinese.

	Dad's work	Where he works	Mum's work	Where she works
1				
2				
3				

教 jiāo	to teach
开车 kāi chē	to drive
讲 jiǎng	to talk about
问 wèn	to ask
医院 yī yuàn	hospital
病人 bìng rén	patients
看病 kàn bìng	see a doctor/ see a patient

 a 起床 qǐ chuáng
 b 吃早饭 chī zǎo fàn
 c 上班 shàng bān
 d 下班 xià bān

/fan xue 放

 e 回家 huí jiā
 f 吃晚饭 chī wǎn fàn
 g 看电视 kàn diàn shì
 h 听音乐 tīng yīn yuè
 i 睡觉 shuì jiào

 2 Listening

Listen to the description of Li Dong's father's day. Answer the questions in English.

1 What time does Li Dong's father get up?
2 How does Li Dong's father go home?
3 What does he eat for dinner?
4 Does he watch TV or listen to music after dinner?
5 What time does Li Dong's father go to bed?

GRAMMAR: Subject + time + verb

Follow the pattern *subject + time + verb (action)* when talking about daily routine. For example:

妈妈六点半起床。 Mum gets up at 6.30. (Literally: Mum 6.30 gets up.)

Subject + (time) + how + verb
tiao

3/03/17

GRAMMAR: Time + manner + place

Remember the word order *time + manner + place*. For example, if the question is 你每天怎么来学校？ (How do you come to school every day?), the answer could be 我每天 (time) 坐公共汽车 (manner) 来学校 (place)。 I come to school by bus every day. (Literally: I every day take the bus come to school.) Note the use of the question word 怎么 to mean 'how' when asking about means of transport.

3 Speaking

Interview your classmates. Copy the chart below and record your results.

Get up at...	Go to school by...	Get home at...	Watch TV/listen to music at...	Go to bed at....

1 你几点起床？ (e.g. 我六点三刻起床。)
2 你怎么来学校？ (e.g. 我坐公共汽车来学校。)
3 你几点回家？ (e.g. 我四点回家。)
4 你每天在家看电视还是听音乐？ (e.g. 我每天在家听音乐。)
5 你几点睡觉？ (e.g. 我十一点差一刻睡觉。)

4 Writing

Write a short paragraph about a set of imaginary parents. Include their names, age, job and a brief account of their daily routine.

週末 zhōu mò

3 我的朋友 wǒ de péng you My friends

Describing people

1 Reading

Read the text about Xiaoli and answer the questions in English.

小丽是我的朋友,今年十六岁。她是中国人,
住在法国。她的个子很高。她的头发是黑色的,
短短的。她的眼睛是棕色的,不大,但是很好看。
小丽喜欢看电影,我和小丽有的时候去电影院看
电影。小丽也爱游泳,星期六我们常常去游泳池。

1 What is Xiaoli's nationality?
2 Is she tall or short?
3 Describe Xiaoli's physical appearance.
4 What do Xiaoli and I sometimes do?
5 What does Xiaoli love doing?

头发 tóu fa
头 tóu
耳朵 ěr duo
鼻子 bí zi
牙齿 yá chǐ
臂 bì
眼睛 yǎn jing
嘴 zuǐ
肚子 dù zi
手 shǒu
腿 tuǐ
脚 jiǎo

个子 gè zi	height
棕色 zōng sè	brown
游泳池 yóu yǒng chí	swimming pool

GRAMMAR: Describing height

To describe a person's height you need to say, literally 'His/her height tall/short'. Use 个子 for height, plus the appropriate verb-adjective.
For example:
弟弟的个子很矮。 My brother is short.
(Literally: My brother's height short.)

2 Listening

Listen to the description of two people.
Draw pictures of them and label them. (1–2)

3 Speaking

Draw and describe a caricature or an alien.

- Firstly, sketch a picture of a weird person or alien, and write a description of it.
- Describe your person to a classmate and ask them to draw what they hear.
- Lastly, compare the original piece of art with your classmate's version.

它的个子…
它有… (colour) 的 … (body part).
它的… (body part) … (adjective; such as long, small, big).
它没有… (body part).

GRAMMAR: Adverbs

Make your description clearer by using the following adverbs before some verb-adjectives:
很 very
比较 (bǐ jiào) quite
非常 (fēi cháng) extremely
For example:
他的头非常大。
His head is extremely big.
它有红色的眼睛。
It has red eyes.

4
Speaking

What animal sign are you? 你属什么？
Interview your classmates.
Ask and answer questions
in Chinese.

> Q: 你的生日是几月几号？
> A: 我的生日是…月…号。
> Q: 你属什么？
> A: 我属… (animal) …。

CULTURE

What Chinese animal sign were you born under? Many Chinese people believe that your animal sign says a lot about your character and they will often ask you 你属(shǔ)什么？

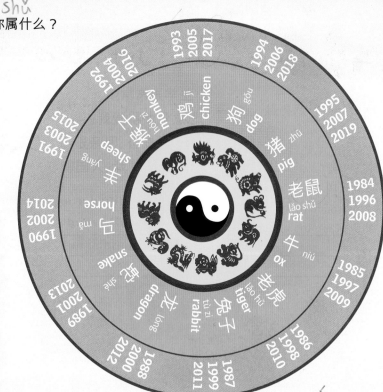

5
Reading

Research the characteristics of people born under each of the animal signs.

6
Listening

Listen to descriptions of Wang Long, Li Ming and Xiaolan.
Make notes under the headings 王龙, 李明 and 小兰. (1–3)

胖 pàng | 瘦 shòu | 漂亮 piào liang | 好看 hǎo kàn | 酷 kù | 懒 lǎn | 聪明 cōng míng | 高 gāo | 矮 ǎi

7
Writing

Write a short paragraph about the appearance and personality of one of your friends. Use the framework to help you.

> 我的朋友叫…
> 他/她比较…(choose an adjective)
> 她也… (a different adjective)
> 她不…(adjective) 也不… (contrasting adjective)
> 她非常… (adjective)

EXAM TIP

Higher marks are awarded for a wide variety of adverbs. Try to go beyond 'very' (很) and use 'quite' (比较) sometimes, and 'extremely' (非常) at other times.

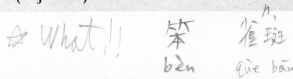

4 爱好 ài hào Hobbies

Asking yes/no questions

a 看书 kàn shū

b 看电视 kàn diàn shì

c 看电影 kàn diàn yǐng

d 听音乐 tīng yīn yuè

e 做运动 zuò yùn dòng

f 玩儿电脑 wánr diàn nǎo

g 跳舞 tiào wǔ

Listening

1 Listen to find out what these teenagers do in their spare time. Write down the letter (a–g) for the activity each person does. (1–5)

1 Zhang Wen   3 Chen Ming   5 Wang Li
2 Mao Lan   4 Liu Hong

Reading

2 Read Chen's diary opposite for Saturday. Answer the questions in English.

1 When does Xiao Chen read?
2 What does Xiao Chen do from 11am to 12 noon?
3 What does he have for lunch?
4 When does Xiao Chen play sports?
5 How long does he spend listening to music?

星期六
早上: 九点 ~ 十点半
看中文书
十点半 ~ 十一点
喝茶
十一点 ~ 十二点
玩儿电脑
十二点 ~ 十二点半
吃牛肉面

下午: 十二点半 ~ 一点半
看电视
一点半 ~ 三点半
做运动
四点 ~ 五点半
听音乐

GRAMMAR: Yes/no questions

To ask somebody whether or not they do a certain activity, you can use a positive/negative questioning style. First say the verb (看 = watch), then follow this directly with the negative form of the verb (不看 = don't watch).

For example:
你每天晚上看不看电视？ Do you watch TV (or not) every day?

EXAM TIP

Make sure that you understand the two main types of basic questions – both those ending in 吗 and 'yes/no' questions. Both types will be asked in the the speaking assessment.

3
Writing

Copy the grid and use the new grammar to fill it in.

Person	Specific time phrase	Verb (positive)	Verb (negative form)	Noun
你 You		玩儿 play	not play	电脑? computer?
You		read	不看 not read	中文书? Chinese books?
他 He	今天晚上 this evening	listen	not listen (to)	音乐? music?
妹妹 Sister	tomorrow	watch	不看 not watch	TV?
She	星期天 On Sundays	做 do / play	not do / play	sports?

4
Speaking

Interview your classmates to find out what they do in their free time. Use the diary in Activity 2 and the questions opposite to help you.

你有空的时候喜欢做什么?
What do you like doing in your free time?

你几点…?
What time do you…?

5
Listening

Listen to the dialogue and answer the questions in English.

1 What question does Zhang Hai ask Xiaohong at the beginning of their conversation?
2 What is Xiaohong's response?
3 Why can't Xiaohong go to the cinema on Sunday?
4 What does Xiaohong often do?
5 What is Zhang Hai's problem?
6 When does Xiaohong invite Zhang Hai to her house? To do what?

6
Writing

Write a diary about a typical day in your life giving times for the activities that you do.
Use the framework to help you.

我七点半起床, 七点三刻吃早饭。我常常吃面包,
有的时候喝牛奶。我八点半上学。我天天四点回家,
然后看电视。我们家五点半吃晚饭。吃饭以后我玩儿
电脑, 听音乐或者看书。我常常十点睡觉。

GRAMMAR: Time/action

When writing in Chinese, remember that a point in time always comes before the action. For example:
妈妈六点回家。 = Mum comes home at 6 o'clock. (Literally: Mum 6 o'clock comes home.)

然后 rán hòu	then
或者 huò zhě	or

5 国籍 guó jí Nationalities

Talking about places you have visited

Listening

Listen to some neighbours introducing themselves.
Answer the questions in Chinese. (1-4)

1 Mao Li 是德国人、中国人、西班牙人还是英国人？

2 Chris 说西班牙语还是德语？

3 住在英国的中国人是 Hannah 还是 Mao Li?

4 谁是学生, Peter, Chris 还是 Hannah?

5 Hannah 是二零零七年还是二零零五年来英国的?

EXAM TIP

Remember when you are making a negative statement about a past event, use 没.

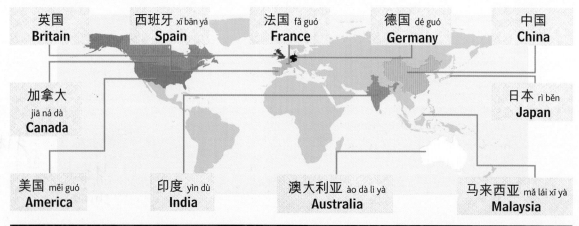

英国 Britain	西班牙 xī bān yá Spain	法国 fǎ guó France	德国 dé guó Germany	中国 China
加拿大 jiā ná dà Canada				日本 rì běn Japan
美国 měi guó America	印度 yìn dù India	澳大利亚 ào dà lì yà Australia		马来西亚 mǎ lái xī yà Malaysia

---

GRAMMAR: 'has/have been'

To say you had the experience of going to a place, put 过 guò after the verb 去 (to go).

For example: 我去过马来西亚。= I have been to Malaysia.

To turn this into a negative statement, put 没 (not) in front of the verb and put 过 after the verb.

For example: 哥哥没去过日本。My brother hasn't been to Japan.

Reading

Read the text about Mr Li and his family.
Answer the questions in English.

李先生六十三岁。他是老师。他住在香港。他有一个
姐姐和一个弟弟, 他们很喜欢旅游, 去过很多国家。
李先生去过法国、美国、加拿大和澳大利亚, 没去过
印度, 也没去过西班牙和德国。李先生的姐姐去过日本
和马来西亚。他的弟弟去过英国、澳大利亚和美国,
没去过中国。

| 旅游 lǚ yóu | to travel |
| 国家 guó jiā | countries |

1 Where does Mr Li live?

2 Which countries has Mr Li been to?

3 Which countries hasn't he been to?

4 Which countries has Mr Li's sister visited?

5 Where hasn't his brother been to?

3
Reading

Read the text about Wang Ming's grandmother and answer the questions in English.

现在 xiàn zài	now
台湾 tái wān	Taiwan
伦敦 lún dūn	London

王明的奶奶住在澳大利亚, 今年五十六岁。
她以前是医生, 现在不工作了。她爱旅游,
也很喜欢游泳。她去过很多地方。她去过
香港, 台湾和北京。她的妈妈是英国人,
但是她没去过伦敦。

1   Where does Wang Ming's grandmother live?
2   What was her occupation?
3   What two things does she like doing?
4   Which places has she visited?
5   Why is it a little surprising that she hasn't been to London?

4
Speaking

Interview five classmates to find out which countries they have visited. If they haven't visited any countries, ask them to think about where they would like to visit and make up the answers! Record your results in a chart. Report your findings to the rest of the class.

Interviewing:
Q: 你去过什么国家？Which countries have you visited?
A: 我去过....和… I have been to …and …
Reporting your results:
她 / 他去过…和…

5
Writing

**Write a short paragraph about where the members of your family have or haven't visited.
Use the expressions to help you.**

我爸爸 / 妈妈 / 姐姐 / 哥哥 / 妹妹 / 弟弟 / 奶奶 /
爷爷 叫…
他 / 她喜欢…
她 / 他去过….和…
她 / 他没去过…

TASK AND PREPARATION

Your Chinese friend has asked you to help him with his research into David Beckham for a school project. You collect some resources from the Internet about David Beckham's personal information, family life and football career. Use the Internet resources to help you answer the questions.

- Ask your Chinese friend what the Chinese public think of your chosen English celebrity.
- Present as much information as you can about the chosen celebrity.
- Give opinions about how celebrities can influence young people in England.

Your teacher will play the part of your Chinese friend and will start the conversation.

www.davbckhm.cn   搜索

Name	David Beckham
Date of birth	2nd May 1975
Place of birth	Leytonstone, London
Parents	Sandra and Ted
School	Chingford High School – No GCSEs
1991	Manchester United trainee
1995–2003	Plays for Manchester United
1996	First senior cap for England
1998–2006	Plays in three World Cups
1999	Marries Victoria Adams ('Posh Spice')
Children	Brooklyn (98), Romeo (02) Cruz (05)
2003-2007	Plays for Real Madrid
2007-2008	Plays for Los Angeles Galaxy
2009-now	Plays for AC Milan
Lifestyle	Hairstyle, outfit, cars, Home: 'Beckingham Palace'

1 **Listening** You will hear a model conversation between Jack and his Chinese friend. Listen to the first part of their conversation and match the Chinese pinyin with the three English terms.

1	màn lián	a	GCSE
2	zhōng xué huì kǎo	b	The World Cup
3	shì jiè bēi	c	Manchester United

2 **Listening** Listen to the first part of the conversation again and answer the questions.

1 How does Jack's Chinese friend start the conversation?
2 How does he answer the question when asked if he likes Beckham?
3 What does he mean by 你听说过曼联吗？which he asks after answering a question?
4 What extra information does he give about when Beckham was born?

3 **Listening** Think about how Jack used the verbs 踢 and 考 in a 得 structure, and then listen to the first part again and check how well you have translated the following sentences.

1 He plays football very well.   2 His exam results were not good.

4 **Listening** In the second part of the conversation, Jack will be asked about Beckham's family life. Write down four questions in Chinese you think Jack might be asked and answer them in Chinese. And then listen and check how well you predicted.

5
Listening

The following sentences come up in the text. Have a go at translating them, and then listen to the third part of the conversation and check if you used the correct structures.

1 Example:
He played football for eight years for Manchester United. 他在曼联踢了8年足球。
a He played football for four years in Spain.
b He played football for three months in Italy.

2 Example:
He spends a lot of money on clothes. 他买衣服花很多钱。
a He spends a lot of money on cars.
b He spends a lot of money on houses.

6
Listening

In the third part Jack talks about how Beckham, as a role model, encourages young people about what they can achieve if they try hard. Translate the following sentences using the given words, and then listen and check your translation.

1 His influence *on* young people is very big. （对）
2 He likes to do things *for* young people. （为）
3 They want to try as hard *as* Beckham. （跟…一样）

YOUR TURN NOW

Prepare your answers to the task, and then have a conversation with your partner.
Award each other one star, two stars or three stars for each of the following categories:

- pronunciation
- confidence and fluency
- range of time frames

- variety of vocabulary
- using sentences with more complex structures
- taking the initiative

Note down what you need to do next time to improve your performance.

ResultsPlus
Maximise your marks

To aim for a **Grade C** you need to:
- ensure you have shown you can use time references for different time frames. Check the examples to see what Jack said: 他也参加了中学会考/他踢过世界杯/他们都想跟他一样成功.
- remember to give opinions where possible. Jack uses 我觉得… to talk about how he thinks Beckham has influenced English young people.

If you are aiming for a grade **higher than Grade C** you need to:
- add complexity to the meaning you try to convey by using small words such as 'on' as in 'influence on somebody', 'for' as in 'do something for somebody', and adverbs such as 'always', 'often' and 'again'.
- communicate relevant and detailed information. Notice how Jack makes the most of the stimulus.
- show you can interact naturally by taking the initiative and asking questions as well as giving answers.

If you want to get an **A or A* grade** you need to :
- communicate comprehensive information. 得 is useful for this purpose. Note how Jack says 'He plays football well' and 'His exam results were not good'.
- use more complex structures. For example, 他买汽车花很多钱 'He spends a lot of money on cars'.
- use structures such as 'go somewhere/to do something with somebody' to add further complexity. Listen where Jack talks about how Beckham spends his free time with his family.

写作 xiě zuò Writing

Preparing for an extended writing task about a famous personality

PREPARATION

Warm Up! This article is about the Chinese rock star Cui Jian. There is a lot about him in English on the Internet. Have a look before you read this article.

中国摇滚乐之父: 崔健

崔健是1961年出生的。他在北京长大, 从十四岁起, 他跟父亲学习小号演奏。1981年, 他参加了北京歌舞团。

1986年, 崔健写了第一首摇滚歌曲"不是我不明白"。1986年, 在北京举行的演唱会上, 当他跳上北京工人体育馆的舞台的时候, 观众还不明白发生了什么事情。当音乐开始, 崔健唱出"我曾经问个不休, 你何时跟我走..."时, 观众变得非常安静。十分钟后, 歌曲唱完了, 在热烈的欢呼声和掌声中, 中国出现了第一个摇滚歌星。

从此, 崔健开始了他的摇滚新长征,他到现在还在演奏。除了摇滚音乐以外, 他也很喜欢中国民歌。

我明年准备去北京听他的一个音乐会。因为现在没有钱买飞机票, 所以我得每天兼职送报!

You may not know the words 摇滚 and 长征. Find out what they mean with the help of a dictionary. Work with a partner to find out why 新长征 is used here.

Find the characters in the text which mean:

1 trumpet player   4 audience   7 folk songs
2 rock song   5 when the song was over   8 part-time
3 stage   6 cheering and applause

Look at how conjunctions are used in this article. Find and copy out sentences using 在...中 and 除了...以外.

Answer these questions in English.

1 What is Cui Jian often called?
2 How old was he when he joined the Beijing song and dance troupe?
3 What was the name of his first rock song?
4 What happened after this appearance?
5 What kind of music does he like as well as rock music?
6 What would the author like to do in the future?

YOUR TURN NOW

Write a short article about a well-known personality of your choice. Write between 100 and 150 characters (less than half the length of the article about Cui Jian). You could include information about the following:

- where he/she was born and spent his/her childhood
- his/her achievements
- his/her future career
- your own opinion of this personality

TIP

The article about Cui Jian is there to stimulate your imagination, but it also includes a lot of general phrases which you could use to help you. Have a look for a few before you start writing. Use a dictionary or the Internet to help you with the research about the personality you have chosen. With good preparation, you will be surprised how much you can say using the vocabulary and structures you have learned.

CHECK

Check the characters and word order. Make sure you have not made any errors with characters that sound the same, for example 以 and 已 in the words 以前 and 已经. Make sure you haven't accidentally used 是 when you meant to use 很, for example 他很有名.

ResultsPlus
Maximise your marks

To aim for a **Grade C** you need to:
- show you can write clearly about your chosen personality and express points of view. The author writing about Cui Jian talks about:
  - his childhood
  - his adult career
  - the author's own hopes for the future
- make use of past, present and future time frames

To aim **higher than a Grade C** you need to:
- look at the examples of connecting words in the article and try to include some of them in your own work

To produce your best written Chinese and to aim for an **A* grade** you need to :
- add some extra interest, as the author does here with lines from some of Cui Jian's songs
- demonstrate awareness of the difference between 的 and 得, for example when the author says 观众变得非常安静.
- demonstrate an awareness of how to use 了, both straight after the verb and at the end of a sentence.

我 wǒ Me

我	wǒ	I/me	我是英国人。	wǒ shì yīng guó rén	I'm British.
我叫…	wǒ jiào…	I'm called…	我是中国人。	wǒ shì zhōng guó rén	I'm Chinese.
我十六岁。	wǒ shí liù suì	I'm sixteen years old.	蓝/棕/黑/绿色的眼睛	lán / zōng / hēi / lǜ sè de yǎn jing	blue / brown / black / green eyes
我住/家在…	wǒ zhù / jiā zài…	I live in…	我的头发很长/短。	wǒ de tóu fa hěn cháng / duǎn	I have long / short hair.
我的生日是八月三号。	wǒ de shēng rì shì bā yuè sān hào	My birthday is 3rd August.	我个子很高/矮。	wǒ gè zi hěn gāo/ǎi	I'm tall / short.
我有一个弟弟叫大海。	wǒ yǒu yí ge dì di jiào dà hǎi.	I have a younger brother called Da Hai.	我有一只猫。	wǒ yǒu yì zhī māo	I have a cat.
			我没有狗。	wǒ méi yǒu gǒu	I don't have a dog.

我喜欢做的活动 wǒ xǐ huan zuò de huó dòng Things I like doing

你喜欢做什么？	nǐ xǐ huan zuò shén me?	What do you like doing?	看电影	kàn diàn yǐng	watching films
我很喜欢…	wǒ hěn xǐ huan…	I really like…	听音乐	tīng yīn yuè	listening to music
我喜欢…	wǒ xǐ huan…	I like…	玩儿电脑	wánr diàn nǎo	playing on the computer
看书	kàn shū	reading	做运动	zuò yùn dòng	doing sport
看电视	kàn diàn shì	watching TV	我不喜欢跳舞。	wǒ bù xǐ huan tiào wǔ	I don't like dancing.

什么时候… shén me shí hou… When do you do it?

常常	cháng cháng	often	有(的)时候	yǒu (de) shí hou	sometimes
天天/每天	tiān tiān / měi tiān	every day/every single day	星期六	xīng qī liù	on Saturdays

我的家人 wǒ de jiā rén My family

弟弟	dì di	younger brother	奶奶	nǎi nai	grandmother
妹妹	mèi mei	younger sister	爷爷	yé ye	grandfather
哥哥	gē ge	older brother	她很胖。	tā hěn pàng	She's fat.
姐姐	jiě jie	older sister	他很好看。	tā hěn hǎo kàn	He's very good looking.
妈妈	mā ma	mother	他不太忙。	tā bú tài máng	He's not very busy.
爸爸	bà ba	father			

工作 gōng zuò **Jobs**

他/她是/当…	tā / tā shì / dāng	He / She is a …	售货员	shòu huò yuán	shop assistant
医生	yī shēng	doctor	服务员	fú wù yuán	waiter / waitress
老师	lǎo shī	teacher	司机	sī jī	driver
工程师	gōng chéng shī	engineer			

日常活动 rì cháng huó dòng **Daily routine**

起床	qǐ chuáng	get up	吃晚饭	chī wǎn fàn	eat dinner
吃早饭	chī zǎo fàn	eat breakfast	睡觉	shuì jiào	go to bed
上班	shàng bàn	go to work	我七点起床。	wǒ qī diǎn qǐ chuáng	I get up at 7 o'clock.
上学	shàng xué	go to school	她每天都五点半回家。	tā měi tiān dōu wǔ diǎn bàn huí jiā	She goes home at 5.30 every single day.
回家	huí jiā	go home			

我的朋友 wǒ de péng you **My friends**

我的朋友很漂亮。	wǒ de péng you hěn piào liang	My friend is very pretty.	她比较懒。	tā bǐ jiào lǎn	She's quite lazy.
			他非常酷。	tā fēi cháng kù	He's really cool.

你去过什么国家？ nǐ qù guò shén me guó jiā? **Where have you been?**

我去过法国和德国。	wǒ qù guò fǎ guo hé dé guó	I've been to France and Germany.	我没去过日本。	wǒ méi qù guo rì běn	I haven't been to Japan.

2 学校 xué xiào SCHOOL

复习 Review – Talking about school subjects

Reading

1 Match the characters to the symbols.

| 1 英语 | 2 体育 | 3 数学 | 4 科学 | 5 音乐 | 6 历史 | 7 汉语 | 8 地理 |

Reading

2 Read the text about a school day. Choose whether the statements are true (对) or false (不对).

星期三, 张红有七节课。第一节课是体育, 她不太喜欢, 因为她不喜欢运动, 也不喜欢体育老师。第二节课是英语, 张红很喜欢学习英语, 她每天晚饭后都在家看英语书。第三节课是汉语, 她喜欢汉语老师, 也喜欢跟中国人说汉语。第四节课是历史, 张红说历史非常有意思, 她喜欢看历史书。第五节课是音乐, 张红爱听音乐, 但是她不喜欢上音乐课。第六节课是科学, 她很喜欢学习科学。第七节课是数学, 她说数学很容易, 所以她喜欢这节课。

节 jié	*measure word for counting lessons*
学习 xué xí	to study
容易 róng yì	easy

1 Zhang Hong really likes the PE teacher.
2 Her second lesson of the day is English, which she likes a lot.
3 She likes the Chinese teacher.
4 She says that history lessons are extremely boring.
5 She doesn't like reading history books.
6 Her fifth lesson is French.
7 She really doesn't like studying science.
8 The last lesson of the day is Maths.

Reading and Writing

3 Copy and fill in Zhang Hong's timetable in Chinese according to the passage above.

第一节课	第二节课	第三节课	第四节课	第五节课	第六节课	第七节课

Reading

Copy and fill in the grid below in English for subjects Zhang Hong likes and dislikes. Include reasons where given.

Subjects she likes	reason	Subjects she dislikes	reason

Listening

Listen to and read the following dialogue. Write down the missing characters for the gaps.

(Write them in pinyin as you hear them, then try to write the characters after hearing the dialogue twice.)

赵明：<u>陈龙</u>，你好吗？

陈龙：哦，我很 <u>1</u> 。你呢，赵明？

赵明：我很 <u>2</u> 。你为什么很累？

陈龙：今天的课没有意思。

赵明：是吗？你今天上了什么 <u>3</u> ？

陈龙：历史、 <u>4</u> 、数学、宗教和 <u>5</u> 。每节课我们都要看书。

赵明：哦，很累很累！

陈龙：你呢？今天 <u>6</u> 了什么课？

赵明：我很 <u>7</u> 今天的课。我有 <u>8</u> 、法语、 <u>9</u> 、美术和汉语。

陈龙：太好了！

宗教 *zōng jiào* RE

Speaking

Interview your classmates. Ask about five lessons they like and dislike, and which teachers they like and dislike. Use the example to help you. Record your results in a chart like the one below.

Q: 你喜欢不喜欢… (subject) 课？　　A: 喜欢 / 不喜欢。

Q: 你喜欢不喜欢… (subject) 老师？　　A: 喜欢 / 不喜欢。

	喜欢	不喜欢
课		
上课的老师		

Writing

Complete the sentences to say how you feel about certain lessons and teachers.

a 我喜欢 (subject)

我很喜欢…

我爱…

我不太喜欢…

我很不喜欢…

b (subject) 老师 (adjective)

…老师很好。

…老师不太好。

…老师很有意思。

…老师没有意思。

…老师…。

Saying where things are

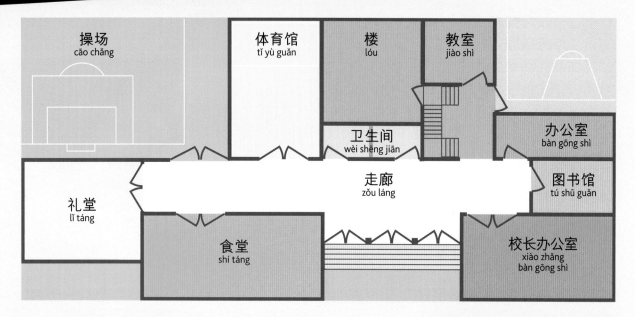

Reading

Read the text about Mao Xi's school and answer the questions in English.

毛希的学校在英国。这所学校很大,有一千五百个学生和九十五个老师。学校除了有一个体育馆以外,也有两个大操场。学校的食堂比较小,所以有的学生在食堂吃午饭,有的学生在教室吃。学校的图书馆不大。礼堂也比较小。每个走廊都有卫生间。

所 suǒ	*measure word for buildings*
除了...以外 chú le... yǐ wài	apart from
有的 yǒu de	some
走廊 zǒu láng	corridor

1 How many students and teachers are there in the school that Mao Xi attends?
2 What does the school have two of?
3 Describe the canteen.
4 If students don't eat lunch in the canteen, what is the alternative?
5 Which three rooms are smaller than you might expect?

EXAM TIP

If you use the 'apart from' structure, you will be awarded higher marks.

GRAMMAR: 'Apart from'

To say 'apart from' or 'besides', use the following structure:
除了 *item or activity* 以外, *subject* 也... . In some cases, the subject can also come before. For example:
除了大礼堂以外, 学校也有很大的体育馆。Apart from having a large assembly hall, the school also has a very big gym.
妹妹除了汉语以外, 也学习西班牙语。Besides studying Chinese, my sister is also studying Spanish.

2
Writing

Write five sentences following the pattern below.
Use vocabulary from this unit.

Apart from, 除了	noun or verb	以外,	subject	also 也	verb	remainder of sentence
除了	说法语	以外,	爸爸	也	写	汉字。

3
Listening

Listen to the dialogue between two teachers and write down the missing characters for the gaps 1–5.

张老师：周老师，你们学校大不大？

周老师：我们的学校非常 __1__ 。

张老师：是吗？有多少个学生？

周老师：有 __2__ 个学生。

张老师：哦，真大！

周老师：你们学校有几个 __3__ ？

张老师：我们有一个图书馆。你们呢？

周老师： __4__ 大图书馆以外，每个走廊都有小图书馆。很方便！

张老师：真好！

周老师：我们还有两个 __5__ 和一个很大的食堂。

张老师：你们学校太大了！

方便 fāng biàn | convenient

GRAMMAR: Talking about where something is

When using relative place words say 在 (place or object) *relative place word*.
For example:
体育馆在操场(的)对面。
The gym is opposite the playground.

4
Reading

Read the text about the layout of a school corridor. Write down the Chinese numbers 一 to 十二 (1 to 12) as on the plan of the corridor. Write down the subject taught in the room next to the correct number.

这是我们学校一年级的走廊。老师在一号教室教数学。数学教室对面是办公室。办公室右边有一个科学教室。科学教室右边是地理教室。地理教室对面是英语教室。英语教室左边是历史教室，右边是宗教教室。宗教教室对面是法语教室，法语教室右边有两个美术教室。在六号教室，老师教音乐，音乐教室左边是戏剧教室。

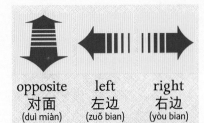

opposite 对面 (duì miàn) | left 左边 (zuǒ bian) | right 右边 (yòu bian)

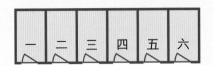

一 二 三 四 五 六

七 八 九 十 十一 十二

戏剧 xì jù | drama

5
Speaking

Describe an imaginary corridor in a school to your partner. Your partner should draw what you describe. Use the place words in Activity 4 to help you.

6
Writing

Write a short paragraph about the layout of your school. Use the panel to the right as a framework.

除了…以外，学校也有…

…对面 / 右边 / 左边 有…

学校没有…

2 学校的一天 xué xiào de yì tiān My school day

Expressing opinions

化学 (huà xué)	物理 (wù lǐ)	经济 (jīng jì)	生物 (shēng wù)	电脑 (diàn nǎo)	手工 (shǒu gōng)

① **Listening**

Listen to the description of Xiao Ming's timetable. Copy and complete the timetable in Chinese.

学期 xué qī	school term
休息 xiū xi	break, rest
东西 dōng xi	things, items

Xiao Ming's Monday – 小明的星期一

第一节课	第二节课	休息	第三节课	第四节课	午饭	第五节课

② **Speaking**

Interview your partner about one day of their timetable and compare it with yours. Copy and complete a timetable for your partner. Add ☺ or ☹ to say whether they like the lesson or not. Use the questions to help you.

Q: 星期一第一节课是什么？
What do you have first period on a Monday?
A: 第一节课是…课。
Q: 你喜欢不喜欢那节课？
A: 喜欢。/ 不喜欢。
Q: 第二节课呢？
A: 第二节课是…课。

第一节课	第二节课	第三节课	第四节课	第五节课	第六节课	第七节课

亲切 (qīn qiè)	严格 (yán gé)	有趣 (yǒu qù)	好玩儿 (hǎo wánr)	厉害 (lì hai)	友好 (yǒu hǎo)

GRAMMAR: Expressing opinions

To express opinions, you can use the verb 觉得 (jué de). This verb means to 'think' or 'consider'. The verb is placed directly after the person, as in English.
For example: 我觉得英语老师很有趣。= I think the English teacher is very funny.

EXAM TIP

Use the structure 我觉得 (I think) with 因为 (because) plus a reason to express your opinions about anything. Examiners will be looking for this!
For example: 我觉得汉语老师很厉害, 因为她常常给我们很多作业。= I think the Chinese teacher is awful, because she often gives us a lot of homework. 我觉得体育老师很友好, 因为他经常问"你怎么样？" = I think the PE teacher is friendly, because he often asks 'How are you?'

3 **Read the text about Li Ming's teachers.**
Reading **Copy and complete the chart in Chinese.**

我很喜欢上学, 因为我有很多很好的老师。生物老师很严格,
但是我觉得他很有意思。戏剧老师非常好玩儿, 她常常跟学生
在一起玩儿。我很不喜欢电脑课的老师, 因为我觉得他没意思,
我也不喜欢用电脑。我觉得经济课的老师很亲切, 但是她的课
没有意思。我最喜欢德语老师,因为他是德国人, 我觉得他很
有趣, 他的每一节课都很好玩儿!

什么课的老师？	李明觉得他 / 她…	other information/comments

4 **Write a short paragraph about a day at school.**
Writing **Use the vocabulary from this unit to help you.**
Use the structures as a guideline and read the text in Activity 3 again to help.

我星期…上…课。
我很喜欢 / 不太喜欢 / 爱…课, 因为我觉得老师…
我认为…课没有意思, 但是老师…
我最喜欢的课是…, 因为…

5 **Read the text and answer the questions in English.**
Extra Reading 我上的这个学校有点儿奇怪。我们每天十点钟上课。
每节课是两个小时, 一天只有三节课。星期一十点,
我们上化学课, 我觉得化学课的老师非常严格。十二点
到十二点半, 我们吃午饭, 然后上第二节课, 是美术课,
这节课不太好, 因为我不喜欢画画儿。美术老师讲课也
没意思, 所以我们觉得两个小时很长! 两点半到三点
我们休息, 休息的时候我跟朋友们一起听音乐。三点
到五点我上电脑课, 这节课是我最喜欢的课, 因为我觉得
电脑很有意思。电脑课的老师也很亲切, 我很喜欢她。

奇怪 qí guài	strange
只 zhǐ	only

1 Name two things that are a little strange about Lu Jing's school.

2 What lesson does she have first on a Monday and what does she think of the teacher of that lesson?

3 What time is lunch at this school?

4 What does she think of art lessons and how does she feel about the art teacher?

5 How long does break time last and what does she do during that time?

6 What is her favourite lesson and why?

7 Why does she like that lesson's teacher?

Making comparisons

GRAMMAR: Simple comparisons

To make simple comparisons use the pattern A 比 (bǐ) B + *adjective*. For example: 学校的体育馆比礼堂大。
The school's gym is larger than the assembly hall.

Listening

1 Listen to and read the text.
Choose the best response, a or b.

一年以前, 我跟父母一起来到了英国。妈妈在这儿的一所大学工作, 我在一所中学上三年级。因为英语不好, 去年一年我觉得很不容易。现在好多了。

我的英国学校比中国的小。我现在的学校有一千个学生, 在中国的时候, 我的学校有两千五百个学生。在英国, 一个班只有二十到三十个学生, 英国的班比中国的班小。

在中国, 我们七点半上学, 五点放学。中国的学生每天都有很多作业。英国的学生九点上学, 三点半放学。他们的作业比中国学生的少。

中国的学生都在食堂吃午饭, 英国学生有的在食堂吃, 有的在教室里吃。中国食堂的饭比英国食堂的好吃。

到 dào	(from…) to…

1   英国的学校比中国的   a 小   b 大
2   英国学校的班比中国的   a 小   b 大
3   英国学生的一天比中国学生的 a 长   b 短
4   英国学生的作业比中国学生的 a 多   b 少
5   英国学校的饭比中国的   a ☺   b ☹

Reading

2 Find the phrases in the text which mean…

1   with my parents   4   from 20 to 30…
2   it wasn't easy   5   some British students…
3   it's fine now

Listening

3 Listen to a passage about Liu Wen and answer the questions in English.

1   What did Liu Wen do in China last year?
2   Why wasn't it easy for him to do this?
3   How was the students' spoken English compared to Liu Wen's spoken Chinese?
4   What did he say about Maths lessons?
5   What lessons did he think were boring?

GRAMMAR: The use of 了 after a verb

Talking about events which have already happened using 了 (le). When an event has happened/an action has been completed, and the object of the sentence has a number before it, put 了 after the verb and before the number. For example:
今天早上我吃了三碗米饭和一条鱼。I ate three bowls of rice and a fish for breakfast today.
我昨天买了六本书。
I bought six books yesterday.

4

Speaking

Tell your classmate what you did at school yesterday using 了 where necessary. Use the expressions to help you. Record your classmates' comments in your book.

我昨天上了五节课, 有英语、地理、...、...和...课。

英语课比...课好玩儿 / 有意思 ...

在汉语课上, 我们写了...

在美术课上, 我们画了...

CULTURE: SCHOOL IN CHINA

In general, pupils in China first go to primary school (小学) at the age of six or seven and study for six years. They then have three years at a junior high school (初中) and three years at a senior high school (高中), leaving at 18 years old.

The average size of a class in many schools is between 35 and 50 pupils! Classrooms are crammed full of desks with very little room for pupils to move around. Between lessons the teachers move around rather than the pupils, which means that generally, pupils have most of their lessons in the same classroom with the same classmates.

Chinese pupils do morning exercises outside every day, as well as eye exercises in the classroom to relax their eyes.

5

Writing

Write a short paragraph comparing your school with one in China.

First research more details about Chinese schools and then compare a few different aspects which interest you. Use the framework to help you. You may want to research the following:

- the school buildings
- school food
- lessons
- sport

This could be your title: 英国的学校和中国的学校

英国的学校比中国的学校...

英国的学校食堂比中国的...

在英国, 学生...点钟上课, 可是在中国他们...

在...作业很多, 但是在...

每天学生都上...节课。

4 校服 xiào fú School uniform
Talking about school uniforms

夹克 jiā kè
领带 lǐng dài
T 恤 T xù
裙子 qún zi
袜子 wà zi
运动鞋 yùn dòng xié
衬衣 chèn yī
毛衣 máo yī
裤子 kù zi
皮鞋 pí xié

 1 Writing

Copy and complete the texts to describe the pictures above.

1 女学生穿蓝 a ___、黄 b ___、戴蓝黄 c ___。
她也穿蓝 d ___、蓝 e ___ 和白 f ___。

2 男学生穿黑 a ___、白 b ___、戴红黑 c ___。
他也穿黑 d ___、黑 e ___ 和黑 f ___。

女 nǚ	female
戴 dài	to wear (of accessories)
男 nán	male

2 Listening

Listen to the dialogue between Li Hua and Xiao Lan about school uniforms. Answer the questions in English.

1 What does Xiao Lan really dislike about her school uniform?
2 What colour are the skirts and sweaters at Xiao Lan's school?
3 Whose school uniform includes wearing a tie, Xiao Lan's or Li Hua's?
4 What two colours of skirt can students at Li Hua's school choose to wear?
5 What colour blazer is worn at Li Hua's school and what does Xiao Lan think about this?

Speaking Interview your classmates about the design and colours of their primary school uniform. Use the questions to help you. Record your results in Chinese.

1 你上的小学有没有校服?
2 校服的裤子/裙子是什么颜色的?
3 衬衣是什么颜色的?
4 有没有领带?
5 学生穿皮鞋还是运动鞋?

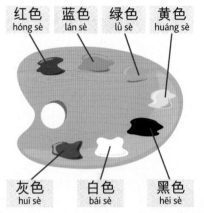

红色 hóng sè
蓝色 lán sè
绿色 lǜ sè
黄色 huáng sè
灰色 huī sè
白色 bái sè
黑色 hēi sè

 Writing Draw a picture to represent your classmates' school uniform and write sentences in Chinese to describe it.

For example:

他穿黄色的衬衣、蓝色的裤子。他没有领带。

 Reading Read the text about a student's ideal school uniform and answer the questions in English.

我们学校的校服很好看! 女学生穿绿色的长裙子和白T恤。
她们也穿蓝色或者黑色的长毛衣。她们穿运动鞋。
男学生穿蓝裤子、黑T恤和黑毛衣。他们也穿运动鞋。

1 What colour skirt do the girls wear?
2 Do the girls wear a black or white T-shirt?
3 What choice of colour do the girls have for their sweaters?
4 What kind of shoes do both the girls and boys wear?
5 Do the boys wear blue or black trousers?

 Writing Write a short paragraph about a school uniform you would like to wear. Include both boys' and girls' uniforms, then draw an illustration to go with the description. Use the structures to help you.

我们学校的校服很….
女学生穿…的裙子或者裤子,…的衬衣。
男学生穿…
我觉得我们的校服…,因为…

Talking about school in more depth

1
Reading

Read about Zhang Jian's timetable. Copy and complete the grid in English. Write any extra information about her timetable in English.

星期五我有五节课。在课间休息以前我上两节课，经济课和美术课。美术课很好，因为我们现在画狗和猫。休息以后我们上英语课，然后有西班牙语课。西班牙语课的老师是南美人，我觉得他很**帅**。午饭以后，我们在操场踢足球或者打篮球。最后一节我们上地理课。我觉得地理课非常好，因为我喜欢旅游。

帅 shuài	smart (look)

Period 1	Period 2	Break	Period 3	Period 4	Lunch	Period 5

2
Reading and Writing

Translate the following text from Chinese into English.

上星期，我们班上课的地方很奇怪。我们在礼堂上了音乐课和英语课，在校长办公室上了数学课。我们的班很大，有四十个学生，所以在体育馆上了历史课、汉语课和戏剧课。上物理课的只有十二个人，我们在科学教室上了物理课。我们的学校没有日语教室，所以在法语教室上了日语课。我们的日语老师是日本人。我很喜欢学习日语，就是因为不容易！

3
Writing

Copy the grid and write out the words in the box under the correct headings.

严厉　手工　经济　食堂　操场　亲切　办公室　生物
有趣　戏剧　图书馆　化学　好玩儿　走廊　教室

School subjects	Places around school	Adjectives to describe teachers

4
Listening

Listen to Xiaohong talking about school and answer the questions in English.

1 What doesn't Xiaohong particularly like about school?
2 What time does Xiaohong have to get up?
3 How does Xiaohong get to school?
4 Which teacher isn't strict?
5 What does Xiaohong think of homework?

5
Writing

Write down a word(s) for each gap. It can be a school subject, a place in school or an adjective. You can make the text as strange as you want. When you have finished, translate the passage into English.

我在中国上学。我的学校很 ___1___ 。我的班 ___2___ 。
我很喜欢上体育课,因为体育课的老师非常 ___3___ 。
我们有时候在 ___4___ 上体育课,有时候在 ___5___ 上课。
休息的时候,我和朋友常常在 ___6___ 吃水果。我们在
___7___ 上美术课。我不太喜欢美术课,因为老师很
___8___ 。我也不喜欢画画儿! 星期四最后一节课是
___9___ 课。我觉得那节课 ___10___ ,因为老师 ___11___ 。

6
Speaking and Listening

Write a short presentation using the comparative structure 比 to compare your teachers with each other and to compare the subjects you take at school. Present your speech to your classmates. Ask them questions about it to check that they have been listening.

EXAM TIP

To gain top marks, use a wide vocabulary, give your opinions and reasons for your opinions.

Some key expressions and words you could use:

I think/feel... 我觉得 / 想 / 认为....

Because... 因为...

Sometimes... 有时候...

Every day... 天天 / 每天

Example of a comparative sentence:

我认为数学比美术好,因为美术老师没意思。 I think Maths is better than Art, because the Art teacher is boring.

7
Writing

Imagine you have been appointed as the Headteacher of a new school. In Chinese, write a description of the new school. Here are some ideas of what you could include:

Layout

Which rooms would you put next to each other?
(Use the relative place words from Unit 1 of this chapter)
Would you have more than one playing field and gym or none at all?
Would you have a large or small canteen?

Timetable

What would a typical day's timetable be in your school?
When would you have breaks?
What time would the school day start and finish?
(You can use Units 1 and 3 of this chapter to help you form sentences about timetables.)

Comparisons

Write some sentences comparing the school that you have just designed to your school. You can compare the teachers, lessons, school design and timetable.

LISTENING

Warm-up! You are going to hear Xiaohua and her uncle talking about Xiaohua's school. Write down all the school subjects you hear in the passage.

Chose the correct answer for each question.

1 In which year of junior high school is Xiaohua?
   a first   **b** second   **c** third

2 How many boys are there in her class?
   a 13   **b** 14   **c** 15

3 Which subject did Xiaohua not mention?
   a geography   **b** physics   **c** maths

4 What is her favourite subject?
   a history   **b** English   **c** PE

5 What is the colour of her school uniform skirt?
   a white   **b** black   **c** blue

6 On which of these days does Xiaohua have homework?
   a Tuesdays   **b** Wednesdays   **c** Thursdays

TIP

- Go over the questions before listening. Think about the type of words you need to listen out for in order to answer the questions.
- Eliminate obvious incorrect answers first.
- Listen for key words, which are usually stressed and pronounced louder than other words.
- Pay attention to the information concerning who, what, when, where, how and why.
- Write down important words while listening.

GRAMMAR: 几 and 多少

几 is only used for numbers less than ten, while 多少 can be used for both large and smaller numbers. For example:
你有几个哥哥？
中国有多少人？
你们学校有多少学生？
几 must be followed by a measure word but for 多少 the measure word is optional.
For example: 几块钱？多少钱？

READING

Read the passage about Deng Xiaoping. Note down the words you are not familiar with and try to work out their meaning.

邓小平5岁的时候, 老师给他起的名字叫邓希贤。他的脸圆圆的, 个子不高, 又聪明又好学, 写得字也很漂亮, 老师很喜欢他。有一天、天气很不好, 妈妈说, 雨太大, 不要去上学了。邓小平说："不行, 我不能旷课。"16岁的时候, 邓小平跟同学一起去法国, 他们是坐船去的, 39天才到法国。在那里, 他先学习法语, 后来去工厂上班。他回国以后, 为他的国家和人民做了很多事。

DENG XIAOPING

Deng Xiaoping (1904–1997) was a member of the Chinese Communist Party from an early age. He played a major role in the development of the People's Republic and is generally known as the architect of China's 'reform and opening up' campaign after 1978. He is credited with advancing China to become one of the fastest growing economies in the world, and with raising the standard of living of her people.

Reading

Choose the correct answer for each question.

1 Who gave Deng Xiaoping his name when he was small?
   a his father   **b** his mother   **c** his teacher

2 Deng Xiaoping had
   a a round face   **b** big eyes   **c** a straight nose

3 How could you describe his personality?
   a optimistic   **b** fond of learning **c** gentle

4 His mother didn't want him to go to school one day, because it was
   a raining   **b** windy   **c** snowing

5 With whom did he go to France?
   a his parents   **b** his classmates **c** his friends

6 What did he do in France initially?
   a travel   **b** study   **c** work

TIP

How to improve your understanding of a passage
- Spend some time working out the title or the opening sentence since this will give you a clue as to what the text is about.
- Find connecting words and phrases. These join sentences in a logical way. For example, showing cause and effect (因为…所以) or a contrast (但是).
- Look at the sentence structure, especially when you come across a long sentence – don't jump to conclusions.
- Distinguish between facts and opinions.

GRAMMAR: 'when' and 'both'

- …的时候 is equivalent to 'when'. The difference is that the clause that follows 'when' in English comes *before* 的时候 in Chinese.
For example:
我年轻的时候 = when I was young
他来的时候 = when he came

- 又…又 is similar to 'both…and' except that it can only be used to connect two adjectives.
For example:
我又饿又累。= I am both hungry and tired.
(but *not* 又老师又学生 'both teachers and students')

口语 kǒu yǔ Speaking

Preparing for a speaking task (presentation)

TASK AND PREPARATION

You are going to visit a school in China. Prepare a presentation about your school to give when you are there. You could include:

- Basic information about your school
- School facilities
- Main features of your school
- A typical school day
- Extra-curricular activities available in your school
- How students get to school
- School uniform
- Any school link in China
- Your education plans for the future.

1
Listening

You are going to hear a presentation. Below are some of the sentences Kate uses to give basic information about her school. Guess how the sentence halves will match up, and then listen to Part 1 of the presentation and check your answers.

1 最小的学生 …   4 女老师 …   a … 回家。   d … 十一岁。

2 最大的学生 …   5 校长每天很早 …   b … 少。   e … 多。

3 男老师 …   6 校长每天很晚 …   c … 来学校。   f … 十八岁。

2
Listening

In Part 2 of her presentation Kate tries to make it easier to remember the school facilities by grouping together two types of the following facilities:

- 馆   • 场   • 堂

Predict which facilities she includes, and then listen to check your predictions.

3
Listening

Kate also uses 'repetition' to help her remember – putting together sentences with the same structure. Try to work out how Kate will say the following sentences which share the same structure in Chinese, and then listen to check.

1 We go to school five days a week.   2 Everyday we have five lessons.

4
Listening

Kate uses the verb phrase 骑自行车 for 'by bicycle' as in 'go to school by bicycle'. The verb phrase goes before the main verb of the sentence 上学 ('go to school'). Find out from the presentation how to say the following sentences.

1 They go to school on foot.   2 They go to school by school bus.

5
Listening

In Chinese, clothes and accessories are so different that they need two different verbs for 'to wear'. Match 1–3 with a–c. Listen to Part 3 and check.

1 穿   a 黑色的皮鞋

2 戴   b 蓝色的外套

3 脚上穿   c 红色的领带

6
Listening

Kate takes every opportunity to express her personal opinions. Listen to the questions and answers on Kate's presentation and fill in the gaps according to the English clues in brackets.

我认为 ___1___ 穿校服。
(Everybody should wear school uniform.)

我觉得走路上学 ___2___ 。
(Walking to school is healthy.)

学校食堂的饭菜 ___3___ 。
(The food in the dining hall is not bad.)

中文和日文 ___4___ 。
(Neither Chinese nor Japanese is easy.)

我觉得做作业 ___5___ 。
(It is important to do homework.)

我认为我们学校 ___6___ 。
(Our school is the best school in town.)

YOUR TURN NOW

Prepare a presentation about your school.

- You can write down your presentation in pinyin. Highlight tone marks so that you can practise your presentation with the right tones. Maybe you could find a Chinese native speaker to practise with.
- Make yourself a prompt sheet (A5 size, containing no more than 30 English words or up to 50 Chinese characters, which can be written in pinyin if you prefer). Practise your presentation until you are fluent.
- Record your presentation and play it to your partner. Discuss with your partner what questions the teacher could ask you about your presentation.

Award each other one star, two stars or three stars for each of the following categories:

- pronunciation
- confidence and fluency
- range of time frames

- variety of vocabulary
- using sentences with more complex structures
- taking the initiative

Note down what you need to do next time to improve your performance.

ResultsPlus
Maximise your marks

To aim for a **Grade C** try to include the following:

- take every opportunity to give personal opinions. You can use 我觉得… or 我认为… if you like.
- try to use different time frames. Kate uses both past and future time frames when she talks about her experience of learning Japanese and Chinese.

If you are aiming higher than a **Grade C** you need to:

- produce comprehensive answers. Note how Kate talks about what she thinks of homework.
- always justify your opinion and further develop your answer to include other relevant points. Listen to where Kate explains why she likes her DT teacher.

To produce your best spoken Chinese and to aim for an **A or A*,** you need to :

- convey complex ideas. When complex structures are difficult to handle, try using a series of simpler sentences which together convey a complex idea. This can reduce hesitation and help to make the presentation flow. For example, 日文老师是一个女老师, 很年轻, 也很漂亮。做老师以前, 她在伦敦大学读书, 学了四年的日文, 她的日文非常好。
- use a variety of adverbs to make your description more vivid and interesting. Kate uses three different adverbs in this short section of the presentation: 她工作很忙, 每天很早来学校, 很晚回家。

写作 xiě zuò Writing

Preparing for an extended writing task about school

PREPARATION

1
Reading

Warm Up! Tell a partner three things in Chinese about the school you attend.

Read the article about Peking University High School and complete Activities 2–5.

> 　　去年夏天，我去北京大学附属中学学了四个星期的中文课。走进校园的南门就能看到有两排参天大树，让人感觉冬暖夏凉。学校有两座六层的教学楼，它们在校园的北边，还有一座两层楼在校园的南边，离南门很近，是办公楼。学校的图书馆是新的，在校园的最北部。图书馆是老师和学生们最爱去的地方，因为那里可以看书，上网，非常方便。在校园的西南是学生宿舍和食堂的大楼。学校有3000多学生，因为学校的饭菜很好吃，所以他们都在学校吃午饭。教学楼和办公楼中间有一个小花园，也有一个很大的篮球场。学生们都说："北大附中是一个成长的好地方。" 我将来很想有机会去北大附中学习中文。

2
Reading

Find the Chinese characters in the text which mean:

1 campus
2 classroom building
3 office building
4 library
5 basketball court
6 garden
7 canteen
8 dormitory

3
Reading

Three ways of describing location are used in this article – 在、有 and 是. Find and copy out a sentence using each.

4
Reading

Using the information in the text, make a sketch of the school campus.

5
Reading

Work on some descriptive phrases. Find the characters for the following:

1 two rows of big trees towering in the sky
2 warm in summer and cool in winter
3 the students' favourite place
4 a good place to grow up in

YOUR TURN NOW

Your teacher has asked you to write a short article about your partner school for the school magazine. Write between 100 and 150 characters, about half the length of the article opposite. The article concentrates on describing the location (since that is the trickiest part), but your writing could include information about some of the following:

- location of the school and description of the site
- the school day
- subjects studied by the students
- extra-curricular activities
- school uniform
- something that happened last year
- something that will happen next year

TIP

Use the vocabulary in this chapter to help you. Make sure the article doesn't just become a list by using comments and opinions as well as descriptive sentences. Structure your text; organise your writing into paragraphs.

CHECK

Check the characters and word order. Make sure that you have not accidentally missed out components of characters that you know well. Make sure that you remember that 都 and 也 come directly before a verb.

ResultsPlus
Maximise your marks

To aim for a **Grade C** you need to:
- use a variety of structures. In the article, the author refers to location using:
  a sentences with 在,是 and 有;
  b sentences with 离...很近/远

To aim higher than a **Grade C** you need to:
- make sure the word order is correct, for example the difference between the position of 'time when' before the verb and 'time how long' after the verb when talking about when a lesson starts and how long it lasts
- make sure you use connecting words. Even simple ones like 也 enable you to build up a more complex sentence
- use different time frames. The task you are set for your controlled assessment may not obviously require different time frames but in any task you must demonstrate that you can use past, present and future time frames

To produce your best written Chinese and to aim for an **A* grade** you need to :
- show a high level of accuracy in the characters you write. Test yourself regularly on the characters you will need to use to write this assessment
- prepare some more advanced descriptive words to use, for example light/dark blue uniform, words such as 好吃 or 方便 which are in the article. Try to use your vocabulary in an imaginative and interesting way
- express some opinions about your school

科目 kē mù Subjects

我最喜欢的课是...	wǒ zuì xǐ huan de kè shì...	My favourite subject is...	化学	huà xué	chemistry
			经济	jīng jì	economics
数学	shù xué	maths	手工	shǒu gōng	design & technology
科学	kē xué	science	电脑	diàn nǎo	ICT
历史	lì shǐ	history	今天第一节课是...	jīn tiān dì yī jié kè shì...	Today's first period is...
地理	dì lǐ	geography			
汉语	hàn yǔ	Chinese	戏剧课以后我们上...课。	xì jù kè yǐ hòu wǒ men shàng... kè	After drama we have a ... lesson.
英语	yīng yǔ	English			
体育	tǐ yù	PE	昨天我上了化学课。	zuó tiān wǒ shàng le huà xué kè	Yesterday I had chemistry.
戏剧	xì jù	drama			
物理	wù lǐ	physics	你喜欢不喜欢...课？	nǐ xǐ huan bù xǐ huan...kè?	Do you like... lessons?
生物	shēng wù	biology			

我觉得... wǒ jué de... My opinion (I think...)

我喜欢...	wǒ xǐ huan...	I like...	容易	róng yì	easy
我很喜欢...	wǒ hěn xǐ huan...	I really like...	难	nán	difficult
我爱...	wǒ ài...	I love...	老师很亲切。	lǎo shī hěn qīn qiè.	The teacher is very kind.
我不太喜欢...	wǒ bú tài xǐ huan...	I don't really like...			
我很不喜欢...	wǒ hěn bù xǐ huan...	I really don't like/I hate	严格	yán gé	strict
			有趣	yǒu qù	funny
因为...	yīn wéi...	because (it's)...	友好	yǒu hǎo	friendly
有意思	yǒu yì si	interesting	好玩儿	hǎo wánr	amusing
没（有）意思	méi (yǒu) yì si	boring	帅	shuài	smart (look)

我的学校 wǒ de xué xiào My school

有一千五百个学生。	yǒu yì qiān wǔ bǎi ge xué shēng.	There are 1,500 students.	教室	jiào shì	classroom
			卫生间	wèi shēng jiān	toilet
我是十年级的学生。	wǒ shì shí nián jí de xué shēng.	I'm a Year 10 student.	图书馆	tú shū guǎn	library
			走廊	zǒu láng	corridor
我们学校有大...	wǒ men xué xiào yǒu dà...	Our school has a big...	校长办公室	xiào zhǎng bàn gōng shì	Headteacher's office
学校的礼堂比较小。	xué xiào de lǐ táng bǐ jiào xiǎo.	The school's assembly hall is quite small.	在图书馆对面有卫生间	zài tú shū guǎn duì miàn yǒu wèi shēng jiān.	There's a toilet opposite the library.
体育馆	tǐ yù guǎn	gym	在...左边有...	zài...zuǒ bian yǒu...	To the left of the... there's a...
操场	cāo chǎng	sports ground	在...右边有...	zài...yòu bian yǒu...	To the right of the... there's a...
食堂	shí táng	canteen			
礼堂	lǐ táng	assembly hall	我们学校没有...	wǒ men xué xiào méi yǒu...	Our school doesn't have a...
办公室	bàn gōng shì	office			

学校比较 xué xiào bǐ jiào Comparing schools

他的学校比我的大。	tā de xué xiào bǐ wǒ de dà.	His school is bigger than mine.	多/少	duō/shǎo	lots; many; much/ few; little
我做的作业比他做的少。	wǒ zuò de zuò yè bǐ tā zuò de shǎo.	I do less homework than him.	好吃/难吃	hǎo chī/nán chī	tasty/disgusting
大/小	dà/xiǎo	big/small	长/短	cháng/duǎn	long/short

校服 xiào fú School uniform

我们的学校有/没有校服。	wǒ men de xué xiào yǒu/méi yǒu xiào fú.	Our school has/ doesn't have a school uniform.	领带	lǐng dài	tie
			袜子	wà zi	socks
			鞋子	xié zi	shoes
女学生穿…	nǚ xué shēng chuān…	Girls wear…	皮鞋	pí xié	leather shoes
男学生穿…	nán xué shēng chuān…	Boys wear…	运动鞋	yùn dòng xié	trainers
夹克	jiā kè	blazer	我觉得我们的校服好看/不好看。	wǒ jué de wǒ men de xiào fú hěn hǎo kàn/bù hǎo kàn.	I think our uniform looks good/looks awful.
衬衣	chèn yī	shirt			
裙子	qún zi	skirt	我不喜欢穿校服。	wǒ bù xǐ huan chuān xiào fú.	I don't like wearing school uniform.
裤子	kù zi	trousers			
T恤	T xù	T shirt			

复习 Review – Sports and hobbies

1
Reading

Read the texts about Li Daming, Li Xiaoming, Liam, Lulu and Chrissy. Match each child with an activity.

 a  b  c  d 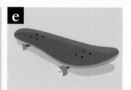 e

我叫李大明, 我有一个双胞胎弟弟, 他叫李小明, 我们都喜欢运动。我喜欢打网球, 我弟弟喜欢跑步。

我叫 Liam, 我喜欢运动。我最喜欢玩儿滑板。我一般下午玩儿滑板。我妹妹不喜欢运动。Lulu 喜欢看书, Chrissy 喜欢看电视。

双胞胎 shuāng bāo tāi	twin(s)	玩儿滑板 wánr huá bǎn	to skateboard	一般 yī bān	generally; habitually

2
Speaking

Interview your classmates to find out which sport is the most popular. Copy and fill in the grid.

	喜欢	不喜欢
打球	|||	
跑步		
玩儿滑板		

打球 dǎ qiú	to play ball games

你喜欢什么运动?

你不喜欢什么运动?

3
Writing

Write a short paragraph based on your survey in Activity 2.

For example, if the survey shows that five people like to play ball games, you write:

五个人喜欢打球。

4

Reading

Read the sentences on different topics.
Match the sentences (1–6) with the correct topics (a–f).

a pets	b hobbies	c colours	d drinks	e subjects	f food

1　我喜欢看书，不喜欢看电视。
2　我喜欢小狗，不喜欢小猫。
3　我喜欢吃肉，不喜欢吃鱼。
4　早上我喜欢喝茶，晚上我喜欢喝水。
5　我喜欢红色，不喜欢白色。
6　我喜欢英文，不喜欢音乐。

5

Listening

A boy, Li Ming, and a girl, Liu Hong, are having a telephone conversation. Listen and choose the correct answer for each question.

在 zài	(before a verb) indicating an action in progress
不行 bù xíng	no (for refusing)

1　What is Li Ming doing?
a　Li Ming is playing on the computer.
b　Li Ming is playing with his younger sister.

2　Why did Liu Hong ring Li Ming?
a　Liu Hong wants Li Ming to go to the cinema with her.
b　Liu Hong wants Li Ming to go swimming with her.

3　Why can't Li Ming go out with Liu Hong?
a　Li Ming has to stay with his younger sister at home.
b　Li Ming is not interested in the suggestion.

6

Reading

Read the text about Wang Hong's pets and answer the questions in Chinese.

王红很喜欢宠物，她家有一只小猫，一只小狗，两只小鸟和三条金鱼。王红家的小猫喜欢看电视，小狗喜欢跑步，小鸟喜欢唱歌，金鱼喜欢游泳。

条 tiáo	measure word for fish and other long narrow things, e.g. trousers, skirts, roads, snakes, etc.

1　王红家有什么宠物？
2　王红家的宠物有什么爱好？

1 运动中心 yùn dòng zhōng xīn The sports centre

Talking about sports facilities

1 **Listening**

You will hear six verb phrases. Match the characters on the left with those on the right to form the verb phrases. Then match the phrases with the pictures.

1 游 yóu   **a** 步 bù

2 骑 qí   **b** 足球 zú qiú

3 玩儿 wánr   **c** 网球 wǎng qiú

4 打 dǎ   **d** 自行车 zì xíng chē

5 跑 pǎo   **e** 泳 yǒng

6 踢 tī   **f** 滑板 huá bǎn

GRAMMAR: To play

In English 'to play' can be used with any ball games, e.g. 'to play football', 'to play table tennis', etc. In Chinese the verb used for 'to play' is different for some ball games. 踢 (tī), 'to kick', is used to refer to football, but 打 (dǎ), 'to hit', for table tennis. For example:
打乒乓球 = to play table tennis (literally 'to hit a table tennis ball')
踢足球 = to play football (literally 'to kick a football')

可以 kě yǐ	may; can
交 jiāo	to make (friends)

2 **Speaking**

Match the questions to the answers a–d and then answer the questions in full sentences. Then ask your classmates questions 1–4. Substitute football with another sport if you want to.

1	When?	你一般什么时候踢足球？	**a**	同学
2	Who?	你一般跟谁一起踢足球？	**b**	星期六上午
3	Where?	你一般去哪儿踢足球？	**c**	因为踢足球可以交朋友
4	Why?	你为什么喜欢踢足球？	**d**	公园

GRAMMAR: Question words

In English 'wh' question words (when, who, where, why, what, etc.) usually go at the beginning of the sentence. In Chinese this is not necessarily the case.

For example: They can be at the beginning, e.g. 谁去？ (Who goes?)

They can be in the middle, e.g. 你为什么喜欢打网球？ (Why do you like playing tennis?)

They can be at the end, e.g. 他是谁？ (Who is he?)

EXAM TIP

When you answer a 'wh' question in Chinese (except 'why' questions), you can often use the same structure as the question sentence. You simply replace the question word with the answer, for example:
你是哪国人？ 我是英国人。

3
Listening

Listen to the information about the opening hours of a swimming pool. Write down the days of the week in English and note the times.

4
Reading

Read the conversation. Work out on which day of the week this conversation might have taken place (using the information from Activity 3).

A: 我们去游泳, 好吗？

B: 现在几点了？

A: 两点一刻。

B: 太晚了, 游泳池关门了。

| 晚 wǎn | late |
| 关门 guān mén | to close (*literally* door) |

GRAMMAR: The use of 了

了 (le) can also be used at the end of a sentence to indicate a new situation, progression or a change of state.

For example:

现在三点了。　　It is 3 o'clock now. (It wasn't some time ago.)

游泳池关门了。　The swimming pool has closed. (It was open earlier.)

5
Reading

Read the text and complete it with the correct times and prices. Use the English leaflet to help you.

运动中心从星期一到星期天每天都开放。星期 __a__ 到星期 __b__ 的开放时间是早上六点半到晚上九点半, 星期天是上午 __c__ 点到晚上 __d__ 点。运动中心有健身房、游泳池、羽毛球场和足球场, 运动中心内还可以打乒乓球。健身一次 __e__ 英镑, 游泳一个小时 __f__ 英镑, 打羽毛球、打乒乓球、踢足球都是一个小时 __g__ 英镑, 学生半价。

中心 zhōng xīn	centre
开放 kāi fàng	to open
时间 shí jiān	time
健身房 jiàn shēn fáng	gym
场 chǎng	ground
次 cì	*measure word for 'occurrence', 'time'*
英镑 yīng bàng	pound sterling
半价 bàn jià	half price

Sports Centre

Monday – Saturday
6.30am – 9.30pm
Sunday 9.00am – 8.00pm

Gym
£6.00 per visit

Swimming pool
£2.00 per hour

Badminton,
Football
& Table Tennis
£3.00 per hour

* Students half price

6
Writing

Design and write a leaflet in Chinese based on what you have read in Activity 5. Use the English leaflet in Activity 5 as a guide.

| 一次 | per visit |
| 一个小时 | per hour |

Frequency and duration of activities

1
Reading

Match the activities with the pictures.
Two pictures are missing.

上网 shàng wǎng	to surf the Internet
比赛 bǐ sài	match, competition

1 打电话   2 踢足球   3 骑自行车   4 玩儿滑板
5 上网   6 游泳   7 跑步   8 看足球比赛

2
Listening

Write down numbers 1–8. Listen to the eight sentences. Write the English for each activity you hear. (1–8)

周末 zhōu mò	weekend
很少 hěn shǎo	rarely; infrequently

3
Writing

Write sentences about the activities in Activity 1.

Write the activities you do every day next to   每天…
Write the activities you often do next to   常常…
Write the activities you rarely do next to   很少…
Write the activities you do at the weekend next to 周末…

4
Speaking

Interview your partner. Find out if you take part in similar activities.

你每天 (常常、很少、周末) 做什么？

GRAMMAR: Word order – frequency

As with time and manner words, frequency words such as 每天,
常常, and 很少 go before the verb in a sentence, following the pattern
subject + frequency + action.
For example:
我每天跑步。   I go for a run every day.
我和妈妈常常一起上网。 Mum and I often surf the Internet together.
他很少看电视。   He very rarely watches TV.

5 Read the speech bubbles and arrange them into a dialogue.

Reading

a 你周末也跑步吗？

c 你周末一般几点起床？

e 六点半起床？

b 我一般六点半起床。

d 对，六点半。我每天早上跑一个小时步。

f 我周末也跑步。

GRAMMAR: Word order – duration of time

一个小时 (yī gè xiǎoshí) is a time expression which shows duration. In Chinese such expressions come after the verb and before the object of the verb (where there is an object). For example:

跑一个小时(的)步 to jog for an hour   打半个小时 (的) 乒乓球 to play table tennis for half an hour

---

6 Write down 1–5. Listen to five people talking about family activities.

Listening Make a note in English of how long each person does their activity. (1–5)

EXAM TIP

Examiners will be impressed if you can demonstrate your knowledge and use of the number 'two' in Chinese. Be aware that when 'two' is followed by a measure word, the usual 二 (èr) becomes 两 (liǎng), for example, 两个小时 (two hours).

钓鱼 diào yú	to go fishing
弹 tán	to play (a musical instrument)
吉他 jí tā	guitar

---

7 Interview your classmates about the following

Speaking activities: 踢足球、打网球、游泳、钓鱼、弹吉他. Make a chart to record your results. Use the questions below. (If you don't like doing a certain activity, simply say 我不喜欢…)

名字	你喜欢 ……… 吗？	你一般什么时候 ……… ？	多长时间？
Tom	踢足球	我一般周末踢足球。	我一般踢一个小时。

| 多长时间 duō cháng shí jiān | how long? |

GRAMMAR: Asking how long

多长时间 is useful to ask about duration of time. It can make a question by itself in certain contexts. It can also be part of a question sentence, coming in between the verb and the object. For example:

星期天你玩儿多长时间滑板？ How long do you skateboard on Sundays?

---

8 Write a short paragraph about your classmates'

Writing hobbies. Use the framework to help you. Replace the underlined words to make your own version.

王东喜欢打网球。他每个星期天都打网球。

他一般打 一个小时 网球。

3 爱好和兴趣 ài hào hé xìng qù Hobbies and interests

Talking about hobbies and interests

1
Listening

Listen to and read the Chinese rap. Find the words in the rap to match the meanings of these words:

we three	very	with

together	short (height)	short (length)

练 liàn	to practise
体操 tǐ cāo	gymnastics
参观 cān guān	to visit
博物馆 bó wù guǎn	museum

你是我的朋，
你是我的友，
我们三个都是好朋友。
朋友他很胖，
朋友他很瘦，
我跟朋友一起踢足球。
朋友他很矮，
朋友他很高，
我跟朋友一起练体操。
朋友头发长，
朋友头发短，
我跟朋友参观博物馆。

2
Reading

Read the sentences about Wang Long. Match the items in his schoolbag to his hobbies. For example the first one is 1c.

王龙有什么爱好？

1 他的书包里有游泳衣。	a 他喜欢看足球比赛。
2 他的书包里有运动鞋。	b 他喜欢看书。
3 他的书包里有iPod。	c 他喜欢游泳。
4 他的书包里有球票。	d 他喜欢打网球。
5 他的书包里有小说。	e 他喜欢听音乐。

票 piào	ticket
小说 xiǎo shuō	novel

3
Listening

Listen to the dialogue and write down the correct characters for each blank.

A: 小文明天过生日，我应该送他什么礼物呢？

B: 他有什么爱好？

A: 他喜欢 ___1___ 。

B: 送他 ___2___ 吧。

过 guò	to celebrate (birthdays and festivals)
应该 yīng gāi	should
送 sòng	to give
礼物 lǐ wù	gift, present
吧 ba	(see grammar box)

GRAMMAR: 吧 Sentences

吧 (ba) can be used at the end of a sentence to make a suggestion to somebody to do something. For example:
我们星期六参观博物馆吧。 Let's visit the museum on Saturday.

4
Speaking

Ask for advice about what birthday present to give to Xiaowen. Follow the example dialogue in Activity 3 and use the pictures and notepad to replace the blanks to make five short dialogues.

小文喜欢 ...

音乐 CD ？　　小说 ？
运动鞋 ？　　游泳衣 ？
足球票 ？

5
Reading

Read the quiz and choose the answer that applies to you.

1　放学回家...	2　周末...	3　过生日...
a 上网跟朋友聊天	**a** 去朋友家玩儿	**a** 请朋友来家玩儿
b 去运动中心游泳	**b** 去公园玩儿滑板	**b** 跟爸爸去看比赛
c 去卧室听音乐	**c** 在家看小说	**c** 去参观博物馆

Count how many **a**, **b** and **c** you have to find out what kind of person you are.

Mostly **a**　你喜欢交朋友
Mostly **b**　你喜欢做运动
Mostly **c**　你喜欢安静

GRAMMAR: Word order – coming and going

去(qù) and 来 (lái) are verbs of movement. When stating the purpose of going or coming, you can use the structure *subject* + 去 or 来 + (*somewhere*) + *action*. For example:

我去公园玩儿滑板。　　I go to the park to skateboard.
我们去打篮球。　　　　We go to play basketball.
我朋友来我家吃晚饭。　My friends come to my house for supper.

聊天 liáo tiān	to chat
请 qǐng	to invite
安静 ān jìng	quiet

6
Writing

Write a short paragraph about how you celebrated your birthday. Use the framework to help you.

我...月...号过生日。...(下午; 晚上)... (我跟...一起去...; 我请朋友来家玩儿)。
他们送了我很多生日礼物。
我喜欢...(看书; 听音乐; 打网球; 看电影), 所以...
(爸爸; 妈妈; 姐姐; 朋友们) 送我...(小说; 音乐CD;
网球拍; 电影DVD)。

Talking about keeping fit

Reading

Read the statements about Li Dahong's favourite things. Match the statements with the pictures.

1 我喜欢唱歌。我会唱中文歌, 也会唱英文歌。
2 我也喜欢打太极拳。我每天都打太极拳。
3 我还喜欢健身。我星期一和星期三去健身房。
4 我最喜欢吃烤鸭。在北京的时候, 我天天吃烤鸭。

| 太极拳 tài jí quán | tai ch'i |
| 还 hái | also, in addition |

a   b   c   d

2
Listening

Listen to the dialogue and identify the missing words. Write these in pinyin while listening and then write the characters later.

放学回家以后, 你最想做什么?

a 我最想在家看电视。
b 我最想跟朋友去 ___1___ 。
c 我最想 ___2___ 跟朋友聊天。
d 我最想 ___3___ 跟朋友聊天。
e 我最想给朋友 ___4___ 。
f 我最想跟朋友去 ___5___ 。

羽毛球 yǔ máo qiú	badminton
给 gěi	to; for; to give
发邮件 fā yóu jiàn	to send emails
遛狗 liù gǒu	to walk a dog

GRAMMAR: Would like to

想 (xiǎng) literally means 'to think', but when it appears in front of other verbs it means 'would like to' or 'want to'.
For example:
我想吃烤鸭。 I would like to/I want to eat roast duck.

3
Speaking

Interview your classmates.

放学回家以后, 你最想做什么?

Record your results in a chart.
Report back to the class.

___ 最想…。

EXAM TIP

To really impress the examiner and aim for higher marks, use superlatives such as 最 to state what you enjoy doing most.

Writing

Identify the missing words by looking at the pictures. Then write the Chinese characters for those words.

a 我下午三点一刻放学, _____1_____。

b 回家以后, 我喜欢 _____2_____、看电视。

我一般发半个小时邮件,看一个小时电视。

c 六点半吃 _____3_____,

d 晚饭以后, 我去卧室看 _____4_____,

我喜欢看小说。

e 有的时候我还给朋友 _____5_____,

我朋友也常常给我打电话。

f 我一般 ___6___ 睡觉。

 Reading

Read the text about Li Dahai and his grandfather. Answer the questions in English.

我叫李大海, 今年十五岁。我爱去健身房。
健身房对面是超级市场, 先买东西, 然后
健身, 很方便。跑步的时候, 我可以听音乐,
很有意思。

我是李大海的爷爷。我不去健身房,
我去公园。早上公园不要门票。跳一会儿舞,
打一会儿太极拳, 然后跟朋友一起喝茶、
聊天, 很舒服。

a Where does Li Dahai go to keep fit?

b Name the two reasons why he prefers to go there.

c Where does Li Dahai's grandfather go to keep fit?

d Name the two reasons why his grandfather prefers to go there.

超级市场 chāo jí shì chǎng	supermarket
先 xiān	first
门票 mén piào	entrance ticket
一会儿 yí huìr	a short while
舒服 shū fu	comfortable

GRAMMAR: First... then...

先... 然后... (xiān ... rán hòu...) means 'first (I do one action)..., and then (I do something else)... ' Both parts of the structure are followed directly by a verb. The structure is used to indicate the sequence of a series of actions. For example:

我先看电视, 然后吃晚饭。 First I watch TV, and then I have supper.

我先去北京, 然后去上海。 First I go to Beijing, and then I go to Shanghai.

 Writing

Write a paragraph about what you usually do at home after school.

回家以后,	(After getting home,)
我先..., 然后...。	(first I ..., and then I ...)
我有的时候..., 有的时候...。	(I sometimes ..., sometimes ...)

5 奥运会 ào yùn huì The Olympic Games
Talking about sports in more detail

Listening

Listen to the passage. Choose the right answer for each question.

1 奥运会每几年举行一次？
   四年还是五年？

2 每次奥运会一般有多少天？
   十六天还是二十九天？

3 北京奥运会是哪一年？
   2007年还是2008年？

4 开幕式是哪一天？
   7月7号还是8月8号？

5 开幕式北京时间几点开始？
   晚上6点还是晚上8点？

6 在北京奥运会上，英国最年轻的运动员多大？
   十四岁还是十八岁？

奥运会 ào yùn huì	Olympic Games
举行 jǔ xíng	to hold
开幕式 kāi mù shì	opening ceremony
开始 kāi shǐ	to start
年轻 nián qīng	young
运动员 yùn dòng yuán	athlete

Reading

Read the text and answer the questions in English.

　　2012年奥运会在伦敦举行。这将是伦敦第三次主办奥运会。2012年的奥运会有一百九十多个国家和地区参加。英国运动员在上次奥运会得了十九块金牌。

　　英国的游泳和自行车项目都非常好，这次奥运会英国想得更多的金牌。因为伦敦2012年有奥运会，所以现在更多的英国人喜欢运动。

第三次 dì sān cì	the third time
主办 zhǔ bàn	to host
参加 cān jiā	to participate in
得 dé	to win; to gain
块 kuài	*measure word for pieces, e.g. money, medals, cake, etc.*
金牌 jīn pái	gold medal
项目 xiàng mù	event
更多 gèng duō	even more

1 How many times have the Olympic Games been held in London before 2012?

2 Approximately how many countries and regions will take part in the 2012 Olympic Games?

3 How many gold medals did Team GB win in the 2008 Olympic Games?

4 Find the two events in the text at which Team GB are very strong.

5 What is the impact of the Olympic Games on the life of the British people?

GRAMMAR: Measure word 次

The measure word for 'occasion', 'occurrence', 'time' is 次 (cì).
For example:

一次	once (one time)	这次	this time
两次	twice (two times)	上次	last time
每次	every time	下次	next time

GRAMMAR: Using 第

第一 (dì yī), as in 第一节课 (the first lesson), can go before 次 and form a phrase 第一次, and it means 'the first time'. In the same structure, 'the second time' is 第二次 and 'the third time' is 第三次.

EXAM TIP

Measure words are an important element of Chinese grammar. The most commonly used measure word is 个. In the writing exam it is better to use the measure word 个 for everything than not to use any measure word at all. For example, in case you cannot remember the measure word for 'a gold medal', which is 一块金牌, it is better to say 一个金牌 than to say 一金牌.

3 Writing Read the texts about football and basketball. In Chinese, write down what Li Dong and Alfie Roberts think of the ball games and what they think of each other.

李东觉得…
Alfie Roberts 觉得…

我不喜欢看中国的足球比赛，中国的足球比赛没意思。我喜欢看英格兰的足球比赛。我很喜欢看 Roberts 踢足球，我觉得他是英格兰最好的足球运动员。

我喜欢踢足球，我对打篮球也很有兴趣。我喜欢看李东打篮球。李东跑步跑得不快，可是他的个子比我高，我觉得他是中国最好的篮球运动员。

英格兰 yīng gé lán	England
得 de	linking word between a verb and an adverb
快 kuài	fast

4 Speaking Tell your partner about a sports personality you know about. You can use the texts in Activity 3 as a guide.

我觉得 …

口语 kǒu yǔ Speaking

Preparing for a speaking task (picture-based discussion)

TASK AND PREPARATION

Prepare a discussion based on a photograph of a hobby you enjoy.
You could include information about the following:

- What the photo shows
- When you started doing the activity and what made you begin it
- When and where you do the activity, and with whom
- Why you enjoy the activity
- Where you buy the clothing/equipment for the activity
- Whether you expect to continue with it in the future and why

1
Writing
Warm-up! Choose a photograph showing one of your hobbies. Write down some key words to remind you of things you could include in a discussion.

2
Writing
Make a list of eight questions which you think you could be asked about your hobby.

3
Listening
You will hear a model conversation between Peter and his teacher, based on the photograph above. Look at the following phrases.
For which of the bullet points in the task above do you think each phrase will be used?

1 上小学   2 在家里   3 中国功夫电影   4 学功夫   5 我爷爷

4
Listening
Listen to the first and second parts of the conversation and fill in the gaps.

1 照片上你在做什么?
我 ___a___ 学功夫。

2 这张照片是在哪儿拍的?
这张照片 ___b___ 在中国拍 ___c___ 。

3 你是从什么时候开始喜欢学功夫的?
从上小学 ___d___ 时候开始, 我很喜欢电影里 ___e___ 功夫表演。

4 你在哪儿学功夫?
我 ___f___ ___g___ ___h___ 跟我 ___i___ 学功夫。

5 你为什么喜欢学功夫?
___j___ ___k___ 学功夫, ___l___ ___m___ 我的身体很好。 ___n___ ___o___ 喜欢功夫,
我在网上交了很多喜欢功夫 ___p___ 中国朋友。

5
Listening
Listen to the second and third parts of the conversation and answer the questions.

1 When talking about where he learns Kung Fu, Peter includes both 'where' and 'with whom'. Which does he say first?

2 What is the reason he gives for not being able to learn Kung Fu everyday?

3 In his answer about when he learns Kung Fu, Peter uses a measure word twice. What is it, and for what nouns?

4 Note down in Chinese the sentence structure the interviewer uses when asking 'Have you thought of going to China to learn Kung Fu?'

5 What are the two things Peter says he wants to do when he goes to China?

6 Before each of the two things he wants to do, he uses a word starting with the character '一'. What is it?

7 Write down an example sentence in Chinese for the present, past and future timeframes.

YOUR TURN NOW

Prepare a picture–based discussion on a hobby.
• Use the ResultsPlus and the work you have done in Activities 1–5 to help you.
• Think of the questions you could be asked about your hobby and try to think about how you would answer them.
• Check the tones of individual words and try to get the tones right when you practise.

ResultsPlus
Maximise your marks

To aim for a **Grade C** you need to:
• talk about the past and the future as well as the present. When you do so, make sure you use the right time words. Also make sure you use the correct suffixes after the verbs, if necessary. Peter uses 年轻的时候 to indicate the past and 现在 to indicate the present. He also used 过 after the verb 学 to indicate past experience.
• try to expand the phrases a bit. Peter says 'Learning Kung Fu is my favourite hobby' (学功夫是我最大的爱好) instead of simply 'Learning Kung Fu is my hobby' (学功夫是我的爱好).

If you are aiming for a grade **higher than Grade C** you need to:
• try to use some more complex expressions. Peter uses the expression 是…的 as in 这张照片是在中国拍的. The 是…的 expression can help to emphasise the part immediately after the 是, for example 在中国. Peter uses the 的 structure a few times. For example, 上小学的时候; 去年去中国的时候; 喜欢功夫的中国朋友.
• be prepared to respond to more complex questions forms. Peter responds well to 你有没有想过去中国学功夫？with 想过。

If you want to get an **A*** you need to:
• take the initiative and develop elaborate responses. Peter answers the question 'Do you learn Kung Fu everyday?' (你每天都学功夫吗？) with more than simply 不是的. He explains why not and states how often and how long (上学太忙, 不能每天都学。我每个星期五学一个小时。)
• give reasons for your statements. For example, when explaining why he enjoys learning Kung Fu, Peter says 因为学功夫, 所以我的身体很好。因为喜欢功夫, 我在网上交了很多喜欢功夫的中国朋友。
• include some conjunctions such as 因为… 所以… and 一边… 一边….

写作 xiě zuò Writing

Preparing for an extended writing task about hobbies

PREPARATION

1
Speaking

Warm-up! Tell a partner three things you could say about tennis in Chinese.

Read the text about tennis and answer the questions.

> 我家住在上海。上个星期六下午, 我和一个同学在公园里打了一场网球。那天的天气很热, 但是因为我热爱网球, 所以我还是打了一个多小时, 流了一身汗水, 感觉很舒服。
>
> 我开始学打球的时候, 我们学校没有网球场, 只有一堵墙。那时, 个别初中学生用那堵墙来练球, 虽然单调但是很快乐。
>
> 几年以后, 上海市政府在公园里开了网球俱乐部, 来打球的人有暑假留校的学生, 也有外面进来的市民, 场面非常热闹。我十三岁生日的那天, 父母给我买了新球拍, 整筒的网球和背包, 奶奶还为我付了俱乐部的会员费。
>
> 我每个星期打两次网球。虽然我练球的机会不多, 但是我去年赢了俱乐部的青年比赛。我也特别爱看双人比赛。希望将来有机会去上海看<u>大师杯</u>网球比赛, 也去英国看<u>温布尔登</u>比赛。
>
> 赵东

2
Reading

- Copy out the three phrases which include the character 热.
  What do they mean? Does the radical in 热 help you to work out the meaning?
- Find the three characters in the first paragraph with the water radical 氵.
  Write down their meanings using a dictionary if necessary. The first one is 海.

3
Reading

Find the characters in the text which mean:

1 I played tennis for over an hour. (para 1)
2 monotonous (para 2)
3 My parents bought me a new racket. (para 3)
4 I play tennis twice a week. (para 4)
5 Last year I won the club's youth tournament. (para 4)
6 I like watching doubles. (para 4)
7 I hope in the future to have the opportunity to… (para 4)

4
Reading

Look at how Zhao Dong uses time words in his article.

- Write down what time frame(s) (future, present, past) each paragraph is written in and find and copy out a time word/phrase in each.
- Find where 了 is used and try to work out why it is used with a partner.

5
Reading

Find the four correct statements.

1 Zhao Dong plays tennis every Saturday.
2 He doesn't like playing tennis in hot weather.
3 He used to play tennis against the wall.

4   Shanghai municipal government opened his tennis club.

5   His club is just for high school students.

6   He doesn't have many opportunities to practise.

7   He'd like to watch Wimbledon doubles in the future.

YOUR TURN NOW

A Chinese friend has asked you to write a short article for the school magazine about your favourite hobby. Write 100–150 characters, about half the length of Zhao Dong's article. You could include information about the following:

- Recent experience of your hobby
- How often you do it
- Hopes for the future
- How you started
- What you need for it

TIP

- Use the vocabulary in this chapter to help you. There is no need to include specialist vocabulary, but you might like to use one or two specialist words; use a dictionary or the Internet to help you with your research. Keep it simple and don't use anything you are unsure how to use.
- Structure your text; organise what you write into paragraphs.
- Use ResultsPlus to help you prepare.

CHECK

Check the characters and the word order. Make sure that you have not accidentally missed out components of characters which you really know.

Check that you have written the characters correctly for your sport/hobby. Some characters can be especially tricky, e.g. 游泳 swimming.

ResultsPlus
Maximise your marks

To aim for a **Grade C** you need to show you can write about past, present and future events. Zhao Dong talks about:

- Present events when referring to his practice
- Past events when referring to his recent match with a friend and when talking about how he started tennis and his club
- Future events when he talks about tournaments he would like to see
- You also need to include some opinions.

To aim higher than a **Grade C** you need to ensure that:

- word order is correct. For example, note the difference between the position of 'time when' before the verb and 'time how long' after the verb when Zhao Dong talks about when he played his tennis match and how long he played it for.
- conjunctions are used. For example, Zhao Dong uses 'because' 因为

To produce your best written Chinese and to aim for an **A* grade** you need to:

- demonstrate use of 的 clauses. Look at the example in the text when Zhao Dong says 来打球的人 or 从外面进来的市民.
- write characters with a high level of accuracy.

运动 yùn dòng Sports

去健身房	qù jiàn shēn fáng	to go to the gym	打羽毛球	dǎ yǔ máo qiú	to play badminton
练体操	liàn tǐ cāo	to practise gymnastics	玩儿滑板	wánr huá bǎn	to skateboard
打太极拳	dǎ tài jí quán	to practise tai ch'i	钓鱼	diào yú	to go fishing

爱好和空闲时间 ài hào hé kòng xián shí jiān Hobbies and leisure

参观博物馆	cān guān bó wù guǎn	to visit a museum	弹吉他	tán jí tā	to play the guitar
交朋友	jiāo péng you	to make friends	看小说	kàn xiǎo shuō	to read a novel
上网	shàng wǎng	to surf the Internet	过生日	guò shēng rì	to celebrate a birthday
聊天	liáo tiān	to chat	送礼物	sòng lǐ wù	to give a present
发邮件	fā yóu jiàn	to send emails	遛狗	liù gǒu	to walk a dog

其它动词 qí tā dòng cí Other verbs

不行	bù xíng	no (for refusing)	开始	kāi shǐ	to start
关门	guān mén	to close	主办	zhǔ bàn	to host
请	qǐng	to invite	参加	cān jiā	to participate in
举行	jǔ xíng	to hold (a meeting, etc.)	得(金牌)	dé (jīn pái)	to win (a gold medal)

买票 mǎi piào Buying tickets

英镑	yīng bàng	pound sterling	票	piào	ticket
半价	bàn jià	half price	门票	mén piào	entrance ticket

什么时候/多长时间 shén me shí hou/duō cháng shí jiān When/how long

一般	yì bān	generally; habitually	多长	duō cháng	how long
周末	zhōu mò	weekend	时间	shí jiān	time
很少	hěn shǎo	rarely	一会儿	yí huìr	a short while

量词 liàng cí Measure words

条	tiáo	measure word for fish and other long, narrow items	块	kuài	measure word for pieces (medals, cake, etc.)
次	cì	measure word for 'occurrence', 'time'			

形容词 xíng róng cí **Descriptive Words**

晚	wǎn	late	年轻	nián qīng	young
安静	ān jìng	quiet	更多	gèng duō	even more
舒服	shū fu	comfortable	快	kuài	fast

能愿动词 néng yuán dòng cí **Modal Verbs**

...做什么？	zuò shén me	what to do?	可以	kě yǐ	may; can
喜欢	xǐ huan	to like	应该	yīng gāi	should
想	xiǎng	would like to			

副词/介词 fù cí/ jiè cí **Adverbs/Prepositions**

在	zài	*(before a verb) indicating an action in progress*	先	xiān	first
			更(多)	gèng (duō)	even (more)
			给	gěi	to; for
还	hái	also			

专有名词 zhuān yǒu míng cí **Proper Nouns**

奥运会	ào yùn huì	the Olympic games	英格兰	yīng gé lán	England
伦敦	lún dūn	London			

去哪儿做什么 qù nǎr zuò shénme **Where to go and what to do**

去健身房跑步	qù jiàn shēn fáng pǎo bù	to go to the gym to run
去公园打太极拳	qù gōng yuán dǎ tài jí quán	to go to the park to practise Tai Chi
去伦敦参加奥运会	qù lún dūn cān jiā ào yùn huì	to go to London to participate in the Olympic Games

复习 Review – Understanding basic information about media

1
Reading

Read the dialogue and match the family members with the pictures.

1 爸爸
2 妈妈
3 哥哥
4 弟弟

A: 爸爸喜欢什么？
B: 爸爸喜欢看杂志。
A: 他喜欢看什么杂志？
B: 他喜欢看《你好》杂志。
A: 妈妈喜欢什么？
B: 妈妈喜欢看报纸。
A: 她喜欢看什么报纸？
B: 她喜欢看《太阳报》。
A: 哥哥喜欢什么？
B: 哥哥喜欢看电影。
A: 他喜欢看什么电影？
B: 他喜欢看007。
A: 弟弟喜欢什么？
B: 弟弟喜欢看电视。
A: 他喜欢看什么电视？
B: 他喜欢看《猫和老鼠》。

杂志 zá zhì	magazine
报纸 bào zhǐ	newspaper
太阳报 tài yáng bào	the Sun newspaper
007 líng líng qī	Double 'O' Seven
猫和老鼠 māo hé lǎo shǔ	Chinese for 'Tom and Jerry'

2
Listening and Reading

Listen to the conversation whilst reading the speech bubbles. Write down the numbers in the correct sequence. One sentence is not needed.

1 我天天看电视。

2 今天的电视节目好看吗？

3 电视节目很好看。

4 我不想看电影。

5 你天天看电视吗？

3 Listening

Listen to the passage and write down the missing words from those in the box.

我们一家人都爱看新闻。

我爷爷看 __1__ 上的新闻，

我爸爸在 __2__ 上看新闻，

我哥哥在 __3__ 看新闻，

我姐姐用 __4__ 看新闻，

我喜欢听他们讲新闻。

手机　电视　报纸　网上

手机 shǒu jī	mobile phone
网上 wǎng shàng	online
新闻 xīn wén	news
用 yòng	to use
讲 jiǎng	to talk about

4 Speaking and Listening

Interview your classmates and find out how they keep up with the news. Use the vocabulary and structures in Activity 3 to help you. For example,

Q: 你喜欢怎么看新闻？

A: 我喜欢在网上看新闻。

5 Listening

Listen to the dialogue and match the times with the programmes.

动画片 dòng huà piān	cartoon

a 7:00

b 8:00

c 9:00

d 10:00

e 11:00

1 音乐节目

2 《学中文》

3 新闻

4 体育节目

5 动画片

6 Speaking

Look again at Activity 5. Talk about when the programmes are on. Use the framework to help you.

A: 今天有什么好的电视节目？

B: 今天有…。

A: 几点钟有…?

B: …点钟有…。

7 Writing

Find out the time of some television programmes from your local newspaper. Write a short paragraph about when the programmes are on. Use the framework to help you. You may need to write some of the programme titles in English.

今天有很多好的电视节目。

… 点有 …

……

中 央 电 视 台

中央电视台-1(综合频道)

7:00 朝闻天下

8:33 天天饮食

9:23 连续剧:敌营十八年
　　　(30~32)

12:39 今日说法

13:09 连续剧:大理公主(30、31)

15:05 走近科学

16:07 半边天

17:41 动画城

18:18 大风车

19:38 焦点访谈

19:55 连续剧:叶挺将军(17、18)

21:43 专题节目

22:36 专题片:汉字五千年(4)

1 BBC 和 CCTV BBC hé CCTV BBC and CCTV

Giving opinions about the media

广播 guǎng bō	broadcast
'老大哥' lǎo dà gē	'Big Brother'
浪费 làng fèi	wasteful; to waste
知道 zhī dào	to know
网站 wǎng zhàn	website

1
Listening and Reading

Read the passages and decide if the opinions are positive, negative or neutral. You may want to listen to the passages before you read them. (1-4).

1 爸爸开车的时候喜欢听广播,他有时候听体育新闻,有时候听音乐。

2 什么电视?《老大哥》?我觉得看这个节目是浪费时间! 我不想看。

3 《猫和老鼠》是一个美国动画片,很有趣! 我和妹妹很喜欢看。

4 你知道这个网站吗? 我经常上这个网站,可以学中文,也可以看新闻。

2
Listening

Listen to the dialogue between Tom and Zhang Long and answer the questions in English. Tom is an English student who is hosting Zhang Long, a student from China visiting the UK.

1 What does Zhang Long immediately think of when he sees the sign for CCTV?

2 According to the dialogue, what media does Zhang Long associate with the BBC?

3 What else can BBC stand for, according to Tom?

3
Reading

Read the dialogue and answer the questions in English.

A: Zhang Long, the Chinese visitor

B: Tom, the English host

A: 英国有CCTV的电视节目吗?

B: 有,是英文的,但是晚上有《跟我学中文》,我常常看这个节目。

A: 英国的电视上有什么体育节目?

B: 有很多,有赛车、赛马,也有球赛。中国有没有BBC广播?

A: 有。我常常听BBC英文广播,因为我想学英文。英国有中国的广播吗?

B: 没有。

赛车 sài chē	car racing
赛马 sài mǎ	horse racing

1 Which programme does Tom say he often watches on CCTV?

2 According to Tom, what sports programmes are on television in the UK besides ball games?

3 Why does Zhang Long often listen to BBC radio?

4
Reading

Read the text about Wang Xiaolong and answer the questions in English.

我叫王小龙，我是北京人，我来伦敦两年了。我觉得伦敦报纸太多了。在地铁上，人人都看报纸。北京也有很多报纸，但是北京的报纸没有伦敦多。有的北京人不想花钱买报纸，他们上网看报纸。在伦敦，很多旧报纸都没有回收，太浪费了！

1　How long has Wang Xiaolong lived in London?
2　What is his impression of London?
3　According to Xiaolong, why don't some people in Beijing want to buy newspapers?
4　What does Xiaolong think we should do with old newspapers?

| 地铁 dì tiě | underground train | 旧 jiù | old |
| 花钱 huā qián | to spend money | 回收 huí shōu | to recycle |

GRAMMAR: Comparisons using 没有

没有 (méi yǒu) can be used in comparisons to say 'X is not as... as Y'. The 没有 comes between the two items being compared, with the adjective after the second item. For example:

| X | 没有 | Y | Adjective | Translation for the whole sentence |
| 英国 | 没有 | 中国 | 大。 | The UK is not as big as China. |

EXAM TIP

有 (yǒu), which means 'to have', has one distinctive feature in that, unlike all other verbs, its negative can only be formed with 没 (méi), not with 不 (bù). Examiners will be looking out for accurate use of this negative. For example: 我没有钱。
I don't have any money.

5
Speaking and Listening

Interview your classmates and find out the answers to the following questions.

你喜欢看电视吗？　你喜欢看什么电视节目？
你喜欢听广播吗？　你喜欢听什么广播节目？
你喜欢上网吗？　你喜欢上什么网站？

6
Writing

Write a short paragraph about what you think of a TV programme. Use the framework to help you.

这个电视节目叫 ...。　This programme is called ...
... 点有这个节目。　The programme is at ...o'clock.
我觉得这个节目 ...　I think this programme is ...
(有意思、没意思、很好看、不好看、有趣、浪费时间)

2 电视 diàn shì Television

Giving opinions about programmes

1
Reading
Copy the characters in the right order from the earliest invention to the most recent one.

a 手机 **b** 电脑 **c** 电灯 **d** 电视

2
Writing
Copy out the sentences and choose the right invention from Activity 1 to fill in the blanks.

经常 jīng cháng	often

1 因为有 ____, 我晚上可以看书。

2 因为有 ____, 我可以看外国新闻。

3 因为有 ____, 我可以上网学中文。

4 因为有 ____, 我可以经常打电话。

3
Speaking
Which invention do you value the most? Why? Say two sentences in Chinese.

4
Reading
Read the texts. Match the people with the pictures.

 **a**  **b**  **c**

1 李大海: 周末有《超级女生》*, 这个节目很像英国的 X Factor, 也是一个音乐节目。我爱看《超级女生》。

2 王小文: 我在看美国篮球比赛, 这个节目不错, 我们班同学都爱看这个节目。我们很少看足球比赛, 我们经常看篮球比赛。

3 刘大明: 我姐姐爱看Harry Potter, 可是我不爱看, 我爱看中国小说, 像《男生日记》*、《女生日记》。

*《超级女生》(chāo jí nǚ shēng) *Super Girl*, a music programme on TV in China

*《男生日记》(nán shēng rì jì) *A Boy Student's Diary*, by Yang Hongying, a Chinese novelist

像 xiàng	for example; to be similar
不错 bú cuò	not bad (literally, not wrong)
日记 rì jì	diary

5
Reading
Read the texts in Activity 4 again and answer the questions in English.

1 What is the name of the programme which is the Chinese equivalent of *X Factor*? When is it broadcast?

2 According to the text, which sports programmes are more popular in China, football matches or basketball matches?

3 Who likes to read *Harry Potter*?

4 Is *A Girl Student's Diary* an English novel or a Chinese novel?

6
Speaking

Interview your classmates until you find two students who have the same likes and dislikes.

你喜欢不喜欢看…？

	Tom				
音乐节目					
篮球比赛					
足球比赛					
Harry Potter					

7
Reading

Read the descriptions. Match the descriptions 1–3 with the programmes a–c in the box.

a Friends   **b** X Factor   **c** Match of the Day

1 这是一个体育节目, 节目在周末, 节目里有英格兰的足球比赛。
2 这是一个美国电视剧。电视剧里有六个好朋友, 他们住在纽约。
3 这是一个音乐节目, 节目里很多人参加比赛, 他们唱流行歌曲。

电视剧 diàn shì jù	TV soap
纽约 niǔ yuē	New York
唱 chàng	to sing
流行歌曲 liú xíng gē qǔ	pop song

GRAMMAR:
the preposition 里

…里 (… lǐ) is a preposition. Unlike in English, this preposition goes after the noun in Chinese. For example: 节目里 = in the programme

年轻人 nián qīng rén	young people
这些 zhè xiē	these

8
Listening

Listen to the passage and write down the missing words. Write the words in pinyin while listening and write the characters later.

我觉得年轻人看电视太 __1__ 了, 看书太 __2__ 了。有的电视节目很好, 但是很多电视节目 __3__ 好, 看这些节目是浪费时间。因为他们看电视太多, 所以他们 __4__ 时间做作业, 晚上很 __5__ 才睡觉。很多年轻人 __6__ 看书, 他们觉得看书没意思。我年轻的时候很爱看书, 我觉得看书是最好的 __7__ 。

9
Writing

Write a short paragraph about what you think of young people surfing the net. Use the vocabulary and structures in Activity 8 to help you.

我觉得	I think…
上网	to surf the net
可以	can
但是	but
因为…, 所以…	because…, therefore…

EXAM TIP

Candidates in Writing and Speaking assessments very often lose marks because they use 是 when they do not need to. Remember to omit 是 if it is followed by a verb-adjective. For a simple statement such as 'the programme is very good', it is correct to say 节目很好 but it is wrong to say 节目是很好.

3 上网 shàng wǎng Surfing the net
Talking about preferences

① Reading

Look up the single characters and try to work out the meaning of their combinations.

电 (diàn/electronic) + 脑 (nǎo/brain) = 电脑 (computer)

网 (wǎng) + 友 (yǒu) = 网友 (......1......)

短 (duǎn) + 信 (xìn) = 短信 (......2......)

手 (shǒu) + 机 (jī) = 手机 (......3......)

② Reading

Read the statements and write down the letter that applies to each according to what you have tried.

For example, write 1a if you have tried writing a blog.

你试过吗? **a** 试过 **b** 没试过

试 shì	to try
博客 bó kè	blog
网友 wǎng yǒu	e-pal
照片 zhào piàn	photo
短信 duǎn xìn	text message

1 写博客   4 用手机发邮件   7 在网上看电影

2 交网友   5 用手机发短信   8 在网上看报纸

3 用手机发照片   6 用手机看新闻   9 在网上看电视

③ Speaking

Look again at the list in Activity 2. Interview your partner to find out if you have tried the same things.

你试过什么?   你没试过什么?

④ Reading

Read the texts and answer the questions in Chinese.

刘小明: 在英国它叫iPod, 在中国它不叫iPod, 它叫MP4。MP4比MP3好, 用它可以听音乐、看电影。我们都有MP4。

李大海: 在英国你们用MSN, 在中国我们用QQ。我的QQ号是228576538。除了上网聊天以外, 我也用QQ玩儿电脑游戏。

张文: 我用中国手机。我经常用手机发短信, 有时候发中文短信, 有时候发英文短信。英国的手机可以发中文短信吗?

1 为什么刘小明觉得MP4比MP3好?

2 李大海用QQ做什么?

3 张文经常用手机做什么?

4 张文想知道什么?

MP4 pronounced 'MP sì'	MP4
MP3 pronounced 'MP sān'	MP3
QQ pronounced as in English	software similar to MSN
游戏 yóu xì	game

5
Speaking

Interview your classmates.

Answer the questions in Chinese. For example:

Q: 你有没有iPod？你经常用iPod做什么？

A: 我有iPod。我经常用iPod听音乐。

1 你有MSN吗？你每天都上网聊天吗？你一般在什么时候上网聊天？

2 你有手机吗？除了打电话以外,你一般用手机做什么？

3 在学校里,你可以用手机吗？

4 你的手机可以发中文短信吗？

6
Listening

Listen to the passages. Match the speakers, 1–3, with their opinions a–c. (1–3)

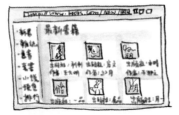

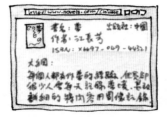

a I like reading novels online, though my eyes suffer.

b I enjoy writing blogs, as they can be read by many people.

c I prefer to buy books online, as it is very convenient.

1 Liu Dong 　　 2 Li Wen 　　 3 Zhang Ming

对…有兴趣 duì…yǒu xìng qù	to be interested in …
网络文学 wǎng luò wén xué	net novel
对…不好 duì…bù hǎo	to be no good for …

7
Writing

Listen again to the passages in Activity 6 and write down the words in the blanks. You may want to write the words in pinyin while listening and write the characters later.

刘东觉得 ___1___ 买书很方便。

李文觉得网上看小说对眼睛 ___2___ 。

张明觉得写博客比写 ___3___ 有意思。

8
Writing

Write a short paragraph about what you think of these Internet-related activities. Use 对…有兴趣 appropriately.

　buying books online
　reading novels online
　writing blogs

EXAM TIP

It helps to impress examiners if you use 对…（没）有兴趣 in addition to 爱 and 喜欢 when talking about likes and dislikes, as variety is always better than repetition.

4 电影和音乐 diàn yǐng hé yīn yuè Film and music

Talking about films and music

Reading

Read the text in the speech bubbles. Match the
Chinese characters with the English words.

1	花	a	interesting
2	钱	b	spend
3	安静	c	money
4	舒服	d	quiet
5	有意思	e	comfortable

我在网上看电影。我不去电影院，我不想花钱。

王龙

我去电影院看电影，虽然很贵，但是很有意思。

张文

我喜欢在家看电影DVD，很安静，很舒服。

陈海

GRAMMAR: 虽然..., 但是...

虽然 has the same function as 'although'. In English 'but' is not needed in the second half of the
sentence. However, in Chinese 虽然 is usually followed in the second half of the sentence by 'but' 但是.

For example:

虽然很贵，但是很有意思。*Although* it is expensive, *(but)* it is interesting.

Speaking and Listening

Interview your classmates. Record your results.

What is the most popular way of watching films?

你喜欢去哪儿看电影？

在网上....

去电影院....

在家看DVD....

3
Listening

Listen to the dialogue. Choose the correct answer for each question.

张 zhāng	measure word (usually flat things like tables and tickets)
《功夫熊猫》 gōng fu xióng māo	'Kung Fu Panda'
开演 kāi yǎn	to start (film)

1 How many tickets are wanted?

a 一张   b 两张   c 三张

2 For what time are the tickets?

a 晚上七点   b 晚上六点   c 晚上八点

3 How much is one ticket?

a 四块   b 十块   c 二十块

4
Reading

Read the dialogue. Give a brief summary of what the student says about Chinese film and music.

A: 你觉得中国电影怎么样？

B: 我觉得中国电影不错。我最喜欢看张艺谋导演的电影。

A: 你最喜欢的中国演员是谁？

B: 我最喜欢的中国演员是章子怡。我有她的电影DVD。

A: 你喜欢中国音乐吗？

B: 喜欢。我会唱《茉莉花》。我有很多中国音乐CD。

A: 你会中国乐器吗？

B: 会一点点，我会二胡。

张艺谋 (zhāng yìmóu)	Director
章子怡 (zhāng zǐyí)	Actress
《茉莉花》 (mò lì huā)	song "Jasmine flower"
二胡 (èr hú)	Chinese 'violin', with two strings

导演 dǎo yǎn	director (of a film); to direct (a film)
演员 yǎn yuán	actor; actress
乐器 yuè qì	instrument

5
Writing

**Write a short paragraph about your experience of going to the cinema.
Use the vocabulary and structures in this unit to help you.**

1 Which day did you go to the cinema?   (星期六、星期天、昨天)

2 With whom?   (爸爸、妈妈、朋友)

3 What time did you arrive at the cinema?   (到)

4 What time did the film start?   (开演)

5 What was the name of the film/the director?   (导演)

6 How much was the ticket?   (电影票、贵、张)

7 What did you think of the film?   (觉得、不错、棒、好看、有意思)

棒 bàng	excellent

GRAMMAR: Using 的 as a linking word

In 我喜欢的电影 'the film that I enjoy', 的 (de) is used to join the two parts - 'I enjoy' and 'film'.

Moreover, in Chinese 'that I enjoy' goes before 'the film', i.e. 'I enjoy' + 的 + 'film'.

Talking about people's lives

Listening and Reading

Listen to and read the text. Answer the questions in English.

郎朗很年轻, 但是很有名, 他弹钢琴弹得非常棒, 他去过很多国家演出。两岁的时候, 他看了美国动画片《猫和老鼠》, 在动画片里小猫Tom会弹钢琴, 他觉得很有意思, 开始对钢琴有兴趣。从小学到大学, 郎朗学钢琴学得非常刻苦, 所以现在非常成功。

Name: 郎朗 (láng lǎng)

1 How does the text show that Lang Lang is well known?

2 What inspired him to become interested in the piano?

3 What has made him so successful?

名人 míng rén	celebrity
钢琴 gāng qín	piano
演出 yǎn chū	to perform
刻苦 kè kǔ	hardworking
成功 chéng gōng	to succeed, successful

GRAMMAR: The use of 得

得 is used to express the manner in which an activity is carried out. The main verb of the sentence is repeated and the repeated verb directly followed by 得: *verb + object + verb + 得 + adverb*. For example:

他弹钢琴弹得非常棒。 He plays the piano very well.

她说英文说得不太好。 She doesn't speak English very well.

Sometimes the object of the verb is placed before the verb to avoid the repetition of the verb: 他钢琴弹得很好。You need to be able to recognise both, but you can stick to just one way yourself.

Speaking

Look at the table. Work in pairs. Say how well Wang Xiaolong could and can do certain things, using 得 appropriately.

✔ = 还可以   ✘ = 不太好

✔✔ = 非常好   ✘✘ = 不会

	说中文	弹钢琴	打网球	玩滑板	游泳
五年以前	✘✘	✘	✘✘	✔	✘
现在	✔✔	✔	✘✘	✔✔	✔✔

For example,

五年以前王小龙不会说中文, 现在他说中文说得非常好。

3
Reading

Read the text. Choose the correct answer a–c for each sentence.

我叫王小丽, 我认识章子怡。我们是同学。1990年到
1996年, 我们在同一所中学读书, 我们都学习跳舞,
我们都喜欢音乐。中学毕业以后, 她上了大学,
学戏剧, 我没有上大学, 我去了幼儿园, 教小孩子跳舞。
章子怡演的第一个电影是《我的父亲母亲》, 导演是
张艺谋。那是1998年, 她在上大学二年级。演了这个
电影以后, 她成了名人。

1 王小丽和章子怡是 _____ 。	a 幼儿园同学	b 中学同学	c 大学同学
2 在大学里章子怡学 _____ 。	a 音乐	b 跳舞	c 戏剧
3 王小丽在幼儿园教 _____ 。	a 跳舞	b 戏剧	c 音乐
4 1996年到1997年, 章子怡上大学 _____ 。	a 一年级	b 二年级	c 三年级

Name: 章子怡 (zhāng zǐ yí)

认识 rèn shi	to know, be familiar with
同 tóng	same
毕业 bì yè	to graduate
幼儿园 yòu ér yuán	nursery
成 chéng	to become

EXAM TIP

Watch out! Chinese sentence structure is often different from English. In English you say, 'We study in the same school.' In Chinese you need to change the structure to say 'We in the same school study.' (我们在同一个学校读书。)

4
Reading

Copy the sentences and fill in the blanks with the right characters from the text.

影迷 yǐng mí	movie fan
农民 nóng mín	peasant
学院 xué yuàn	college
摄影 shè yǐng	photograph, photography
后来 hòu lái	later on

我是张艺谋的影迷。他导演的电影我都喜欢。他年轻的
时候做过农民, 还做过工人。1978年他上北京电影学院,
学摄影。毕业以后, 他做过摄影, 也做过演员, 后来
开始做导演, 现在是中国最有名的导演。

1 张艺谋1978年上 __1__ 。
2 上大学以前他做过 __2__ 、 __3__ 。
3 大学毕业以后他做过 __4__ 、 __5__ 。
4 他现在是 __6__ 。

5
Writing

Write a short paragraph about a celebrity of your choice.

Making comparisons

Reading

Read the sentences 1–6. Which sentences do you think might refer to Lucy and which to Wang Hong?

王红, 19岁, 中国南方, 工人。

Lucy, 18岁, 英国北方, 学生。

1 现在是晚上八点, 她在学电脑。她对电脑很有兴趣。

2 她住在工厂里, 八个人住在一起。

3 今年九月她要去中国。她想一边工作, 一边学中文。

4 她跟父母住在一起, 她的卧室很大。

5 她每天工作11个小时。星期六晚上她还要去学英语、学电脑。

6 她每天上午九点上学, 下午四点放学, 周末她去超级市场当售货员。

GRAMMAR: 'while.../at the same time...'

一边..., 一边... (yì biān... yì biān...) literally means 'while..., at the same time... '. Each is followed by a verb, and the construction indicates two actions are being carried out at the same time. For example:

我一边吃饭, 一边看电视。I watch television while eating.

妈妈一边喝茶, 一边跟爸爸聊天。Mum chats with dad while drinking tea.

生活 shēng huó	life
南方 nán fāng	south
卧室 wò shì	bedroom

Speaking

Work in pairs. Make twelve cue cards. Each one should have an activity written on it in Chinese. Pick up two cards at random and make a sentence with the structure: 一边..., 一边.... Report back to the class to see who has come up with the funniest sentence.

3
Reading and Speaking

Read the text and then perform a role play. One student plays Tom, the other plays Ma Wenshan. Find out what Tom/Ma Wenshan was doing at a particular time.

Example:
Tom: 星期一早上6点半的时候你在做什么？
Ma: 星期一早上6点半的时候我在走路去学校。你呢？
Tom: 我在游泳池练跳水。

这是2008年6月的一个星期。

Tom, 15岁、一个喜欢跳水的英国男孩		
星期一	早上6点半	在游泳池, 练跳水
星期二	上午9点	在学校, 上数学课
星期三	晚上7点	在厨房, 做作业
星期四	下午5点半	又在游泳池, 练跳水
星期五	晚上6点	在飞机上, 去美国比赛

马文山、14岁、一个喜欢游泳的中国男孩		
星期一	早上6点半	走路去学校
星期二	上午9点	和同学在操场上玩
星期三	晚上7点	吃晚饭
星期四	下午5点半	和朋友在河里游泳
星期五	晚上6点	帮助妈妈做晚饭

GRAMMAR: 在 to show continuity of an action

在 (zài), or sometimes 正在 (zhèng zài), is used before a verb to show that something is/was going on at a particular time. For example: 那是1998年, 她在上大学。 = That was 1998. She was studying at university.

跳水 tiào shuǐ	to dive
河 hé	river

4
Listening

Listen to the dialogue. Choose the correct answer(s) for each question.

1 What did Xiaodong think of his day at home?
  a 很忙   b 很开心   c 没意思

2 What were Xiaodong's friends busy with during the day?
  a 学钢琴   b 玩儿电脑游戏   c 做作业

3 According to Xiaodong's dad, what was his life like when he was younger?
  a 经常不回家吃晚饭   b 爸爸妈妈很少担心他
  c 跟朋友出去玩儿很长时间

开心 kāi xīn	happy
担心 dān xīn	to worry

5
Listening and Speaking

Listen again to the dialogue in Activity 4. Discuss with your classmates in Chinese which lifestyle you prefer, the dad's or the son's.

6
Writing

Re-read the text in Activity 3. Write a short paragraph about what you did at specific times over the last week.

星期一早上6点半我在睡觉。……

EXAM TIP

It is advisable to write short simple sentences and to write them correctly. However, examiners will be impressed and award higher marks if you can use some conjunctions such as 虽然..., 但是, 因为..., 所以, 一边... 一边.

LISTENING

1
Listening

Warm-up! You are going to hear five people talking about their strategies for learning Chinese. Write down all the media you hear them mention.

2
Listening

Listen again and match each person to the media they prefer.

1	Tom	a	book
2	Jenny	b	film
3	Jack	c	TV
4	Mary	d	radio
5	Peter	e	newspaper
		f	Internet

3
Listening

Warm–up! You are going to hear Ling Ling talking about her mobile phones. Think about how you use your mobile phone.

4
Listening

Now listen to Ling Ling. Look at the statements below. Only four are correct. Write down the letters that represent the correct statements.

a Ling Ling was given a mobile phone for her birthday.

b She didn't like the colour very much.

c She was very excited about it.

d She doesn't like the design of her current mobile phone either.

e She can't surf the Internet on her mobile phone.

f She uses it to listen to music.

g She uses it to send 30 to 40 texts everyday.

GRAMMAR: 一...就 and 还是

一...就: 一 and 就 are both followed by verbs and one action occurs immediately after the other. The second action is usually the result of the first. For example:
我一看书就明白了。这个孩子一看见妈妈就笑。

还是 is used to form 'yes/no' questions (吗 cannot be used in this kind of question). For example:
你吃饺子还是吃面条？

> **TIP**
> - Listen carefully for the names of speakers so that you know who is speaking.
> - Match the ones you know first. If you are unsure of an answer, mark it and return to it later.
> - Be sure to make notes while listening so you don't miss a detail needed for the matching exercise.

> **TIP**
> - Read the instructions and the statements first. Try to predict what words you are likely to hear.
> - With the predicted words in mind, pay attention to the specific information you need to decide about the statements.
> - A statement that is only partly true should be considered false.

READING

5
Reading

Match the questions and the answers below.

An interview with a singer

问:

1 你从多大开始唱歌？
2 爸爸妈妈支持你当歌星吗？
3 你每天都有演出吗？
4 你去过国外演出吗？
5 你有什么兴趣爱好？
6 你将来想做什么？

答:

a 周末没有。
b 我喜欢看电影、电视。
c 大概三岁吧。
d 我希望自己能成为一名电影明星。
e 我上学时反对、现在没问题了。
f 还没有。希望明年能去。

TIP

The following strategies are helpful when matching questions and answers.

- If the questions and answers contain words of similar or contrary meanings, they are probably, but not always, a match.
- Do the easiest first and the hardest last.
- You don't have to understand every word to be confident in your choice.
- Pay attention to patterns of questions and answers in Chinese. For example, for the question 你吃早饭了吗, the more correct answer is either 吃了 or 没吃呢, rather than 是的 or 不是, the literal translation of 'yes' or 'no'.

GRAMMAR: Synonyms and Antonyms

Synonyms (words with similar meanings) and antonyms (words with opposite meanings) are common in all languages. If you know some, they will be helpful for understanding the listening and reading passages and answering relevant questions. The following are frequently used Chinese synonyms and antonyms:

Words with similar meanings 近义词

说 shuō = 讲 jiǎng = 谈 tán
寒 hán = 冷 lěng
暖 nuǎn = 热 rè
叫 jiào = 喊 hǎn
望 wàng = 看 kàn = 见 jiàn
立刻 lì kè = 马上 mǎ shàng
每天 měi tiān = 天天 tiān tiān
兴趣 xìng qù = 爱好 ài hào = 喜欢 xǐ huan
高兴 gāo xìng = 开心 kāi xīn = 愉快 yú kuài = 快乐 kuài lè
著名 zhù míng = 有名 yǒu míng
希望 xī wàng = 愿望 yuàn wàng
美丽 měi lì = 漂亮 piào liang = 好看 hǎo kàn
觉得 jué de = 认为 rèn wéi = 想 xiǎng
帮助 bāng zhù = 帮忙 bāng máng

Opposites 反义词

多 duō - 少 shǎo   上 shàng - 下 xià   左 zuǒ - 右 yòu
前 qián - 后 hòu   东 dōng - 西 xī   冷 lěng - 热 rè
高 gāo - 低 dī   快 kuài - 慢 màn   好 hǎo - 坏 huài
美 měi - 丑 chǒu   饿 è - 饱 bǎo   爱 ài - 恨 hèn
开 kāi - 关 guān   胖 pàng - 瘦 shòu   真 zhēn - 假 jiǎ
对 duì - 错 cuò   支持 zhī chí - 反对 fǎn duì
有 yǒu - 没有 méi yǒu
高兴 gāo xìng - 生气 shēng qì - 伤心 shāngxīn

口语 kǒu yǔ Speaking

Preparing for a speaking task (open interaction)

TASK AND PREPARATION

You are hosting a Chinese student who is visiting the UK on a school trip. Your visitor wants to go to the cinema next week and needs information about the opening hours of the cinema, tickets and the films being shown. Use the information leaflet to help you answer the questions.

- You will need to ask questions to find out what sort of films your visitor likes.
- You will also need to give opinions on the kinds of films you enjoy watching and talk about films you have seen.

Empire Cinema		Opening hours: 10.00am - 10.00pm Tickets: £6 adults; £4 children or students			
UA 1	The Curious Case of Benjamin Button	A feature film (NEW!)	12A	Everyday	11.30am; 3.30pm; 7.30pm
UA 2	The Forbidden Kingdom	A Kung Fu film	12A	Thu-Sat	2.30pm; 5.30pm; 8.30pm
UA 3	Kung Fu Panda	An animated film	PG	Fri & Sat	10.00am; 1.00pm
UA 4	The Road Home	Chinese film with English subtitles	12A	Tue	3.00pm; 5.30pm

1
Reading

Three kinds of films are included in the leaflet.
Use your previous knowledge to match 1–3 with a–c.

1 Feature Film   a   动画片 dòng huà piàn

2 Kung Fu Film   b   故事片 gù shì piàn

3 Animated Film   c   功夫片 gōng fu piàn

2
Listening

You will hear a model conversation between Tom and his teacher, who is playing the role of Tom's Chinese visitor. Listen to the first part of the conversation and fill in the gaps.

    __1__ 是一部故事片。   __2__ 是一部功夫片。   __3__ 是一部动画片。

3
Listening

Listen to part 1 again and make notes in English about:

1 the questions Tom is asked   2 how he answers them.

4
Listening

Listen to part 2 of the conversation and fill in the gaps.

1 在中国, 新电影 __a__ 老电影 __b__ 。

2 __c__ 你喜欢故事片, 我觉得你 __d__ 看 'Benjamin Button'。

3 我 __e__ 看 'Kung Fu Panda', __f__ 我喜欢动画片。

4 这两部电影我们 __g__ 看, __h__ 吗?

5
Listening

Listen to the part 3 of the conversation and rewrite the sentences using the words and phrases given in brackets.

1 '我的父亲母亲'和 'Benjamin Button'都是故事片。 (跟…一样、也…)

2 'Bolt' 和 'Kung Fu Panda' 都是动画片。 (跟…一样、也…)

3 我们1点看'Kung Fu Panda', 3 点半看'Benjamin Button'。 (先…, 然后…)

Listen to the whole conversation again and answer the questions below.

1 Give three examples of how Tom asks his teacher questions.

2 Give two examples of how Tom asks for agreement after/before he gives suggestions.

3 Give two examples of the Chinese visitor and Tom talking about their experience of the cinema.

4 'Shall we go to the cinema next week?' – How does the teacher make this proposal?

5 'Which film do you think we should see?' – How does the teacher ask for advice?

YOUR TURN NOW

Prepare your answers to the task, and then have a conversation with your teacher or partner.

- Use the ideas in the ResultsPlus to enhance what you say.
- Take the initiative by asking some questions yourself. In this way you can take control of the conversation and talk about your preferred topics.

Award each other one star, two stars or three stars for each of the following categories:

- pronunciation
- confidence and fluency
- range of time frames
- variety of vocabulary
- using sentences with more complex structures
- taking the initiative

Note down what you need to do next time to improve your performance.

ResultsPlus
Maximise your marks

To achieve a **Grade C** you need to:

- include different time frames where possible – cinema experiences in the past, future plans for going to the cinema, and so on.
- use the phrases you know to express what you want to say. For example, 'I want to learn English through watching films,' might be difficult for you to say in Chinese, but you probably know how to say 'I want to learn English while watching films,' (我想在看电影的时候学英文。).
- remember to give opinions about the kinds of films you enjoy watching and what you think about a film you have seen. For example, 我喜欢功夫片 and 我觉得这部电影不错。

To aim higher than a **Grade C** you need to:

- use the structure with 如果 (如果你喜欢故事片)
- vary the ways you ask for advice. How many examples can you find in Tom's conversation?
- give advice where appropriate. 应该 is useful as in 我觉得你应该看'Benjamin Button'。

If you want to get an **A or A***, you need to :

- use comparatives, for example 'Bolt'跟'Kung Fu Panda'一样, and 学生票比大人票便宜。
- show that you can use more complex structures. For example, 先…, 然后… as in 我们先看'Kung Fu Panda', 然后看'Benjamin Button'。

写作 xiě zuò **Writing**

Preparing for an extended writing task about films

PREPARATION

Speaking

1 Warm-up! Tell a partner three things in Chinese about a film you would recommend.

Read the film review and then complete Activities 2–5.

> 　　我想给大家介绍一下张艺谋导演的《一个都不能少》。我先讲讲这部电影里的故事。
>
> 　　水泉小学的高老师要回家看妈妈，村长找来魏敏芝给她代一个月的课。魏敏芝只有十三、四岁，没当过老师，高老师有点儿担心，可是没有办法。
>
> 　　高老师对魏敏芝说，一定要看好学生，一个都不能少。魏敏芝开始上课了，她整天让学生抄课文，每天数人数，谁要把学生叫走，她就跟谁急。学生见她人小，又不会上课，不听她的，教室里总是乱哄哄的。她不管这些，只是站在教室门口，不到时间不让走。
>
> 　　从《一个都不能少》中，我学到了很多知识。农村的孩子不但要学习，而且要种地。对家长来说，种地有时候比学习更重要。虽然魏敏芝是一个没有受过很多教育的女孩子，我还是很佩服她。下个月我们学校准备放几部张艺谋的电影，我已经买好了电影票。张艺谋的影迷们，都跟我一起去看吧！

Reading

2 The director of this film is very famous. Who is he? Work out the pinyin for the name of the director and have a go at translating the name of the film. Once you have done this, read about the plot of the film in English on the Internet and take down the names of some of the director's other films.

3 Find the characters in the text which mean:

Reading

1　to introduce
2　to direct (a film)
3　to tell the story of the film
4　knowledge

5　to admire
6　to show (a film)
7　I have already bought tickets
8　movie fans

4 Find the four correct statements about the text.

Reading

1　Teacher Gao is going home to see his father.
2　Teacher Gao has every confidence in the replacement teacher.
3　The students spend a lot of time copying.
4　Wei Minzhi is very concerned about counting the children.

5　She is not too concerned about noise in the classroom.
6　She lets some children go home early.
7　Children in the countryside have to work in the fields
8　The writer of the review has not bought tickets for the Chinese films next month.

Reading

5 Work with a partner to find all the linking words used in the text. Copy them, translate them and then try to use at least three of them in your own writing.

YOUR TURN NOW

Write a review of a film you would recommend to others. (The text opposite was reading practice. You are not expected to write at this level!) You should include information about:

- The film's title and director
- What it was about
- Why you enjoyed it
- Why you would recommend it

TIP

- Use the Internet and a dictionary to help you work out how to write about the plot of a film you have seen.
- Make sure you don't use vocabulary and structures that you are unsure of.
- Structure your text and organise what you write into paragraphs.

CHECK

Check the characters and word order. Make sure that you have not accidentally missed out components of characters that you know well. Check that you have written the characters correctly for the title of the film you have chosen (if it is a Chinese film). Before you start, make absolutely sure you can write 电影, 电影票, 电影院 and other useful words in Chapter 4.

ResultsPlus
Maximise your marks

To achieve a **Grade C** you need to:

- show you can write about past, present and future events. You can:
    - talk in the present or past time frame when talking about the plot
    - talk in the past time frame when you discuss having seen the film
    - talk in the future when encouraging others to go and see it.

To aim higher than a **Grade C** you need to:

- make sure that word order is correct. For example, note the difference between the position of 'time when' before the verb and 'time how long' after the verb: 代一个月的课.
- use linking words and phrases. For example, the writer of the review uses 虽然… 但是 and 连…也.

To produce your best written Chinese and to aim for an **A* grade** you need to :

- demonstrate use of 的 clauses, e.g. 不听她的 or 是一个没有受过很多教育的女孩子 in the review
- write characters very accurately
- plan how to show off your best Chinese as well as conveying the plot clearly.

媒体 méi tǐ Media

杂志	zá zhì	magazine	广播	guǎng bō	radio
报纸	bào zhǐ	newspaper	网站	wǎng zhàn	website

电视节目 diàn shì jié mù TV programmes

节目	jié mù	programme	电视剧	diàn shì jù	TV Soap
新闻	xīn wén	news	赛车	sài chē	car racing
动画片	dòng huà piān	cartoon	赛马	sài mǎ	horse racing

互联网 hù lián wǎng Internet

网上	wǎng shàng	online	QQ	as in English	software similar to MSN
博客	bó kè	blog			
网友	wǎng yǒu	e-pal	网络文学	wǎng luò wén xué	net novel

休闲 xiū xián Leisure

短信	duǎn xìn	text message	日记	rì jì	diary
MP3	M P sān	MP3	摄影	shè yǐng	photograph; photography
MP4	M P sì	a gadget similar to an iPod	照片	zhào piàn	photo
游戏	yóu xì	game	跳水	tiào shuǐ	to dive

电影 diàn yǐng Film

导演	dǎo yǎn	director (of a film); to direct (a film)	演员	yǎn yuán	actor; actress
			影迷	yǐng mí	movie fan

音乐 yīn yuè Music

唱	chàng	to sing	钢琴	gāng qín	piano
流行歌曲	liú xíng gē qǔ	pop song	演出	yǎn chū	to perform
乐器	yuè qì	instrument			

学习 xué xí Learning process

试	shì	to try	成	chéng	to become
知道	zhī dào	to know	毕业	bì yè	to graduate
成功	chéng gōng	to succeed, successful	认识	rèn shi	to know (be familiar with)

意见 yì jiàn Opinions

不错	bú cuò	not bad	对...有兴趣	duì...yǒu xìng qù	to be interested in ...
对...不好	duì...bù hǎo	to be no good for...			

生活 shēng huó Way of life/Lifestyles

名人	míng rén	celebrity	担心	dān xīn	to worry
生活	shēng huó	life	农民	nóng mín	peasant
浪费	làng fèi	wasteful; to waste	工厂	gōng chǎng	factory
花钱	huā qián	to spend money	超级市场	chāo jí shì chǎng	supermarket
回收	huí shōu	to recycle	地铁	dì tiě	the underground train
刻苦	kè kǔ	hardworking	幼儿园	yòu ér yuán	nursery
友好	yǒu hǎo	friendly	卧室	wò shì	bedroom
忙	máng	busy	贵	guì	expensive
开心	kāi xīn	happy			

量词 liàng cí Measure words

张	zhāng	*measure word (usually for flat things)*	所	suǒ	*measure word (for school, etc.)*

5 我住的地方 wǒ zhù de dì fang WHERE I LIVE

复习 Review – Talking about the home and where things are

1
Reading
Read the characters and match them to the pictures, for example: 1g.

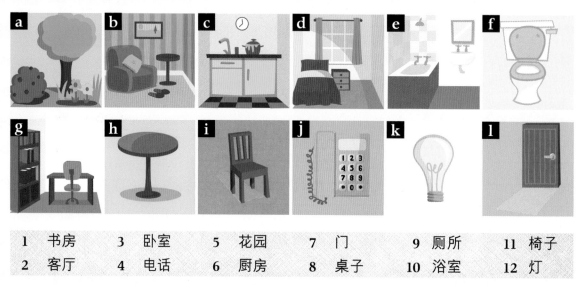

1	书房	3	卧室	5	花园	7	门	9	厕所	11	椅子
2	客厅	4	电话	6	厨房	8	桌子	10	浴室	12	灯

2
Listening
Listen to the passage. Copy out the table and tick the items Zhao Xiaohai, Wang Li and Li Xin have in their rooms. (1–3)

房间 fáng jiān	room
衣柜 yī guì	wardrobe
书架 shū jià	bookshelf

	bed	sofa	table	chair	wardrobe	TV	computer	bookshelf	book
赵小海									
王丽									
李新									

3
Reading
Read about different people's rooms and answer the questions in English.

王海：我的房间不大，里面有床、电视和书架。书架上有很多中文书和英文书。

还 hái	also

小丽：我的房间很大，里面有床、衣柜、桌子和椅子。我的衣柜里有很多漂亮的衣服。

明明：我的房间很小，里面除了有床和衣柜以外，也有很多东西：有很多足球明星的画，还有运动鞋和滑板。

1 Who likes football and skateboarding?
2 Who likes reading books?
3 Who likes fashion?

GRAMMAR: Relative place words

When relative place words are used, for example 'on the right of', 'in front of', they always come after the place being referred to.

Watch out! You do not use 是 in this kind of sentence.

For example:

我在学校。= I am at school.

我在超市前面。= I am in front of a supermarket.

Relative Place Words

里(面/边)	lǐ (mian/bian)	in, inside	前(面/边)	qián (mian/bian)	in front of
外(面/边)	wài (mian/bian)	outside	后(面/边)	hòu (mian/bian)	behind, at the back of
上(面/边)	shàng (mian/bian)	on, above	左(面/边)	zuǒ (mian/bian)	to the left of
下(面/边)	xià (mian/bian)	under, below	右(面/边)	yòu (mian/bian)	to the right of
			旁边	páng bian	beside

4
Speaking

Work with another student. Look at the picture. One student asks where each item or person is, and the other answers.

冰箱 bīng xiāng	fridge
炉子 lú zi	cooker

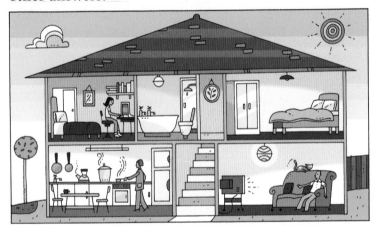

For example:

Q: 王丽在哪儿？
  Where is Wang Li?

A: 王丽在她的房间里。
  Wang Li is in her room.

Q: 冰箱在哪儿？
  Where is the fridge?

A: 冰箱在厨房里。
  The fridge is in the kitchen.

5
Writing

Look at the picture above and write a paragraph about Wang Li's house. Use the framework to help you. Your title could be 王丽的家.

这是王丽的家。王丽的家很大/小，有…个房间。

一楼有…

二楼有…

这是王丽的房间。

她的房间里有… 和…

在卧室的旁边有…

桌子上有…

书架上有…

楼 lóu	floor

EXAM TIP

Remember that 一楼 is the ground floor and 二楼 is the first floor in Chinese.

1 我的家 wǒ de jiā My house
Describing people's homes

1

Reading and Writing

Copy the grid and choose in which of the rooms you will place each object. Some objects go in one room specifically; for others it is up to you to decide. Write the characters for the object under the room you choose for them.

客厅	饭厅	厨房	书房	卧室	卫生间	车库

书架   电视机   电脑   电话   花   冰箱 bīng xiāng

洗衣机 xǐ yī jī   炉子 lú zi   空调 kōng tiáo   CD 机 jī   钟 zhōng   床

2

Reading

Read the questions and match them to the answers.

整齐 zhěng qí	tidy
乱 luàn	messy
外语 wài yǔ	foreign language

1 你的房间里有什么？　　a 不，我的房间很乱。

2 你的房间整齐吗？　　b 我的房间很小，但很舒服。

3 你的书架上有什么书？　c 有很多中文书和法文书，我喜欢学外语。

4 你的房间里有电脑吗？　d 有，我天天上网和朋友聊天。

5 你的房间很大吗？　　　e 我的房间里有桌子、椅子、衣柜和床。

3

Listening

Listen to the dialogue and write down what is in each room of Xiaohai's house.

哇 wā	exclamation word to express amazement
一定 yí dìng	must, for sure
别 bié	do not
忘 wàng	to forget

Room	Items
living room	
kitchen	
bathroom	
bedroom	

4

Listening

Listen to Activity 3 again and answer the questions in English.

1 What impressed Mike about Xiaohai's living room?

2 What are Mike's hobbies?

3 What do both Mike and Xiaohai like watching?

4 What is in the fridge?

5 What, according to this dialogue, is one of the differences between Chinese and English family homes?

GRAMMAR: 住 + type of house

To say what kind of house you live in, you can use
住 + type of house. You don't need to say 住在...
in this situation. For example:
我家住公寓楼。We live in an apartment building.
我家住两层的楼房。We live in a two-storey house.

两层的楼房
liǎng céng de lóu fáng

平房 píng fáng

公寓 gōng yù

5
Speaking

In pairs or small groups describe your homes.
One person describes his or her home and the
others draw a picture. Compare pictures to see
whose matches the description the closest.

一进门 yí jìn mén	as soon as you get in

我家住两层的楼房。一楼有..., 二楼有
我家住平房。一进门是..., ...在左边, ...在右边..., ...在...的旁边。
我家住公寓。客厅里有..., 我的卧室里有...

6
Reading

Read the three advertisements about places to rent.
Look at the requirements each person has and
decide which house is most suitable for them.

房屋	fáng wū	house
出租	chū zū	for rent
层	céng	floor, layer
带	dài	with, equipped with
家具	jiā jù	furniture
希望	xī wàng	to wish; to hope for
工资	gōng zī	salary

房屋出租 1: 两层的楼房, 一楼有一个大客厅, 一个很新的厨房, 有大花园, 但没有车库; 二楼有三个卧室, 一个厕所和一个浴室。不带家具。
每月 ¥3,500。

房屋出租 2: 两层楼房, 花园, 两个车库, 一楼有一个大客厅、一个大饭厅、一个书房、一个厕所和一个厨房; 二楼有三个卧室, 一个厕所和一个浴室。家具有: 床、衣柜、沙发、电视、冰箱、洗衣机和炉子。每月¥4,000。

房屋出租 3: 平房, 一个大卧室, 带空调的客厅, 厨房不很大, 一个小厕所, 家具有床、衣柜、沙发、电视。每月 ¥1,000。

a 赵女士:
这个城市的夏天很热, 我希望我的房子里有空调, 我喜欢看电视, 不喜欢做饭。我的工资不高, 所以我希望我的房子不要太贵。

b 刘女士:
我一个人, 没有丈夫和孩子, 但我有很多朋友, 我喜欢请朋友来我家玩, 我家的客厅一定要很大, 很舒服, 夏天不要太热。

c 王太太:
我家有四口人。我和丈夫都开车。我的孩子们都喜欢看电视, 也喜欢在花园里玩儿。我们只在这个城市住半年, 所以不想买很多家具。

2 我的城市 wǒ de chéng shì My town
Talking about where places are

1
Reading and Writing
Read the questions 1–6. Write down the question numbers and then write the characters for the correct place next to each number.

 银行 yín háng

 邮局 yóu jú

 超市 chāo shì

 电影院 diàn yǐng yuàn

 汽车站 qì chē zhàn

 博物馆 bó wù guǎn

 体育馆 tǐ yù guǎn

 学校 xué xiào

 地铁站 dì tiě zhàn

 动物园 dòng wù yuán

Example: 1 超市

1 我去哪儿买牛奶和面包？

2 我去哪儿可以看到大熊猫？

3 我喜欢运动。我去哪儿打球？

4 我去哪儿寄一张明信片？

5 我喜欢艺术，尤其喜欢看艺术的展览，我可以去哪儿看展览？

6 我下个月要去中国旅游，我去哪儿换钱？

寄 jì	to post, send
张 zhāng	*measure word for postcard , paper, etc.*
明信片 míng xìn piàn	postcard
展览 zhǎn lǎn	exhibition

GRAMMAR: Talking about proximity

To express proximity the structure is: Place A 离 Place B 远/近.
For example:
公园离电影院不远。= The park is not far from the cinema .
学校离我家很近。= The school is very close to my house.

2
Listening
Listen to three people talking about their neighbourhoods. Using the pictures in Activity 1, write down in English the places close to each person's home. (1–3)

1 赵海 zhào hǎi　　2 刘红 liú hóng　　3 王新 wáng xīn

附近 fù jìn	nearby
离 lí	away, from
远 yuǎn	far
近 jìn	close

Speaking

Interview your classmates to find out which places they live near. Record your results in a chart. Use the structures to help you.

教堂 jiào táng	church

place	学校	公园	超市	邮局	医院	教堂	汽车站	银行
person 1								

你家附近有…吗？   Is there a …near your house?

… 离你家近吗？   Is… close to your house?

我家附近有/没有…   There is/isn't … near my house.

我家旁边有…   There is a… next to my house.

我家前面/后面有…   There is… in front/behind my house.

我家离…很远/很近   My house is very far from/close to…

4
Reading and Writing

Look at the picture and fill in the gaps in the description.

小红的家

小红家住在北京的郊区。 __1__ 离她的家不远，所以她每天上学很方便。 __2__ 离小红家也不远，她常常去那儿游泳。 __3__ 在她家旁边，买东西很方便。 __4__ 离她家也很近，她常常坐公共汽车去市中心玩儿。但她家附近没有 __5__ ，所以坐火车很不方便。

5
Writing

Write a short paragraph about the area where you live. Say what amenities can and cannot be found locally. Use the vocabulary and phrases in Activities 3 and 4 to help you.

3 我住的地方 wǒ zhù de dì fang My local area

Using adjectives to give opinions

郊区 jiāo qū

海边 hǎi biān

城市 chéng shì

小镇 xiǎo zhèn

山区 shān qū

农村 nóng cūn

Listening

Listen and note down which type of area each person lives in. (1–6)

极 jí	extremely

GRAMMAR: The use of 极了

Adjective + 极了 = extremely/really: 好极了 = extremely good, brilliant; 美极了 = extremely beautiful, really beautiful. For example: 海边的风景美极了。= The scenery at the seaside is extremely beautiful. 妈妈做的中国菜好吃极了。= The Chinese dish Mum cooks is really delicious.

EXAM TIP

Add 极了 to your list of alternatives to the adverb 很 in order to gain higher marks and avoid repetition.

Reading

Read the sentences and copy out and complete the table in English. The first row has been filled in for you.

1 我叫赵花，我家住在海边，海边的风景美极了。夏天我可以去海边游泳，但是海边有时风很大。

2 我叫王大海，我家住在山区，山区有很多树，空气也很新鲜，但是学校和商店都很少，上学和买东西都很不方便。

3 我叫张丽，我家住在一个小镇上，小镇很安静，但是很没意思。

4 我叫刘明，我家住在城市里，我家附近有很多商店和博物馆，很热闹，也很方便，但是太吵。

5 我叫张新，我家住在农村，农村很安静，空气也很新鲜，但是买东西、看医生都很不方便。

夏天 xià tiān	summer
风 fēng	wind
树 shù	tree
空气 kōng qì	air
新鲜 xīn xiān	fresh
安静 ān jìng	quiet
热闹 rè nao	bustling, lively
吵 chǎo	noisy

Person	Place	Advantages	Disadvantages
赵花	Seaside	Beautiful scenery, can swim in the sea in summer	Strong wind sometimes

Reading

Read the passage and decide whether the statements are true (T), false (F) or not mentioned (NM).

虽然 suī rán	although
空气 kōng qì	air
湖 hú	lake
鸭子 yā zi	duck
散步 sàn bù	to take a walk

我叫刘丽丽，我家在郊区，离市中心很远。我每天坐公共汽车去上学。郊区虽然没有城市热闹，但风景比城市美，有很多树和草，空气也比城市新鲜。我家后面有一个湖，湖里有很多鸭子。我每天晚饭后和爸爸妈妈到湖边散步，看鸭子，很有意思。

1 I live near the city centre.

2 I walk to school every day.

3 There is a lake behind our house.

4 The scenery in the suburbs is better than that in the city.

5 I go for a walk with my parents every evening by the lake.

6 I enjoy living in the suburbs.

Speaking

Pair work. Describe the area where you live to your partner. Use the phrases to help you. Make a table like the one below and fill it in while you listen to your partner's description.

我家住在郊区/海边/城市/小镇/山区/农村。
我家附近/旁边/后面/前面有…
我喜欢/不喜欢…因为这个地方很热闹/安静/吵/方便/有意思/没意思。

Name	Area they live	Local amenities/scenery	Further comments

Writing

Write a short paragraph describing the area where you live. Use the vocabulary and structures in Activity 4 to help you. Include:

• the kind of area you live in

• local amenities

• type of scenery

• your opinion

Listening

Listen to the passage and answer the questions in English.

目前 mù qián	at present
差别 chā bié	difference
交通 jiāo tōng	transportation
机会 jī huì	opportunity

1 Where do most people prefer to live in China?

2 What is the advantage of living in the countryside?

3 What are the disadvantages of living in the countryside?

4 What do a lot of young people from the countryside come to the city for?

Reading

Read the dialogue and complete the following activities:

明明：	你好, 我想借几本日文书, 请问在哪个书架上？
图书馆员：	外语书都在对面的书架上, 在数学书架和科学书架之间。日文书在外语书架的第三层, 在英文书的下面, 法文书的上面。
明明：	我还想要几本日本历史的书, 请问在哪里？
图书馆员：	历史书架在数学书架和美术书架之间, 日本历史书在书架的最下层。
明明：	你们有学习日语的字典吗？
图书馆员：	有, 外文字典都在外语书架的最上层, 但是很抱歉, 我们的字典只能在图书馆看, 不能借。
明明：	没关系, 我就在这里看, 谢谢。

借 jiè	to borrow
几 jǐ	a few *(when used in a statement)*; how many/much *(when used in a question)*
之间 zhī jiān	between
抱歉 bào qiàn	sorry
没关系 méi guān xi	that's fine, no problem

1 Label the book shelves in Chinese characters according to the dialogue, for example.

 A 科学书

2 Where can you find the following books?

 For example:

 Japanese language books B3

 English language books
 French language books
 Japanese history books
 foreign language dictionaries

GRAMMAR: The use of 之间

A is *between* B and C = A在 B和 C之间.
For example: 图书馆在商店和医院之间。= The library is between the shop and the hospital. 中文教室在英文教室和法文教室之间。= The Chinese classroom is between the English classroom and the French classroom.

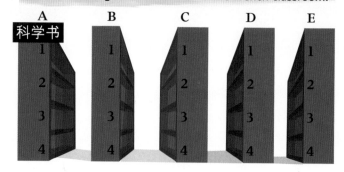

Listening

Listen to the dialogue and answer the questions in English.

1 What is the boy looking for?
2 Where is the office?
3 Where is the library?
4 Where are the boys' toilets?
5 How long has the boy been in the school?
6 Where is the map of the school?

知道 zhī dào	to know
一进门就是 yī jìn mén jiù shì	it is right at the entrance
对 duì	yes, correct
新生 xīn shēng	new student

3
Speaking

Role-play. In pairs one partner is a new student, asking where the places below are in your school, the other gives the locations. See Chapter 2, Unit 2 if you are not sure how to say the places.

Library; Chinese classroom; English classroom; gym; canteen; assembly hall; toilet; head teacher's office

请问，…在哪儿？
Excuse me, where is…?
…在一/二/三 楼，
… is on the ground/first/second floor
…在…的旁边/右边/左边，
…is beside/on the right/left of…
…在 …和…之间
…is between…and…

 4
Listening

Listen to the dialogue and answer the questions in English.

找 zhǎo	to look for
鞋架 xié jià	shoe rack
找到 zhǎo dào	to find
马虎 mǎ hu	careless
先生 xiān sheng	Mr

1 Where are the boy's sports clothes?
   a in his wardrobe **b** behind the door **c** under his bed
2 Where is one of the boy's shoes?
   a under his bed **b** under his table **c** under his chair
3 Where is the other shoe?
   a on the shoe rack **b** in his wardrobe **c** in his bag
4 Where is his tie?
   a on his head **b** around his neck **c** in his hand
5 What does his mum think of him?
   a he is too messy **b** he is too careless **c** he is too lazy

 5
Speaking

Pair work. Look at the picture of Xinxin's messy room and take turns to suggest where each item should go.

他的… 应该放在…。 His… should be put…
For example: 他的书应该放在书架上。
His books should be put on the book shelf.

6
Writing

Look at the picture of Xinxin's room and write the characters to fill the blanks in the paragraph below.

收拾 shōu shi   to tidy

新新的房间

新新的房间很乱：他的书在地上，他的衣服在 ___1___ ，他的裤子在 ___2___ ，足球在 ___3___ ，滑板在 ___4___ ，领带在 ___5___ ，鞋在 ___6___ 。

新新应该好好收拾他的房间。Xinxin should really tidy his room.

7
Writing

Write a paragraph of approximately 100 words about the room, suggesting where each item should go.

5 问路 wèn lù Finding the way

Asking for directions

1 **Reading**

Try to work out which picture goes with which direction.

1 向前直走
2 向前走十分钟
3 第二个路口向右拐
4 向左拐
5 向右拐
6 到十字路口向右拐
7 过了红绿灯向左拐

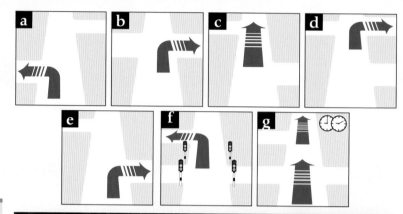

直 zhí	straight
向右 xiàng yòu	towards the right
拐 guǎi	turn
十字路口 shí zì lù kǒu	crossroads
过 guò	after, pass
红绿灯 hóng lǜ dēng	traffic lights

GRAMMAR: Directions

'Turn left' in Chinese is literally 'toward left turn': 向左拐 xiàng zuǒ guǎi. 'Turn right' is 向右拐 xiàng yòu guǎi; 'go straight ahead' is 向前走 xiàng qián zou.

GRAMMAR: 请问，到...怎么走？

To ask for directions politely, you can use the phrase 请问，到...怎么走？= Excuse me, how do I get to...?. For example:
请问，到医院怎么走？= Excuse me, how do I get to the hospital?

2 **Speaking**

With your partner take turns to ask and tell each other how to get to certain places on the map.

Example:
请问，到动物园怎么走？
Excuse me, how do I get to the zoo?
一直走，到第二个十字路口向右拐。
Go straight ahead and turn right at the second crossroads.

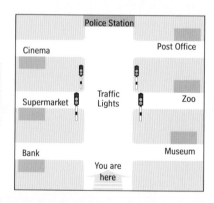

3 **Listening**

Listen and decide which picture is correct for each dialogue. (1–2)

1
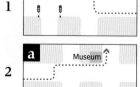

2
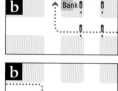

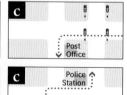

马路 mǎ lù	road
过不去 guò bù qù	cannot get through
警察局 jǐng chá jú	police station

4
Reading

Read the email and answer the questions in English.

www.youremailaccount.cn 搜索

亲爱的大伟：

我们终于要见面了，我好高兴!

明天你坐地铁到前门站下，出了地铁站向左拐，走过一个体育馆，五路汽车站就在体育馆后面，你坐五路汽车到北京动物园站下车，北京动物园就在汽车站对面，我下午两点在动物园门口等你! 我的个子很高，不胖也不瘦。我的头发不长，是黑色的。我明天穿红色的上衣和白色的裙子。

我们明天下午见!

网友：丽丽

七月二十号

1 Where does Dawei need to get off the tube to catch the bus?

2 Where is bus stop no. 5?

3 Describe how to get from the tube station to bus stop no.5.

4 Where is Beijing Zoo?

5 Where will Lili wait for Dawei?

6 What will Lili be wearing tomorrow?

终于 zhōng yú	finally
见面 jiàn miàn	to meet
高兴 gāo xìng	happy
下 xià	to get off (bus, train, tube, etc.)
出 chū	to go out
路 lù	road (here used with number 5 meaning 'bus no. 5')
等 děng	to wait for

 5
Writing

Look at the map in Activity 2. Choose five places and write down directions to each place.

 6
Writing

You are inviting a Chinese friend to your house for the first time. Write an email to direct your friend to your house from the tube station/bus stop.

You could use:

你好!

明天你要来我家，我好高兴!

你在...站下车，下车后...

我们明天见!

你的朋友

EXAM TIP

In your writing, use the six following question words to check that you have covered everything: Who? When? Where? What? Why? How?

Making comparisons

Reading

Fact or opinion? Read the following sentences and decide whether they are fact or personal opinion?

1　香港在中国的东南边，香港人说汉语。
2　西班牙在欧洲的西南边，西班牙是一个美丽的国家，西班牙人非常**热情**。
3　印度是**世界第二人口**大国，但没有中国的人口多，中国是世界第一人口大国。
4　加拿大在**美洲**的北边，加拿大的冬天**特别**冷，夏天也不太热。
5　去年暑假我去马来西亚旅游，马来西亚漂亮极了，你一定要去看看！

热情 rè qíng	warm-hearted
世界 shì jiè	world
第二 dì èr	the second
人口 rén kǒu	population
美洲 měi zhōu	America (continent)
特别 tè bié	especially

Speaking

Pair work. Look at the facts about the different continents. Partner A compares one continent with another in Chinese and partner B guesses which continent it is. Use the example to help you.

	大小	人口
亚洲	44,579,000 sq km	3,879,000,000
非洲	30,065,000 sq km	877,500,000
北美洲	24,474,000 sq km	501,500,000
南美洲	17,819,000 sq km	379,500,000
欧洲	9,938,000 sq km	729,000,000

亚洲 yà zhōu	Asia
非洲 fēi zhōu	Africa

For example:
它比南美洲小，但人口比南美洲多，它是哪个洲？
（欧洲）
It's smaller than South America but has a larger population.
Which continent is it?

Listening

Listen to the conversation between a teacher and her students. Copy and complete the table.

Name	Nationality	Description of country	Reason to be in Beijing
迈克			
丽丽			
大卫			
美美			

介绍 jiè shào	to introduce	亲戚 qīn qi	relative
自己 zì jǐ	self	可能 kě néng	maybe
夏令营 xià lìng yíng	summer camp	听说 tīng shuō	it is said that

Reading

Read the following email and say whether the sentences are true (T), false (F) or not mentioned in the text (NM).

---

www.youremailaccount.cn

亲爱的大山：

你好吗？我来伦敦一个星期了，住在我的朋友Mike 家。
Mike 家在伦敦的郊区，周围到处是绿色的草地和树木，还有各种各样的花，漂亮极了。这儿的空气也比我们那儿新鲜，但这里没有我们那儿热闹，附近没有商店，只有一个教堂和公园。这儿的公园和我们那儿的公园很不一样。这儿的公园不要门票，但里面没有很多好玩儿的东西，也没有我们的公园大。
Mike 的家比我家大，是两层的楼房，带车库，还有一个很大的花园，我天天和Mike 在花园里打羽毛球、打篮球或踢足球。Mike 家有四个卧室，我的卧室没有Mike 的大，但很舒服，也很现代化，里面有电视、电脑、电话和音响。
我现在就在我的房间给你写电子邮件。
快吃晚饭了，我要下楼去了，我们晚上再聊吧。

好友：小海

周围 zhōu wéi	around
到处 dào chù	everywhere
门票 mén piào	entrance ticket
或 huò	or
音响 yīn xiǎng	hi-fi

1 小海喜欢Mike家周围的风景。

2 小海家附近很热闹。

3 小海家附近的公园很大，也很好玩儿，要买门票。

4 小海的卧室太小，所以他不喜欢他的卧室。

5 小海可以在他的卧室里上网聊天。

6 小海和Mike都喜欢运动。

7 小海的家很小，没有车库和花园。

8 小海是在晚饭后写信给大山的。

Writing

Write about a place you have been to and compare it with the place you come from, using phrases from Activity 4 for help.

Speaking

Class debate. Suburbs or city – where do you prefer to live? Divide the class into two groups: A and B. Group A prefer to live in the city while Group B prefer to live in the suburbs.

Each group tries to persuade the other group using comparative sentences; the group that produces more sentences wins the debate. Look at Unit 3 for more help.

EXAM TIP

To get a good grade in the exam, always try to use connective words whenever possible. such as 也, 而且 ér qiě (moreover), 还, 但是/可是 and 因为…所以….

For example: **Group A:** 住在城市比住在郊区方便；(one point)
Group B: 但郊区的空气比城市的新鲜。(one point)

口语 kǒu yǔ Speaking

Preparing for a speaking task (presentation)

TASK AND PREPARATION

Prepare a presentation about your town or village and local area to attract Chinese tourists to visit. You could include:

- Where the town/village is
- What there is to do and see
- Other attractions in the area and your opinions of them
- A comparison with other places you may have lived in the past
- Whether you like living in your area
- Suggestions on how your area could be improved

1
Listening

Chen Dong is delivering a presentation to his teacher about his local area, Wuhan. Listen to Part 1 of the presentation and choose the correct ending for each sentence: a, b or c.

1 武汉是一个…   a 城市   b 小镇   c 山村
2 有一座山在市中心, 山上有…   a 教堂   b 博物馆   c 庙
3 湖边和江边都有很漂亮的…   a 大学   b 公园   c 餐馆

2
Listening

Listen to Part 2 of the presentation and write the words to fill in the gaps.

1 武汉的交通很方便, 除了 __a__ 和 __b__ 以外, 武汉还有很多 __c__ 。
2 往 __d__ 可以去上海, 往 __e__ 可以去香港, 往 __f__ 可以去西安, 往 __g__ 可以去北京。
3 武汉的 __h__ 、 __i__ 、 __j__ 都很好吃。

3
Listening

The following aspects of Wuhan are mentioned in Chen Dong's presentation. Match the aspects (a–f) to the sentences (1–6).

a leisure scene   1 武汉在中国的中部。
b public transport   2 市中心的庙很有名, 游客很多。
c tourist attraction   3 武汉有公共汽车, 有地铁, 也有船。
d food   4 很多人去公园打太极拳、放风筝。
e location   5 武汉有很多大学生, 武汉人都很友好。
f people   6 武汉的鱼、鸡汤、面条都很好吃。

4
Listening

Listen to the questions and answers on the presentation. Answer the questions in Chinese.

1 Where had Chen Dong lived before he started primary school?
2 Where does he live now?
3 How does he compare schools in Wuhan with those in the countryside?
4 Which three places does he recommend to go to enjoy flowers in spring?
5 He suggests everyone in Wuhan learns Putonghua. How does he say that in Chinese?
6 Where does he want to go after he graduates from middle school?

5
Reading

The following are either *adjective* + 的 + *noun* phrases, or *noun* + *adjective* sentences. Change the phrases into sentences and the sentences into phrases. For example:

adjective + 的 + *noun* phrase: 很大的城市 a very big city
noun + *adjective* sentence: 城市很大。The city is very big.

1 很美的风景	3 很有名的面条	5 城市很古老。	7 公园很漂亮。
2 很方便的交通	4 很友好的武汉人	6 东西很好吃。	8 火车站很大。

YOUR TURN NOW

Prepare a presentation about your town or local area.

- You can write down your presentation in Pinyin and highlight the tone marks. Maybe you could find a Chinese native speaker to practise with.
- Make yourself a prompt sheet (A5 containing no more than 30 English words or up to 50 Chinese characters, written in pinyin if you prefer). Practise your presentation until you are fluent.
- Record your presentation and play it to your partner. Discuss with your partner what questions the teacher could ask you about your presentation.

Award each other one star, two stars or three stars for each of the following categories:

- pronunciation
- confidence and fluency
- range of time frames
- variety of vocabulary
- using sentences with more complex structures
- taking the initiative

Also note down what you need to do next time to improve your performance.

ResultsPlus
Maximise your marks

To achieve a **Grade C** you need to:

- ensure that you include plenty of adjectives to describe your area, and use these adjectives correctly. When using adjectives in the noun + adjective structure, be careful not to use 是 as you would use 'is/am/are' in English. For example, the statement 武汉的山是美。 is not correct.
- use different time frames. Chen Dong uses past time frames to say where he used to live and future time frames to say where he wants to go after middle school. For the rest he uses present time frames.

To aim higher than a **Grade C** you need to include some of the following:

- a variety of measure words. Remember it is better to use the most common measure word 个 than not to use any at all.
- try to give advice where appropriate. 可以 is useful for this purpose, e.g. 你可以去东湖划船。
- another example to add complexity to sentences is to include 'place' and 'reason for going' in one sentence, e.g. "我想去北京上大学,因为我想上中国最好的大学。"

If you want to get an **A or A*** you need to :

- use some comparatives. How many examples can you find in Chen Dong's presentation and the follow-up questions and answers?
- show that you can use more complex structures. For example, 武汉除了有公共汽车以外, 还有很多船。 is more sophisticated than 武汉有很多公共汽车, 武汉也有很多船。

写作 xiě zuò Writing

Preparing for an extended writing task to advertise your house and area

PREPARATION

1
Speaking

Warm-up! Tell a partner three things in Chinese about your house and area.

www.writingaboutmyarea.cn   搜索

欢迎您来中国海南岛的三亚度假

介绍三亚的气候: 我家住在中国南方的一个海滨城市三亚。三亚的气候温和，常年气温平均22摄氏度左右。这个城市里有很多椰子树和鲜花。

介绍我家: 我家住在四楼。我们有三间卧室，一个客厅和一个饭厅。除了这些以外，我家还有一个小厨房，两个洗手间和一个挺大的阳台。

在三亚可以做什么: 我家附近有一片很长的海滩，一年四季都有人在海里游泳。住在市中心很方便，比如说，我家附近有三家超市，一个公园，几家茶馆和咖啡厅，一家电影院，两家书店和好几家饭馆。如果你吃够了中餐，你还可以吃麦当劳或者去咖啡厅里吃三明治。

交通方式: 虽然三亚现在已成了一个现代城市，但是你可能想象不到它在二十年前还是农村。小时候，我们没有什么汽车和公共汽车，所以经常骑自行车去上学和见朋友。现在，很多人出门就坐公共汽车和出租车。三亚市长和市民希望这个城市将来成为一流的旅游城市，吸引越来越多的人来居住，生活和享受。

2
Reading

- Find the different measure words in the text. Copy them out and work with a partner to find out what kind of nouns they 'measure'.

- Make a list of all the nouns to describe rooms in a house or places in a town. Test yourself to see if you can write them all.

3
Reading

Find the characters in the text which mean:

1 coastal city
2 on the third floor
3 balcony
4 all year round

5 If you've eaten enough Chinese food…
6 modern
7 When we were small…
8 first rate tourist resort

4
Reading

Look at how the writer uses the verbs 'imagine', 'hope' and 'attract' in the article. Write down a sentence using each of these verbs and think how you might incorporate them into your webpage.

Reading

Find the four correct statements.

1 Sanya has lots of apple trees.
2 The apartment has three rooms.
3 There is no swimming in the winter.
4 There are plenty of supermarkets nearby.

5 McDonalds also has outlets in Sanya.
6 Sanya is a modern city.
7 The city of Sanya has a long history.
8 The mayor has ambitious plans for the city

YOUR TURN NOW

Design a house exchange web page advertising your house and local area.
Write between 100 and 150 characters, under half the length of the web page shown above. You could include information about the following:

- the general area
- your house

- your local area – including how it has changed in the last few years and how it might change in the future

TIP

Use the vocabulary in the web page to help you write yours. There is plenty of vocabulary to refer to in this book, but you might want to use a dictionary to work out how to say one or two additional things. Look up what you want to say in the English–Chinese side of the dictionary. If there is a choice of Chinese words, then look the words up the other way around also in the Chinese–English side of the dictionary to check how they are used; this will help you decide which one you need for your writing.

CHECK

Check the characters and word order. Make sure that you have not accidentally missed out components of characters that you know well. Make sure that you do not use 和 to connect two sentences. Try to make sure that what you have written sounds Chinese rather than a translation of English into Chinese.

ResultsPlus
Maximise your marks

To aim for a **Grade C** you need to.
- show you can use description well.
  - break up the paragraphs, as in the sample text
  - use a variety of adjectives
  - try to build in different time frames.

To aim higher than a **Grade C** you need to:
- ensure that connecting words are used, for example in the web page here 除了…以外 'apart from' and 虽然…但是 'although' are both used

To produce your best written Chinese and to aim for an **A* grade** you need to :
- demonstrate the use of a resultative ending, as for example in the phrase 吃够了.
- try to include phrases such as 越来越 in your writing.
- ensure your word order correctly reflects time + manner + place in that order, for example 经常骑自行车去上学.

我的家 wǒ de jiā **My house**

花园	huā yuán	garden	浴室	yù shì	bathroom
车库	chē kù	garage	一楼有	yī lóu yǒu	there is/are...on the ground floor
客厅	kè tīng	living room			
厨房	chú fáng	kitchen	我家住...	wǒ jiā zhù	I live in...
饭厅	fàn tīng	dining room	平房	píng fáng	single-storey house
卧室	wò shì	bedroom	两层的楼房	liǎng céng de lóu fáng	two-storey house
卫生间	wèi shēng jiān	toilet	公寓楼	gōng yù lóu	flat/apartment building

家具 jiā jù **Household items**

你的房间里有什么？	nǐ de fáng jiān lǐ yǒu shén me?	What do you have in your room?	椅子	yǐ zi	chair
			书架	shū jià	bookshelf
我的房间里有...	wǒ de fáng jiān lǐ yǒu..	In my room, there is/are...	衣柜	yī guì	wardrobe
			床	chuáng	bed
书架上有...	shū jià shàng yǒu...	On the bookshelf, there is/are...	冰箱	bīng xiāng	refrigerator
			洗衣机	xǐ yī jī	washing machine
电视机	diàn shì jī	TV	炉子	lú zi	cooker
电脑	diàn nǎo	computer	空调	kōng tiáo	air conditioner
电话	diàn huà	telephone	CD机	CD jī	CD player
桌子	zhuō zi	table	钟	zhōng	clock

我住的地方 wǒ zhù de dì fāng **Where I live**

我家住在...	wǒ jiā zhù zài...	I live in...	海边	hǎi biān	seaside
我家附近有	wǒ jiā fù jìn yǒu...	there is/are...near my house	城市	chéng shì	city
...离我家不远	...lí wǒ jiā bù yuǎn	...is not far from my house	小镇	xiǎo zhèn	little town
			山区	shān qū	mountainous area
郊区	jiāo qū	suburb	农村	nóng cūn	countryside

有用的形容词 yǒu yòng de xíng róng cí **Useful adjectives**

整齐	zhěng qí	tidy	近	jìn	close
乱	luàn	messy	新鲜	xīn xiān	fresh
舒服	shū fu	comfortable	安静	ān jìng	quiet
现代化	xiàn dài huà	modern	热闹	rè nao	bustling, lively
安全	ān quán	safe	吵	chǎo	noisy
新	xīn	new	方便	fāng biàn	convenient
旧	jiù	old	发达	fā dá	advanced
远	yuǎn	far	热情	rè qíng	hospitable

城市的主要建筑 chéng shì de zhǔ yào jiàn zhù Places in town

银行	yín háng	bank	博物馆	bó wù guǎn	museum
邮局	yóu jú	post office	体育馆	tǐ yù guǎn	gym
超市	chāo shì	supermarket	教堂	jiào táng	church
购物中心	gòu wù zhōng xīn	shopping centre	警察局	jǐng chá jú	police station
电影院	diàn yǐng yuàn	cinema	地铁站	dì tiě zhàn	tube station
汽车站	qì chē zhàn	bus stop	动物园	dòng wù yuán	zoo

方位和方向 fāng wèi hé fāng xiàng Location and direction

请问，...在哪儿？	qǐng wèn, ...zài nǎr?	Excuse me, where is…?	向左拐	xiàng zuǒ guǎi	turn left
			向右拐	xiàng yòu guǎi	turn right
到...怎么走？	dào...zěnme zǒu?	How do you get to…?	向前走	xiàng qián zǒu	go ahead
			过了...向左拐	guò le... xiàng zuǒ guǎi	turn left after…
...在上面	...zài shàng mian	…is on the top			
...在...旁边	...zài...páng bian	…is beside…	红绿灯	hóng lǜ dēng	traffic light
...在...和...之间	zài...hé...zhī jiān	is between…and…	马路	mǎ lù	road
			十字路口	shí zì lù kǒu	crossroads

七大洲 qī dà zhōu The seven continents

亚洲	yà zhōu	Asia	欧洲	ōu zhōu	Europe
非洲	fēi zhōu	Africa	澳洲	ào zhōu	Australia
北美洲	běi měi zhōu	North America	南极洲	nán jí zhōu	Antarctica
南美洲	nán měi zhōu	South America			

6 度假 dù jià HOLIDAYS

复习 Review – Revising weather and transport

1 Reading

Match one or two pictures to each sentence.

1 今天早上伦敦是晴天，但是有风。
2 今天上午北京有小雨，下午雨**转**多云。
3 今天的天气不好，早上很冷，下午有雪。
4 昨天天很热，但今天很凉快。
5 今天是晴天，但明天有雾。
6 今天风很大，但是不冷也不热，很凉快。
7 昨天虽然很冷，但是没有风。
8 今天是晴天，很热**而且**没有风。

转 zhuǎn	change into
天气 tiān qì	weather
凉快 liáng kuai	(pleasantly) cool
而且 ér qiě	in addition

2 Listening

Listen to a student talking about how his family travel and match the pictures to the correct relative.

1 爸爸　2 妈妈　3 哥哥　4 姐姐　5 妹妹　6 我

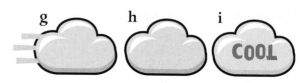

| a 坐火车 zuò huǒ chē | b 坐飞机 zuò fēi jī | c 开车 kāi chē | d 坐公共汽车 zuò gōng gòng qì chē | e 坐地铁 zuò dì tiě | f 骑自行车 qí zì xíng chē | g 走路 zǒu lù |

3 Speaking

Class survey. Find out how your classmates and their families go to school or go to work every day. Copy the table and complete in English.

Name of classmate	How he/she gets to school	One of the family members	How he/she gets to work

| 通常 tōng cháng | usually |
| 一般 yì bān | normally |

How do you…every day/usually? 你每天/通常/一般怎么…?
I go to school by bus every day/usually. 我每天/通常/一般坐汽车去上学。 Places to go:
去上班 qù shàng bān go to work, 去上学 qù shàng xué go to school

EXAM TIP

To gain a higher mark, try to add frequency words (how often?) to your activities. The words we have learned so far to indicate frequency are 天天/每天 (every day), 常常 (often), 通常 (usually), 一般 (normally), and 很少 (rarely). Remember to put the frequency words straight after the subject.

4

Reading

Read the text and answer the questions.

我叫小明。我现在在香港。这是火车站，那是汽车站，飞机场在汽车站的后面。

妈妈要坐火车去北京，爸爸要坐飞机去伦敦，我和姐姐要坐汽车去广州。

1 Where is Xiaoming at the moment?

2 Where is the airport?

3 Where is her mum going? How is she getting there?

4 Where is her dad going? How is he getting there?

5 Where is Xiaoming going? How is she going to get there?

GRAMMAR: Means of transport

In Chinese, you put the means of transport before the action verb.

For example: 我坐飞机去中国。= I go to China by plane ('I by plane go to China').

5

Writing

Write a class survey report based on Activity 3. You may find the following phrases useful:

我们班有...人每天走路上学，...人每天坐公共汽车上学。

我们班有...人的家人通常...去上班。

6

Reading

Put the dialogue between 小红 (xiǎo hóng) **and** 大伟 (dà wěi) **in the correct order.**

a 大伟，你好！你在哪儿？

b 天气预报说香港今天有大雾，飞机要停飞。

c 我明天也要去北京，北京的天气怎么样？

d 我坐火车去。你怎么去香港？

e 我坐飞机去。

f 我现在在北京，但我今天下午要去香港。

g 啊？这太糟糕了！

h 北京这两天天气不太好，常常下雨。你最好带上雨伞。你怎么来北京？

GRAMMAR: The use of 最好

最好 is used before the verb to suggest that someone had better do something: 你最好 = you'd better...

For example:

天很冷，你最好多穿几件衣服。= It's cold today, you'd better put on a few more clothes.

今天有大雾，你最好不要开车去上班，很不安全。= It's foggy today, you'd better not drive to work – it's not safe to do so.

最好的 can mean 'the best'.

For example:

他是我们班最好的学生。= He is the best student in our class.

天气预报 tiān qì yù bào	weather forecast
停 tíng	to stop
啊 ā	exclamation to show surprise
太糟糕了 tài zāo gāo le	too bad
这两天 zhè liǎng tiān	the last few days (not necessarily two days); recently
最好 zuì hǎo	had better, best
雨伞 yǔ sǎn	umbrella

1 天气 tiān qì The weather

Talking about the weather

1 Listening

Listen to the weather forecast and copy and complete the table. The first one has been done for you.

	am	pm	evening	average temperature
Beijing	b	a	d	10°
Hong Kong				
Taiwan				
London				

平均 píng jūn	average
温度 wēn dù	temperature
零下 líng xià	below zero
度 dù	degree

2 Speaking

Look at the map of China and ask your partner about the weather in each city.

...明天的天气怎么样？

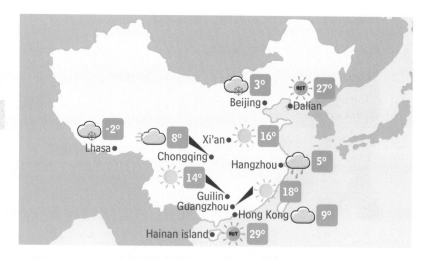

3 Reading

Read the weather in column A and find the activities that 小月 might do at the weekend in Column B.

打算 dǎ suàn	to plan
阴天 yīn tiān	overcast day

小海：小月, 这个周末你打算做什么？

小月：这要看周末的天气怎么样...

Column A

a 要是下大雨, 又很冷,

b 要是有风, 又有太阳,

c 如果是晴天, 又很热,

d 如果是阴天, 但不太冷,

e 如果不下雨, 天又凉快,

Column B

1 我就打算去放风筝。

2 我就想去海边游泳。

3 我就在家看电视。

4 我就打算和朋友一起玩滑板。

5 我会去电影院看电影。

4
Speaking

Work in pairs. Ask each other what you are going to do at the weekend. Answer by combining the weather with the activity. For every reasonable answer, you get a point. See who wins! Use phrases in Activity 3 to help you.

A: 这个周末你打算做什么？
B: 这要看周末的天气好不好。
   要是下大雨, 我就在家听音乐、看电视。

GRAMMAR: 'It all depends'

To say: 'it all depends if…' use 这要看…
For example: 这要看明天的天气好不好。 It all depends if the weather is good or not tomorrow.

GRAMMAR: If… then…

要是/如果… 就…. If… then… For example:
要是明天下雨, 我们就不去踢足球。 If it rains tomorrow, then we will not go to play football.

5
Reading

Read the following text and answer the questions in English.

北京一年有四个季节：春天、夏天、秋天和冬天。
北京的春天常常有风, 早上和晚上都很冷, 但是白天不冷也不热。
   北京的夏天很热, 几乎每天都是晴天, 但有时也会有暴雨。
   秋天是北京最好的季节, 因为北京的秋天不冷也不热, 很凉快, 虽然有时候是阴天, 但是下雨不多。
   冬天是北京最冷的季节。冬天有时会下大雪。

季节 jì jié	season
春天 chūn tiān	spring
夏天 xià tiān	summer
秋天 qiū tiān	autumn
冬天 dōng tiān	winter
几乎 jī hū	almost
暴雨 bào yǔ	rain storm

1　What's the weather like in the morning and evening in spring in Beijing?
2　What's the weather like in summer in Beijing?
3　Which season is the best season in Beijing? Why?
4　What is the winter like in Beijing?

6
Writing

Write a short paragraph about the different seasons where you live.

你好, 我叫…。 我家在…一年有…个季节：…
…的春天/夏天/秋天/冬天…

EXAM TIP

Don't forget to use these frequency words to boost your level: 每天/天天, 常常, 通常, 一般, 有时候, 很少, 几乎不/没有

2 交通 jiāo tōng Transport

Talking about different means of transport

Reading

1 Match the following people's means of transport and their reasons for using them.

1 爸爸坐飞机去德国　　　a 因为她想看大海

2 哥哥骑自行车去学校　　b 这样虽然很贵, 但是很快

3 妹妹坐公共汽车去上学　c 因为她很不舒服, 不能开车

4 妈妈坐出租车去医院　　d 因为这是很好的运动

5 我们班坐旅游车去旅游　e 因为这样又安全又便宜

6 姐姐坐船去澳大利亚　　f 这样我们可以很多人一起玩儿

这样 zhè yàng	in this way, this way	又...又 yòu...yòu	both... and
出租车 chū zū chē	taxi	便宜 pián yi	cheap
旅游车 lǚ yóu chē	coach	船 chuán	ship

Listening

2 Listen to the dialogue and choose the statements that are true.

1 Zhao Yu was planning to take Xiao Xing to the cinema this weekend.

2 Xiao Xing is going to Dalian by plane because it is quicker.

3 Xiao Xing was planning to go to the airport by tube because it is more convenient.

4 Xiao Xing has a lot of luggage.

5 In the end, Xiao Xing decided to drive to the airport herself.

请 qǐng	to invite
慢 màn	slow
行李 xíng li	luggage
换 huàn	to change (tube/ money/clothes)

GRAMMAR: 换 'change'

To change transport: 我每天上班要换三次车, 很不方便。 = I have to change buses three times to get to work everyday. It's very inconvenient.

To change money: 我想用英镑 (yīng bàng)换点人民币 (rén mín bì)。 = I would like to change some Sterling into Chinese currency.

To change clothes: 请等一下, 我需要换件衣服。 = Please wait a moment, I need to change my clothes.

Read the text and answer the questions.

Reading

今天是星期六, 我们一家人打算去剧院看京剧。剧院在市中心, 哥哥想开车去, 可爸爸说市中心停车很不方便, 应该坐地铁去;姐姐说剧院不在地铁站附近, 下了地铁还要走路, 也很麻烦, 应该坐出租车去;妈妈说打的太贵了, 应该坐公共汽车去;哥哥、姐姐和我都说:"坐公共汽车太慢了!"。

妈妈问我:"小红, 你说我们应该怎样去?"

我说:"我认为我们应该先开车到地铁站, 然后坐地铁, 下了地铁再打的。"

哥哥姐姐 很高兴, 他们说:"这样又快又方便。"

爸爸妈妈也很高兴, 他们说:"这样也很省钱。"

1 Who is against going by tube? Why?
2 Who is against going by car? Why?
3 Who is against going by bus? Why?
4 Who is against going by taxi? Why?
5 What is the author's suggestion?
6 Why do they all like this suggestion?

麻烦 má fan	inconvenient
打的 dǎ dī	to take a taxi
认为 rèn wéi	to think; consider
先 xiān	first
省钱 shěng qián	economical

Imagine you are going to travel from London to France. In groups discuss the advantages and disadvantages of using different forms of transport. Use the structures below to help you.

Speaking

快 kuài	fast
便宜 pián yi	cheap
累 lèi	tiring
安全 ān quán	safe

A: 我认为我们应该开车去法国。

B: 为什么?

A: 因为开车比较便宜。

B: 开车虽然便宜, 但是太累了。我认为我们应该…

Look back at Activity 4. Write about the different people's opinions.

Writing

我们下个星期要去法国。我想….., 可是… (someone's name) 认为…..。

3 度假经历 dù jià jīng lì Holiday experiences

Talking about a past holiday

Reading

Read the dialogue between a teacher and a student called 赵阳 (zhào yáng) about holidays and answer the questions.

老师：你上一次度假是什么时候？

赵阳：是去年暑假。

老师：你去了哪里？和谁一起去的？

赵阳：我和我的家人去了台湾。

老师：你们怎样去的？

赵阳：我们坐飞机去的。

老师：你们住在哪儿？

赵阳：我们住在亲戚家。

老师：你们做了什么？

赵阳：我们参观了很多名胜古迹，照了很多照片，
还买了很多东西。

老师：你们在台湾住了多久？

赵阳：我们住了两个星期。

老师：台湾的天气怎么样？

赵阳：天气特别好，几乎每天都是晴天。

老师：你觉得台湾怎么样？

赵阳：我觉得台湾很好玩，台湾的风景很美，
台湾人也很友好，还有很多好吃的东西，
我们玩儿得开心极了。

上一次 shàng yí cì	last time
度假 dù jià	to go on holiday
去年 qù nián	last year
暑假 shǔ jià	summer holiday
名胜古迹 míng shèng gǔ jì	scenic spots and historical sites
照 zhào	to take (a photo)
照片 zhào piàn	photo
玩儿得开心 wánr de kāi xīn	have fun, have a good time

1　When was the last time Zhao Yang had a holiday?
2　Where did he go on holiday?
3　Where did he stay?
4　How long did he stay?
5　What did he do there?
6　What was the weather like there?
7　What did he think about the place?
8　Why did he think that?

EXAM TIP

今年暑假 can mean both 'the summer holiday just gone' or 'this coming summer holiday', depending when the conversation takes place.
The same applies to 今年八月, 今年九月, etc.

Pair work. Role play. Ask and answer questions about holidays.

Here are some additional phrases to help you:

Past time phrases
去年寒假 qù nián hán jià
winter holiday last year
去年八月 qù nián bā yuè
August last year
上个月 shàng ge yuè
last month
今年暑假 jīn nián shǔ jià
this summer holiday

Activities
滑雪 huá xuě skiing
晒太阳 shài tài yáng sunbathe
买纪念品 mǎi jì niàn pǐn buy souvenirs
看精彩的表演 kàn jīng cǎi de biǎo yǎn watch an excellent performance
游泳 yóu yǒng go swimming

Opinions
有趣/有意思
yǒu qù/yǒu yì si interesting
无聊/没意思
wú liáo/méi yì si boring
好玩儿 hǎo wánr fun
太棒了 tài bàng le brilliant
糟糕 zāo gāo awful, terrible
我们玩得很开心!
We had a great time!

Listen to four teenagers talking about where they went on holiday. Copy and complete the table.

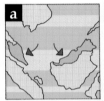 

	Where did they go?	Who with?	What did they do?	How did they feel?
1	b			
2				

Read the postcard. Match the activities with the weather, e.g. 1d.

小红,你好! 我现在在海南岛, 海南岛的天气真好, 几乎天天是晴天! 我现在一边晒太阳,一边给你写信,舒服极了!

上个星期我去了香港,我在香港住了两天。第一天下雨,我去了商店,买了很多东西;第二天白天不下雨了,但是有大风,我就去参观博物馆。晚上风停了,星星和月亮都出来了,我就去坐船看香港的风景,我觉得香港的晚上比白天还好看!

| 星星 xīng xing | star |
| 月亮 yuè liang | the moon |

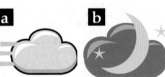 

Write a short paragraph about a past holiday.
Use the suggestions to help you.

For example:
去年暑假我和家人去了…。 我们参观了…,买了…,
吃了…,看了…,还照了…我们在…住了…(duration of time)。我们住在…我觉得…

4 假期计划 jià qī jì huà Holiday plans

Talking about the future

Reading

Read the sentences. Copy and complete the table in English.

1 张伟：去年暑假我和朋友去了北京，明年暑假我想去香港和广州。

2 王月：去年寒假我和家人去了法国和西班牙，明年寒假我打算去德国。

3 赵京：去年春天我和我的男朋友去了台湾，今年春天我们计划去马来西亚。

4 刘海：去年秋天我和我的女朋友去了香港，明年我们打算去澳大利亚。

5 李红：上个周末我和朋友去了电影院，这个周末我们想去听音乐会。

6 陈丽：我去过欧洲和亚洲，没去过非洲和美洲，我将来很想去非洲和美洲。

| 计划 jì huà | to plan to... |
| 将来 jiāng lái | in the future |

Name	Places he/she has visited	Places he/she is planning to visit
张伟	Beijing	Hong Kong and Guangzhou

GRAMMAR: Talking about the future

In Chinese, to indicate past or future, there is no need to change the verb. To indicate the future, simply put a time phrase indicating future, such as 'next year', 'next week', etc.; and use verbs such as 想, 打算, 计划, 要, 将会 jiāng huì (will...).

For example: 下个星期六我打算去博物馆看展览。= I am planning to see an exhibition next Saturday.

	Time phrases	Verbal phrases
Past	昨天, 前天 qián tiān (the day before yesterday), 去年, 上个星期, 上个月, 过去 guò qù (in the past), 以前 yǐ qián (in the past)	Verb + 过, 了
Future	明天, 后天 hòu tiān (the day after tomorrow), 明年, 下个星期, 下个月, 将来 jiāng lái (in the future)	想/打算/计划/要/将会 + verb

Listening

Listen to the passage and answer the questions.

1 Where is Xiao Hong now?

2 Which place has Xiao Hong been to in Europe?

3 What are Xiao Hong's plans for this summer holiday?

4 What activity is mentioned for each of these places?
   a Beijing **b** Chengdu **c** Lhasa **d** Guilin **e** Hainan Island

爬 pá	to climb
长城 cháng chéng	the Great Wall
故宫 gù gōng	the Imperial Palace
大熊猫 dà xióng māo	the Giant Panda
小吃 xiǎo chī	snack

Reading Read the dialogue and answer the questions.

明明：小海, 今年暑假你有什么打算？

小海：我打算先工作一个月, 然后出去旅游。你呢？

明明：我也想去旅游。我打算去香港和 新加坡, 你想去哪儿？

小海：我去过香港, 但没去过新加坡。

明明：我们可以先一起去新加坡。我们可以住在我朋友的家里。

小海：那太好了。然后我们再一起去香港, 正好 我也有亲戚在香港, 我们可以住在我的亲戚家里。

明明：那太好了！ 我想坐飞机去新加坡, 你想怎么去？

小海：好的。我们可以先坐飞机去新加坡, 然后再坐船去香港, 这样既省钱, 又可以看海上的风景。

明明：好！ 我想在新加坡呆 三天, 你打算在香港住几天？

小海: 你想呆几天, 我们就呆几天。

新加坡 xīn jiā pō	Singapore
正好 zhèng hǎo	it happens that...
呆 dāi	to stay for a period of time

1 What's Xiaohai's plan for this summer holiday?
2 Which city has Xiaohai been to before?
3 Where are they going to stay in Hong Kong?
4 How are they going to get from Singapore to Hong Kong? Why?
5 How long are they going to stay in Singapore?

 Writing Fill in the blanks about yourself.

你好, 我叫 ___1___ 。 我是 ___2___ (your nationality)。
我家在 ___3___ 。去年暑假我和 ___4___ 去了 ___5___ 。明年
暑假我 ___6___ 去 ___7___ 。我们打算 ___8___ 去 (how you
get there)。我将会在那儿呆 ___9___ 。我们打算住在 ___10___ 。

Speaking Interview your classmate about their holiday plans.

A: 今年暑假你有什么打算？　B: 我打算和...一起去...

A: 你打算怎么去？　B: 我打算 _____ 去。因为...

A: 你计划在那儿呆住多长时间？　B. 我计划...

A: 你将会住在哪儿？　B: 我将会住在 _____ 。

A: 你想在那儿做些什么？　B: 我想先 _____ ,再 _____ ,
然后 _____ ,最后 _____ 。

GRAMMAR: Question words: a different use

你想呆几天, 我们就呆几天。= We will stay as many days as you want to. (Literally: 'you want to stay how many days, we will stay how many days')

Here the word 几 is no longer a question word.

For example:
你想吃什么, 就吃什么。= Eat whatever you want to eat.

 Writing Write up the results from at least three of your interviews.

Complete the sentences using the words on the right.

订 dìng   单人房 dān rén fáng   双人房 shuāng rén fáng   信用卡 xìn yòng kǎ

1 你好,请问 _____a_____ 在哪里?我想订飞机票。

2 下个月我打算去香港旅游,我想明天 _____b_____ 房间。

3 因为我一个人,所以我打算订一间 _____c_____ 。

现金 xiàn jīn   支票 zhī piào   付款 fù kuǎn   服务台 fú wù tái

4 下个星期我和我的太太两个人去上海玩,我们想订一间 _____d_____ 。

5 出去旅游,需要花很多钱,但是带太多 _____e_____ 很不安全,用 _____f_____ 又不是很方便,我喜欢用 _____g_____ ,既安全,又方便。

6 请问,我怎么 _____h_____ ?您可以用现金,也可以用信用卡。

Read the short emails and answer the questions.

你好。我叫李明。我现在在上海。我下个月想去北京旅游一星期,想订一间单人房,我想从三号住到八号。我的房间里要有电视、电话和空调,还要能上网。请问多少钱一个晚上?我怎样付款?

李明　六月一号

从…到… cóng…dào…	from…until/to… *(time or place)*
能 néng	be able to…
联系 lián xì	to contact
酒店 jiǔ diàn	hotel
这样的 zhè yàng de	this kind of
包括 bāo kuò	to include

李先生,
您好!谢谢您联系我们酒店。您要的房间:单人间,有电视、电话和空调、能上网,这样的房间每天四百元,包括早饭。您可以用信用卡付款,也可以到我们饭店后用现金付款。

张月　北京饭店　六月二号

1 Where is Li Ming?

2 What kind of room is he looking for?

3 How long is he planning to stay?

4 What facilities does he want in his room?

5 How much will his accommodation cost in total?

6 What methods of payment does the hotel accept?

GRAMMAR: 你 and 您

There are two ways of saying 'you' in Chinese: 你 and 您。你 is informal, used for friends and family and for young people. 您 is polite/formal, used for older people or people of higher status, or for customers in a business context.

3

Reading

Match the questions with the answers.

1 请问您贵姓？   a 十号到十三号
2 您的联系电话是多少？   b 我姓赵, 我叫赵明。
3 您打算从几号住到几号？ c 我的手机号码是：0135898869
4 您想订什么样的房间？   d 我想用信用卡付。
5 您打算怎样付款？   e 我想要单人房, 带电视和电话。

| 贵姓 guì xìng | what's your surname? *(polite/formal way of asking)* |
| 号码 hào mǎ | number |

4

Speaking

Role play. One pupil is a customer, the other a hotel receptionist. Try to include these points:

- Say when you want the room.
- Say what type of room you want (single or double)
- Say what facilities you want in your room.
- Find out the cost per night and about methods of payment.

我想订一个单人房/双人房	I would like to book a single/double room.
我想从 …. 住到….	I would like to stay from…until…
我的房间要有/能….	My room should have/be able to…
请问多少钱一个晚上？	How much is the room per night?
怎样付款？	How do I make a payment?
您可以用现金/信用卡/支票付款。	You can use cash/credit card/cheque to make a payment.

5

Listening

Listen to the telephone conversation between a hotel receptionist and a customer. Copy and complete the registration form with the correct information.

登记表 Registration form
姓名 full name: ………………………
联系电话 contact number: ………………………
房间日期 dates for the room: ………………………
房间类型 type of room: ………………………
房间设备要求 equipment requirements: ………………………
价格 price per night: ………………………
付款方式 method of payment: ………………………

登记 dēng jì	registration
表 biǎo	form
类型 lèi xíng	type
设备 shè bèi	equipment
方式 fāng shì	method

6

Writing

You are going to spend a week of your summer holiday in China with your friend. Write an email to a hotel in China to find out the cost of the accommodation.

Remember to include the following:
- How many days you are staying.
- What type of room you would like to reserve.
- What facilities you would like in the room.
- What methods of payment are accepted.

6 旅行安排 lǚ xíng ān pái Making travel arrangements
Talking about sequences of activities

1 Listening Listen to the two dialogues. Which items has each of the speakers lost? (1–2)

不见了 bù jiàn le	disappeared
丢了 diū le	lost

a
b
c
d
e
f
g
h
i

a	b	c	d	e	f	g	h	i
单程 dān chéng	来回 lái huí	照相机 zhào xiàng jī	身份证 shēn fèn zhèng	信用卡 xìn yòng kǎ	旅行箱 lǚ xíng xiāng	护照 hù zhào	地图 dì tú	钱包 qián bāo

2 Reading Read the speech bubbles and answer the questions.

车次	目的地	出发时间	到达时间	站台
T 102	青岛	11: 35	20:30	1
K 579	大连	11: 45	22: 50	4
T 396	重庆	17: 30	10:20	6
K 832	昆明	19: 15	12:18	9

张明: 哥哥，我们的火车晚上五点半出发，第二天早上十点二十到，我们的行李不多，你不用来接我们。

陈红: 妈妈，我们的火车在一站台，快点儿，我们的火车就要出发了！

李海: 爸爸，我们晚上八点半到，我们有很多行李，请到火车站接我们！

王丽: 我们的火车快要出发了，我们去四站台吧。

赵月: 姐姐，我们的车晚上七点一刻出发，我们可以先去吃午饭，再买点儿东西，然后回来等车，好吗？

1 谁去…
   a 青岛？　　b 大连？　　c 重庆？　　d 昆明？
2 谁的家人会去接她/他？
3 谁要去购物？
4 现在大概几点钟？
   a 上午十点　　b 上午十一点半　　c 下午三点

车次 chē cì	train number
目的地 mù dì dì	destination
出发 chū fā	departure
到达 dào dá	arrive, arrival
站台 zhàn tái	platform
接 jiē	to pick someone up

3
Speaking

Role play. One student is a station/airport employee and the other a tourist. Look at the model dialogue and make your own using the timetable in Activity 2.

| 登机口 dēng jī kǒu | *(flight departure)* gate |

A: 请问，下一个去青岛的火车/飞机几点出发？
(Excuse me, when does the next train/plane leave for Qingdao?)

B: 下一个去青岛的车/飞机十一点三十五分出发。

A: 几点到达？ (When does it arrive?)

B: 晚上八点半到。

A: 在 几站台/哪个登机口上车/飞机？ (Which platform/gate does it leave from?)

B: 在一站台/第三登机口上车/飞机。

4
Reading

Read the passage and answer the questions.

你好！我叫大明。我是中国人，但我和爸爸妈妈住在英国的伦敦。我的爷爷奶奶住在中国的香港，今年暑假我要去香港看我的爷爷奶奶。除了看爷爷奶奶，我还想去中国很多地方旅游。我不想去大城市，因为我一直住在大城市：人太多，太吵，夏天又很热，我喜欢风景美的、有山有水的地方。我想先坐飞机去 杭州，因为听说杭州的西湖很迷人，然后坐火车到苏州，苏州的花园很有名，再从苏州到山东的泰山，去看有名的云海和日出，最后再从山东坐飞机回到香港。你觉得我的计划怎么样？

一直 yī zhí	all the time
西湖 xī hú	West Lake in Hangzhou
迷人 mí rén	charming, attractive
泰山 tài shān	Mount Tai
日出 rì chū	sun rise

1 Where is Da Ming's home?

2 Where are Da Ming's grandparents?

3 What is Da Ming's plan for this summer holiday?

4 Why does Da Ming not want to go to big cities?

5 Put these places in the right order according to Da Ming's travel plan: Suzhou, Shandong, Hangzhou.

6 What does Da Ming specifically want to see in each place?

GRAMMAR: The use of 再

再 can mean 'again'.
For example: 再见 = see you again/bye
再 can also mean 'then', showing that one action takes place after the another action has finished.
For example:
我想先去你家, 再去他家。=
I would like to go to your house first, then to his house.

5
Writing

Write a letter to your friend including an itinerary of a planned trip around China. Invite your friend to accompany you on the trip.

亲爱的 ....
暑假快到了，你有什么打算？
我打算去中国旅游。我想去 ....，因为 ....。
我计划先坐 ...... 到 ......，再乘 ...... 到 ......。因为这样可以 ....。
你不是也喜欢 ...... 吗？你想和我一起去吗？
祝　身体健康！　好友：............ 五月三号

LISTENING

1
Speaking

Warm-up! During your last holiday, what kind of weather did you have and what did you do?

2
Listening

You are going to hear Zhang Long talking about his holiday. Match the weather with the day.

Monday	**a** clear
Tuesday	**b** cloudy
Wednesday	**c** rainy
Thursday	**d** sunny
Friday	**e** windy
	f hot

3
Listening

Listen to Zhang Long again and match the places with the days.

Monday	**a** mountain
Tuesday	**b** gym
Wednesday	**c** swimming pool
Thursday	**d** sea
Friday	**e** museum
	f park

GRAMMAR: 在

When 在 is used as a preposition, the 在 phrase generally goes before the main verb. For example: 我在中国学汉语。= I study Chinese in China. 我在家里吃午饭。= I have lunch at home.

TIP

For listening questions which require you to make matches, remember:

• When you are listening, make brief notes particularly concerning time, place and activity.

• When you miss some information the first time you listen, don't worry. Pay attention the second time you listen.

• When you come across new words, don't panic. If you are sure about four of the five pairs in a matching exercise, make the last match with confidence.

• Beware of distractors. When you hear two phrases connected with a word of negation, don't get confused. For example: 昨天我们去爬山了, 没去游泳。 我爱吃菜, 不太爱吃肉。

READING

4
Reading

Warm-up! Find the descriptive words from the travel advertisement below and decide on their meanings.

请到美丽的三亚来

春节到了, 欢迎您到美丽的三亚度假! 这里有雪白的沙滩、蓝蓝的海水、迷人的海底世界; 这里有温暖的气候、干净的空气、美味的椰子。海南东方旅行社愿意为您服务：

1 预订饭店和机票
2 到机场接机
3 选择最好的旅行路线

我们的联系方式是:

电话： 0898-18855510 (早8:00 到晚10:00)
网址： http://travel.sanya.com/
电子邮件： sanyadujia@travel.com
联系人： 王小姐

5
Reading

Choose the five correct statements.

1 This is an advertisement for a holiday over the Chinese New Year.

2 Sanya is a city with beautiful lakes.

3 Food is mentioned in the text.

4 The travel agency can book hotels and air tickets for you.

5 You will need to organise airport transfer yourself.

6 The travel agency chooses the tourist routes for you.

7 You can call the travel agency at any time.

8 You can find more information on the travel agency website.

TIP

How to work out the meaning of new words:

- From the words around them. Certain types of words need to go together. For example, if 美味 comes before and modifies a word, the word probably has something to do with food.
- From the context. If an important word appears in a passage, you can usually find clues from the context. For example, if 美丽 is a new word to you, then the following 雪白 and 蓝蓝 may give you some idea.
- From parallel structures. Parallel structures are formed in the same way, so if you recognize these structures, you will be able to work out the category of the new words at least. For example, if 温暖 is a new word to you, then the parallel structure 干净的空气 may give you some idea that 温暖 is being used as an adjective.

口语 kǒu yǔ Speaking
Preparing for a speaking task (picture-based discussion)

TASK AND PREPARATION

Prepare a discussion based on a photograph or picture/postcard of a holiday destination. You could include:

- A description of the resort, how you got there, who you went with.
- Where you stayed and what it was like.
- The activities you did and your opinions of them.
- What the weather was like.
- Your plans for future holidays.

1
Writing
Warm up! You may be asked why you have chosen this photo. Prepare two possible ways of answering the question.

2
Writing
Prepare some brief notes for each of the bullet points in the task. Altogether you can write up to 50 Chinese characters in bullet point or mind map format. You may refer to this when undertaking your actual assessment.

3
Writing
Make a list of eight questions you might be asked about your photo. Check back later when you have finished listening to the whole conversation to see how many questions you were able to anticipate.

4
Listening
You will hear a model conversation between Sophie and her teacher, based on the photo above. Listen to the first part of the conversation and note down answers to the questions below.

1 What reason does Sophie give for choosing this photo?
2 What are the other five questions that Sophie is asked in this part of the conversation?
3 Note down in characters or pinyin the five questions and answers. What feature do you notice about the sentence structure of the questions and answers in Chinese?

5
Listening
Listen to the second part of Sophie's conversation and fill in the gaps.

你以前去过长城吗?

去 __a__ 好几次。我 __b__ 去北京, __c__ 去北京我 __d__ 要去长城。

十月北京的天气怎样?

十月北京的天气 __e__ ,每天都是晴天,气温 __f__ 20度 __g__ 。

长城上游客多吗?

__h__ 我们周末去长城,长城上游客 __i__ 。

__j__ 是星期三,拍照 __k__ 是早上8点,长城上游客 __l__ 。

长城上风景怎么样?

这是秋天, __m__ 树是红色的, __n__ 树是黄色的, __o__ 树是绿色的。

Listening

Listen to the third part of Sophie's conversation and answer the questions.

1 In this part many time references are used. These include time phrases and function words after or before verbs. Write down four examples of time references from the conversation.

2 When Sophie explains why she enjoys living in her father's home in Beijing, the reasons can be categorised as 'facilities', 'people' and 'activities'. Under 'facilities' she includes 网球场, 游泳池 and 图书馆. Write down details for the two other categories.

3 Sophie says she will go to Guangzhou for her next holiday during the Chinese New Year. How does she express 'during the Chinese New Year' in Chinese? Where does she insert the time phrase in the sentence 我想去广州。?

YOUR TURN NOW

Prepare a picture-based discussion about a past holiday.

- Look back through this chapter for more ideas.
- Practise your discussion with a partner. When you are practising, you might want to prepare some prompt cards to remind you what to talk about. These could be visuals.
- Consider how the discussion might develop and try to prepare appropriate answers. Remember to include a range of time references.
- Check the tones of individual words and get the tones right when you practise the conversation with your partner.

Award each other one star, two stars or three stars for each of the following categories:

- pronunciation
- confidence and fluency
- range of time frames

- variety of vocabulary
- using sentences with more complex structures
- taking the initiative

Also note down what you need to do next time to improve your performance.

ResultsPlus
Maximise your marks

To achieve a **Grade C** you need to.
- show an ability to follow the structure of the question sentence and produce an answer accordingly.
- know which particles to use after and before verbs to indicate time frames. Sophie uses two different particles in 他在拍照 and 去过好几次.

To aim higher than a **Grade C** try to:
- use pronouns to replace nouns previously mentioned. For example 照片上没有我爸爸, 他在拍照。 sounds better than 照片上没有我爸爸, 我爸爸在拍照。
- use more complex structures: 我想春节去广州, 看看中国人怎样过春节。 Sophie uses this structure to explain when she plans to go and why she chooses that time of year to go.

If you want to get **A or A* grade** you need to :
- take the initiative and develop elaborate responses. When asked 长城上风景怎么样, Sophie produces a very comprehensive answer.
- explain reasons from different points of view. When explaining why she enjoys living in her father's home in Beijing, Sophie talks extensively about different factors such as facilities, people and activities.

写作 xiě zuò Writing

Preparing for an extended writing task about a past holiday

PREPARATION

1
Reading

Warm up! Use the Internet to find out about Kunming and Lijiang in Yunnan Province and find them on a map of China

Read the letter from Li Ming to his penfriend and complete Activities 2–5.

亲爱的笔友：

你好！

放寒假时, 我和爸爸妈妈去云南旅行了一个星期。从北京出发, 飞行了三个小时以后, 我们到了昆明。昆明是个好地方, 冬天也很暖和, 听说一年四个季节都跟春天一样。

第二天我们去滇池看鸟。网上说, 那些鸟的名字叫"红嘴鸥", 它们是从北方来昆明过冬的。我站在滇池旁边, 鸟儿们一个接一个地飞过来吃我手里的面包, 真好玩儿！

昆明的石林很有名, 那里的石头多极了, 又高又大, 有的像大象, 有的像兔子, 还有一个石头像美丽的姑娘。

我们还去了丽江古城, 那里没有高楼, 房子的屋顶都是尖尖的。城里有三条小河, 河水都是清清的。

冬天去南方, 真是不错！ 我们一家已经有了明年的计划, 我们打算在下一个寒假时去海南——中国的最南方。朋友说, 海南比云南还要暖和, 各种各样的水果又便宜又好吃！

祝好

李明　三月四日

2
Writing

- There are three different stretches of water mentioned in the text; they all have the water radical 氵. Write down their meanings, using a dictionary if necessary.
- Use the Internet to find the meaning of 石林 and 红嘴鸥.

3
Reading

Find the characters in the text which mean:

1 we went on holiday for a week
2 after a three-hour flight
3 the next day
4 one after the other
5 the roofs of the houses were pointed
6 the river water was clear
7 my family already has a plan for next year
8 all kinds of

4
Reading

The writer uses three different ways to make comparisons in his letter.
Find a sentence using each of these different ways and copy it down.
Work with a partner to make up some sentences of your own using comparison.

Reading

Find the four correct statements.

1 The family on holiday is from Beijing
2 Summer temperatures in Yunnan are similar to those in winter.
3 The birds come to Yunnan to spend the summer there.
4 Some of the stones looked like elephants.

5 There are three rivers in Lijiang.
6 Lijiang is a very modern city.
7 The family plans to go to Hainan in the summer holiday next year.
8 Fruit in Hainan is very expensive.

YOUR TURN NOW

You want to write a letter to a Chinese penfriend about your recent holiday. Write between 100 and 150 characters, less than half the length of the letter opposite. You could include information about some of the following:

- who you went with
- how long you stayed there
- a description of the place where you stayed
- what you did

- your opinions about the place and about the holiday
- your plans for next year's holiday

TIP

Use the vocabulary in this chapter to help you. There is no need to include specialist vocabulary, but you might like to use one or two words, as the writer did here with 红嘴鸥; use a dictionary or the Internet to help you with your research or to find the Chinese name for the place where you went.

CHECK

Check the characters and word order. Make sure that you have not accidentally missed out components of characters that you know well. Make sure you have used a measure word where it is necessary.

ResultsPlus
Maximise your marks

To aim for a **Grade C** you need to.
- show you can write about a past event, using time words and 了 where appropriate.
- give your point of view about the holiday.
- show that you understand that 'when' comes before the verb but 'how long' comes after the verb: 旅行了一个星期.

To aim higher than a **Grade C** you need to:
- refer to a future event even though your writing is about a past holiday.
- give some opinions about what you have done or seen.
- think about your description: 河水都是清清的, 石头又高又大.

To produce your best written Chinese and to aim for an **A* grade** you need to :
- try to use more sophisticated language, as in the use of 越来越 or 屋顶都是尖尖的.
- show that you understand the difference between 的, 得 and 地.
- make sure that you have learnt really well how to write the characters you want to use.

重要语言点 zhòng yào yǔ yán diǎn Key language

天气 tiān qì Weather

天气预报	tiān qì yù bào	weather forecast	很凉快	hěn liáng kuai	very cool
伦敦明天的天气怎么样？	lún dūn míng tiān de tiān qì zěn me yàng?	How is London's weather tomorrow?	很热	hěn rè	very hot
			不太冷	bú tài lěng	not very cold
伦敦明天是晴天。	lún dūn míng tiān shì qíng tiān.	London is sunny tomorrow.	这要看天气怎么样。	zhè yào kàn tiān qì zěn me yàng.	It all depends on the weather.
…是阴天	shì yīn tiān	is overcast	要是天气好，我就…	yào shì tiān qì hǎo, wǒ jiù…	If the weather is good, I will…
…有大雾	yǒu dà wù	is very foggy	春天	chūn tiān	spring
…有大雪	yǒu dà xuě	has heavy snow	夏天	xià tiān	summer
…有小雨	yǒu xiǎo yǔ	is showery	秋天	qiū tiān	autumn
…有风	yǒu fēng	is windy	冬天	dōng tiān	winter
…多云	duō yún	is cloudy	太阳	tài yáng	the sun
多云转晴	duō yún zhuǎn qíng	cloudy becoming clear	星星	xīng xing	star
			月亮	yuè liang	the moon

交通 jiāo tōng Transport

你怎么去上学？	nǐ zěn me qù shàng xué?	How do you go to school?	坐出租车	zuò chū zū chē	by taxi
我坐公共汽车去上学。	wǒ zuò gōng gòng qì chē qù shàng xué.	I go to school by bus.	打的	dǎ dī	by taxi
			骑自行车	qí zì xíng chē	by bike
我…去。	wǒ…qù.	I go by…	开车	kāi chē	drive
坐旅游车	zuò lǚ yóu chē	by coach	太慢	tài màn	too slow
坐飞机	zuò fēi jī	by plane	快	kuài	fast
坐火车	zuò huǒ chē	by train	省钱	shěng qián	economical, money-saving
坐地铁	zuò dì tiě	by tube	太贵	tài guì	too expensive
坐船	zuò chuán	by ship	麻烦	má fan	too inconvenient
坐公共汽车	zuò gōng gòng qì chē	by bus			

假期活动和计划 jià qī huó dòng hé jì huà Holiday activities and plans

去年暑假你去了哪里？	qù nián shǔ jià nǐ qù le nǎ lǐ?	Where did you go last summer holiday?
去年暑假我去了…	qù nián shǔ jià wǒ qù le…	I went to…last summer
今年暑假你有什么打算？	jīn nián shǔjià nǐ yǒu shénme dǎ suàn?	What's your plan for this summer holiday?
我打算和…一起去…	wǒ dǎ suàn hé… yì qǐ qù…	I plan to go…with…
打算	dǎ suàn	intend to, plan
计划	jì huà	to plan
将来	jiāng lái	in the future
度假	dù jià	have a holiday
暑假	shǔ jià	summer holiday
寒假	hán jià	winter holiday
旅行	lǚ xíng	to travel

买纪念品	mǎi jì niàn pǐn	to buy souvenirs
看精彩的表演	kàn jīng cǎi de biǎo yǎn	to watch an excellent performance
参观博物馆	cān guān bó wù guǎn	to visit museums
看名胜古迹	kàn míng shèng gǔ jì	to look at scenic spots and historical sites
滑雪	huá xuě	to ski
晒太阳	shài tài yáng	to sunbathe
照照片	zhào zhào piàn	to take photos
爬长城	pá cháng chéng	to climb the Great Wall
玩得很开心	wán de hěn kāi xīn	had a great time
太棒了	tài bàng le	brilliant
糟糕	zāo gāo	terrible
无聊	wú liáo	boring

旅行安排 lǚ xíng ān pái Travel arrangements

我想订飞机票	wǒ xiǎng dìng fēi jī piào	I want to book a flight ticket.
我想订一间单人房	wǒ xiǎng dìng yì jiān dān rén fáng.	I want to book a single room.
下一个去…的火车/飞机几点出发/到达？	xià yí ge qù…de huǒ chē/fēi jī jǐ diǎn chū fā/dào dá?	When is the next train/flight to… leaving/arriving?
我打算先去…，	wǒ dǎ suàn xiān qù..,	I plan to go to…first
再去…，	zài qù…,	then go to…

然后…，	rán hòu…	then…
最后…	zuì hòu	and finally…
我的…不见了/丢了	wǒ de …bú jiàn le/diū le	I lost my…
单程	dān chéng	single (ticket)
来回	lái huí	return (ticket)
单人房	dān rén fáng	single room
双人房	shuāng rén fáng	twin room

复习 **Review** – Talking about likes and dislikes

1
Listening and Reading

Listen and match the word to the appropriate picture, for example: 1c. (1–10)

1	咖啡
2	水果
3	水
4	鸡蛋
5	茶
6	菜
7	面条
8	肉
9	米饭
10	汽水

a   b   c   d   e

f   g   h   i   j

2
Listening

Copy out the grid, then listen and write the correct letter using the pictures from Activity 1, as in the example. (1–6)

	Like	Dislike
1	d	g
2		

GRAMMAR: The use of 都

You have already learnt that 都 means 'all' or 'both'. But it can also be used to reinforce 'every' 每 (个/只, etc.). 都 must come just before the verb or, in the case of the third example below, the verb–adjective.

For example:

他们都住在中国。 They all live in China.

我爸爸妈妈每天都吃米饭。 My mum and dad both eat rice every day.

每只猫都很可爱。 Every cat is cute.

EXAM TIP

When you come across different ways of saying one word (e.g. restaurant), it is best to choose the easiest to remember and stick to it. For the remainder you just need to be able to understand or recognise them, otherwise you might end up mixing them all together!

3
Reading

Read the passages and then complete the sentences with the correct names.

> 我叫兰花，我十六岁。我住在海南。我们家每天都吃很多菜，也吃肉。我们吃牛肉、猪肉、鸡肉、鸭肉等等。我也很喜欢吃鱼。

> 我的名字叫李丽，我十七岁。我家在北京。我早饭常常吃面包和鸡蛋，我喜欢喝果汁和汽水，我有时候也喝英国茶。我妈妈喜欢喝英国茶，因为她在英国住过。我爸爸喝牛奶。我不喝牛奶因为我觉得牛奶不好喝。

> 我叫毛明，我十五岁。我们家有三口人，爸爸妈妈和我。我和爸爸妈妈常常晚上出去吃饭。爸爸妈妈工作很忙，所以他们都没有时间做饭。我爸爸妈妈喜欢吃南方菜，因为他们是上海人。所以我们常常去上海餐馆。

谁？

1 _____ 住在海南。

2 _____ 爱吃鱼。

3 _____ 常常和爸爸妈妈一起去餐馆吃饭。

4 _____ 不喜欢喝牛奶。

5 _____ 的妈妈喝英国茶。

6 _____ 的爸爸妈妈是上海人，喜欢去上海餐馆。

7 _____ 的爸爸妈妈很忙，没有时间做饭。

8 _____ 每天吃很多肉和菜。

4
Speaking

Interview two or three classmates using the key sentences. Copy this table to record your results. Then report back to the whole class.

	Person 1	Person 2	Person 3
Name			
Age			
Family			
Where they live			
Food/drinks they like/dislike			

Questions	Reporting back to the class
你叫什么？	他/她叫…
你多大了？	他/她今年…岁。
你家里有谁？	他/她家有…
你家在哪儿？	他/她家在…
你喜欢吃/喝什么？(你不喜欢吃/喝什么？)	他/她喜欢吃/喝，不喜欢吃/喝…

5
Writing

Copy out the sentences and complete them, using the pictures to help you.

1 王明住在…，他…岁。他喜欢吃的东西是…，他不喜欢吃…，也不喜欢喝…。

2 小龙今年…岁。他住在…。他喜欢…，他不…。

Now write about yourself.

1 学校的饭菜 xué xiào de fàn cài School meals

Giving opinions

Listening

Listen to the conversation and answer the questions.

1 What does Zhang Wen like about the new school?
2 Does Zhang Wen like the canteen? Why or why not?
3 Does Zhang Wen board at school?
4 Does Zhang Wen have all three meals at school every day?
5 Why does Zhang Wen like to eat at school?
6 According to Zhang Wen, are the school meals expensive?
7 Does Xiao Lan board?
8 Where does Xiao Lan have her lunch and supper every day?

小兰 xiǎo lán

张文 zhāng wén

最近 zuì jìn	recently; lately
不用 bú yòng	need not
特别 tè bié	especially
顿 dùn	*measure word for meal*, e.g.一天三顿饭 three meals a day

GRAMMAR: The use of 菜

菜 cài has several meanings: 1. 'vegetables, greens', for example: 他喜欢吃菜, 也喜欢吃肉。= He likes to eat vegetables and also likes to eat meat; 2. 'dishes', for example: 今天饭桌上有很多菜。= There are many dishes on the dining table today; 3. 'cuisine', for example: 我妈妈喜欢法国菜。= My mum likes French cuisine.

Reading

Read the letter Chen Hai wrote to his parents and complete the sentences.

陈海来到 ___1___ 一个多月了。

陈海的学习 ___2___ 。

陈海常常和他的朋友们一起去 ___3___ , 去 ___4___ 和 ___5___ 。

陈海说学校餐厅的饭菜有时候 ___6___ , 有时候 ___7___ 。

陈海早餐常吃 ___8___ 和馒头。中餐喜欢吃 ___9___ 加一个 ___10___ 和一个素菜。晚餐他吃 ___11___ 或者 ___12___ 。

陈海觉得学校餐厅的牛肉比 ___13___ 的牛肉好吃。

爸爸妈妈:

你们好! 我来到新学校已经一个多月了。我除了学习很忙, 一切都好。

我已经交了几个朋友。我们一起去上课, 一起去运动, 一起去餐厅吃饭。我们学校餐厅的饭有时候好吃, 有时候不好吃。

我早饭常常吃面包或馒头, 喝牛奶、果汁或稀饭。中饭我喜欢吃米饭, 加一个肉菜和一个素菜。我很喜欢吃我们餐厅的炒牛肉。我觉得我们餐厅的牛肉比爸爸做的牛肉好吃。晚饭我有时候吃面条, 有时候吃米饭。

我很好。希望你们都好。

陈海
十月三日

一切 yí qiè	everything; all
馒头 mán tou	steamed bun; steamed bread
稀饭 xī fàn	porridge
素菜 sù cài	vegetarian dish
炒 chǎo	to stir fry
希望 xī wàng	to hope; to wish

GRAMMAR: The use of 几

You have met 几 (jǐ) as a question word, e.g. 你家有几个人 (How many people are there in your family?) or 几点了 (What time is it?). 几 also means 'a few', 'several', 'some', for example: 我有几个好朋友。= I have a few good friends. 他在我家住了几天。= He stayed in my house for several days.

3 **Speaking** Interview two classmates (preferably one who has lunch in the school canteen and another who has a packed lunch). Use the structures below to help you.

| 干净 gān jìng | to clean |
| 带 dài | to bring; to take |

Questions	Answers
你们学校的餐厅怎么样？	大, 不大, 干净, 漂亮, 人很多, 人不多…
你每天在哪儿吃中饭？	我在学校餐厅… or 我自己带中饭…
你为什么去餐厅吃饭？ 你为什么自己带饭？	因为…
你中饭喜欢吃什么？	…
你觉得餐厅的饭怎么样？	…
你觉得餐厅的饭贵不贵？	…

4 **Writing** Write a letter to your school canteen saying what you think could be done to improve their service.

- Introduce yourself
- Say what you think is good
- Say what you think is not so good
- Suggest what they could do to improve their service (e.g. add more vegetarian food or hot food, etc.)

我上十一 年级 。	I am in Year 11.
好/不好的地方	good/bad parts
应该 yīng gāi	should
太 tài	too (as in 'too expensive' or 'too cold')

吃饭 zài cān guǎn chī fàn Eating out in a restaurant

...ood

...ne conversation in a restaurant and choose the correct statements from below.

1 One of the customers ordered orange juice.

2 They ordered two vegetarian dishes.

3 They both wanted boiled rice.

4 The restaurant is not big, but very clean.

5 It was the first time for both of them to eat in this restaurant.

6 The price of the food in this restaurant is reasonable.

汤 tāng	soup
点 diǎn	to order (food/drink)
碗 wǎn	bowl; a bowl of

2 Reading

Read three people's experiences of eating out. Copy and complete the table in Chinese.

a

b

c

张海丽: 上个月, 朋友一家从西安来看我们, 这是他们第一次来北京。我们带他们去了长城和故宫, 还在最有名的烤鸭店"全聚德"吃了北京烤鸭。大家都觉得烤鸭非常好吃, 朋友一家说他们想再来。

赵东: 上个星期六, 我和爸爸妈妈去了一个素食餐馆。这是个新开的餐馆, 离我家不远, 我们是坐地铁去的。这个餐馆人不很多, 很安静, 因为有空调, 所以不热, 这里的菜都是蔬菜或者豆腐做的, 很好吃、很健康, 看起来也很漂亮。

周龙: 昨天我们几个好朋友又去吃麦当劳了, 我们经常去吃。我喜欢麦当劳, 我的朋友有的喜欢麦当劳, 有的喜欢肯德基。我爸爸妈妈说快餐不健康, 让人得肥胖症。但是他们有时候太忙, 不能给我做饭, 所以我只好去吃快餐。

西安 xī ān	(city of) Xi'an
全聚德 quán jù dé	famous roast duck restaurant
蔬菜 shū cài	vegetables
豆腐 dòu fu	tofu/bean curd
麦当劳 mài dāng láo	McDonald's
肯德基 kěn dé jī	KFC
让 ràng	to make; to let; to allow
肥胖症 féi pàng zhèng	obesity
快餐 kuài cān	fast food

GRAMMAR: The use of 让

让 (ràng) as a verb means 'make, let, allow'. It often appears in this structure: 让 + somebody + verb (or verb phrase).

For example:

吃太多快餐让人得肥胖症。= Eating too much fast food will make you overweight.

让我看看。= Let me have a look.

我妈妈不让我去游泳。= My mum doesn't allow me to go swimming.

Which restaurant	Who	When	Opinion

3
Speaking
Interview your classmates about their eating out habits and record your results in a chart.

你上一次去餐馆吃饭是什么时候？   你吃了什么, 喝了什么？

你去了哪个餐馆？它在哪里？   那里的饭菜怎么样？

你怎么去的？   你会再去吗？为什么？

你和谁去的？

4
Reading
A food magazine has carried out a survey asking teenagers when they last ate out. Read the two passages and choose the correct answers.

夜市 yè shì	night market
各种各样 gè zhǒng gè yàng	a wide range of
火锅 huǒ guō	hot pot
为 wèi	for
庆祝 qìng zhù	to celebrate
蛋糕 dàn gāo	cake

星期五晚上, 我和同学去了夜市。夜市上有各种各样的小吃, 有炒面、炒菜、火锅、烤肉, 还有点心等等。我们又饿又渴, 我们吃了好几种东西, 有的好吃, 有的不好吃。我很喜欢夜市, 因为那里很热闹, 很有意思, 而且花钱少。

上个星期六, 我们一家去 "小江南" 餐馆 为爷爷庆祝生日。小江南餐馆在我们这个城市很有名。我们点了很多菜, 那些菜都很好吃。餐馆还给了爷爷一个很大的生日蛋糕, 爷爷很高兴。

周文东

李大海

周文东:

1   a 夜市上东西都好吃。b 夜市上东西都不好吃。
    c 夜市上有的东西好吃, 有的东西不好吃。

2   a 夜市东西很贵。 b 夜市人不多。c 夜市很热闹。

李大海:

1   a 全家去餐馆庆祝爸爸的生日。b 全家去餐馆庆祝
    爷爷的生日。c 全家去餐馆庆祝李大海的生日。

2   a 餐馆给了爷爷一本书。b 餐馆给了爷爷一个鸡蛋。
    c 餐馆给了爷爷一个大蛋糕。

GRAMMAR: The use of 为

1. 'for', for example:
我们为爷爷庆祝生日。=
We celebrate the birthday for granddad (i.e. granddad's birthday).
2. 'for the purpose of' (indicating reason or purpose), for example:
很多人为健康吃素。=
Many people eat vegetarian food for the purpose of being healthy.

5
Writing
Imagine you have been out for a meal on your mum's birthday. What was the restaurant like? What did you eat and what did you think of the food?

妈妈的生日是...   我觉得... 最好吃 / 不好吃

我们去了...   那个餐馆很...

我喜欢/不喜欢那个餐馆的... 因为...

3 健康饮食 jiàn kāng yǐn shí Healthy eating

Talking about diet and healthy lifestyles

Listening

Listen to three people talking about their diet and lifestyles. Copy the grid and put ✔ for 'yes' and ✗ for 'no' in the boxes. (1–3)

a 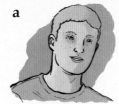 b  c

1  2 3  4 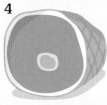 5

	1	2	3	4	5
a					
b					
c					

抽烟 chōu yān	to smoke a cigarette or a pipe
戒烟 jiè yān	to quit smoking

Reading

Read the survey and say which statements are *true* (**T**) and which are *false* (**F**).

性别	年龄	职业	抽烟吗？	喝酒吗？	一般在哪里吃晚饭
男	四十二	老师	是	不	家/学校
女	三十八	医生	不	是	家/餐馆
女	二十八	司机	不	不	餐馆/家
男	二十六	演员	不	是	餐馆/朋友家
男	五十七	工程师	是	不	家/餐馆

GRAMMAR: The use of 对

对 (duì) has many meanings and one of the most common is as a preposition meaning 'for' or 'to'. However, the Chinese word order is different from the English.

For example: 很多人说, 吃素对身体好。= Many people say that eating vegetarian food is good for the health.

抽烟对人不好。= Smoking is not good for you.

1 这个老师喝酒, 但是不抽烟。

2 这个工程师抽烟。

3 这个演员二十多岁, 他喜欢在家吃晚饭。

4 这个女医生有时候喜欢去餐馆吃晚饭, 她不喝酒。

5 这个司机二十多岁, 她不抽烟, 也不喝酒, 她有时候去餐馆吃晚饭。

性别 xìng bié	gender
职业 zhí yè	occupation; profession

3 Interview your classmates about their lifestyle habits
Speaking and record the results in a table.

> 你家谁抽烟？
>
> 你家谁喝酒？
>
> 你和家人常常去餐馆吃饭吗？你们喜欢去餐馆吃什么饭？
>
> 你们家晚上几点吃饭？一般谁做饭？

4 Are these statements facts or just personal opinions?
Reading Read them and write (F) for fact or (O) for opinion.
For example: 成龙不胖不瘦。(O)

区 qū	area; district; region
饮食习惯 yǐn shí xí guàn	eating habits

EXAM TIP

When you give your opinion try and back it up with a reason, e.g. 我觉得… 好/不好, 因为… (I think… is good/bad because…).

1　抽烟喝酒都不健康。
2　在中国很多餐馆不分抽烟区和不抽烟区。
3　你如果想身体好, 就应该有好的饮食习惯。
4　晚饭吃得太多不健康。
5　喝红酒对身体好。
6　在中国很多人喜欢晚上去餐馆吃饭, 因为他们工作太忙, 太累, 不想做饭。
7　每天晚上六点到九点吃晚饭最好。
8　戒烟不容易。
9　我们每个人都应该多吃蔬菜和水果。
10　每天抽一两支烟不会对身体不好。

5 Imagine you have a friend who is a journalist (记者 jì zhě).
Writing Write about him or her using the pictures, and making use of the vocabulary and structures in this unit to help you.

中国
饭馆

4 饮食习惯 yǐn shí xí guàn Eating habits

Talking about regional food

1
Listening

You will hear a list of the most popular dishes in a local restaurant. Match the dishes you hear with the pictures, for example, 1d. (1–8)

a   b   c   d

e   f   g   h

2
Listening

Listen to the telephone conversation between Wang Lan and her father and answer the questions in English.

1 What is the conversation about?

2 Where was the restaurant?

3 What did Wang Lan think of the fish and Ma Po Tofu?

4 What did the restaurant manager say after Wang Lan and friends told him what they thought about the meal.

5 What did Wang Lan think of the food when she was there last time?

6 What was her dad's suggestion to her?

3
Reading

Read the passage and decide which of the five statements below are true.

中国很大, 不同地方的人有不同的饮食习惯, 一般来说, 北方人喜欢面食, 南方人喜欢米饭。不同地方的人也有不同的口味, 比如, 上海人喜甜, 山西人好酸, 四川人和湖南人爱辣, 所以在中国, 如果你去不同的地方, 你会吃到不同口味的饭菜。

1 People from different parts of China have similar eating habits.

2 Southerners prefer wheat.

3 Shanghai people like sour food.

4 Shanxi people like sweet food.

5 Sichuan people like spicy food.

麻婆豆腐 má pó dòu fu	spicy tofu
红烧 hóng shāo	stew with soy sauce
青菜 qīng cài	green leafy vegetables
宫保鸡丁 gōng bǎo jī dīng	Kung Pao Chicken
蘑菇 mó gu	mushrooms

咸 xián	salty
辣 là	spicy
等 děng	to wait
提意见 tí yì jiàn	to make a complaint/ a suggestion
经理 jīng lǐ	manager
对不起 duì bù qǐ	sorry (in apologies)
没关系 méi guān xì	it is ok

一般来说 yì bān lái shuō	generally speaking
口味 kǒuwèi	flavour
好 hào	to like/love
甜 tián	sweet
酸 suān	sour

EXAM TIP

Remember that measure words are not only used between number and objects, they are also used between 这/那 and objects, or between 每 and objects. Always double check whether you have put an appropriate measure word after 这, 那 and 每 in both speaking and writing.

4

Reading

Read the text and complete the sentences.

在中国很多地方, 如果你去餐馆吃饭, 第一个菜常常是凉菜, 凉菜很多, 有肉菜、素菜, 还有海鲜, 什么都有。如果你去广东, 饭前常常有汤, 广东的汤很有名, 广东人会做各种各样的汤, 有些汤里有中药帮助治病。

中餐饭后一般没有甜点, 但是有水果, 水果放在盘子上叫果盘, 在很多餐馆 水果盘是免费的。

中国人认为, 饭后应该活动活动, 这样对身体好。人们常说：“饭后百步走, 活到九十九”。

第一个菜 dì yī ge cài	first course
中药 zhōng yào	traditional Chinese medicine
治病 zhì bìng	to cure disease
甜点 tián diǎn	dessert
放 fàng	to put, place, lay
盘 pán	plate
免费 miǎn fèi	free of charge
活动 huó dòng	to move about; to exercise
活 huó	to live
到 dào	to reach

在中国的很多餐馆, 第一道菜一般是 ___1___ 。

凉菜有 ___2___ , ___3___ 和 ___4___ 。

有些汤帮助治病, 因为汤里有 ___5___ 。

中餐饭后一般有 ___6___ 没有 ___7___ 。

在很多餐馆, ___8___ 是免费的。

中国人说, ___9___ 百步走, 活到 ___10___ 。

5

Speaking

Imagine you have returned from a trip to China.
Tell your classmate about the food.

我… 去了…,	我不喜欢…
我住在…	在中国, 早饭/中饭/晚饭跟我们家一样/不一样
每天的早饭/中饭/晚饭有…	饭前我们…
我最喜欢的是…	饭后我们…

6

Writing

You have just had a meal in a restaurant. You are not happy with the meal and you are writing a letter of complaint to the manager. Make sure you cover all the bullet points.

• when and with whom you had the meal

• what dishes you had

• why you were not happy with the meal

• what you think the restaurant should do

5 节日饮食 jié rì yǐn shí Food and festivals
Talking about celebrations

1 Listening

Write down the numbers 1 to 8. Listen and write the correct letter for each number according to the pictures. (1–8)

a b c d
e f g h

2 Listening

Listen to Xiao Li and Peter talking about celebrating festivals. Copy the grid and note down the similarities and differences between the festivals. (1–2)

Similarities	Differences

春节 chūn jié	Spring Festival/ Chinese New Year
包 bāo	to wrap up/ to make (dumplings)
饺子 jiǎo zi	dumplings
年年有余 nián nián yǒu yú	have more than enough year after year
巧克力 qiǎo kè lì	chocolate
圣诞节 shèng dàn jié	Christmas
火鸡 huǒ jī	turkey
香 xiāng	delicious (literally 'fragrant')

GRAMMAR: The use of 从… 来…

In general, a place is inserted between the two parts of the structure 从 (cóng)… 来 (lái) 'come from…'. For example:
她从美国来。 She comes from America.
你从什么地方来？ 我从山东来。 Where are you from? I am from Shandong.

3 Speaking

Interview your classmate about festivals. Use the structures below to help you ask and answer the questions.

Q: 你最喜欢哪一个节日 (jié rì)？   A: 我最喜欢的节日是…

Q: 你为什么…？   A: 因为

Q: 在….节, 你通常 (tōng cháng) / 一般吃什么？   A: 我们通常 / 一般吃…

Q: 你们去饭馆吃还是…？

Q: 你送礼物 (lǐ wù) 吗？

4
Reading

Read the texts about Chinese festivals and complete the sentences.

春节是中国人最大的节日，每一家都会有很多好吃的东西。北方人春节吃饺子，南方人吃汤圆。家家的饭桌上都有鱼，因为要"年年有余(鱼)"。春节的时候有舞狮、舞龙活动，很热闹。

每年农历五月五日是端午节，也叫"五月节"。端午节一般有龙舟活动，所以也叫龙舟节，每年很多地方会有龙舟比赛。在端午节，大家都吃粽子。你能在商店或饭馆里买到粽子，也有很多人在家里包粽子吃。

中秋节是在农历八月十五日。那一天的月亮又大又圆，一家人坐在一起看月亮、吃月饼。商店里有各种各样的月饼。有些人送月饼给家人和朋友，作为中秋节的礼物。

哪一个节日？

...... 1　北方人吃饺子，南方人吃汤圆。

...... 2　大家吃月饼，看月亮。

...... 3　有龙舟比赛活动。

...... 4　有舞龙和舞狮活动。

...... 5　每一家都吃粽子。

...... 6　家家的饭桌上都会有鱼，因为要"年年有余(鱼)"

汤圆 tāng yuán	stuffed dumping made of glutinous rice flour served in soup
舞狮 wǔ shī	lion dance
舞龙 wǔ lóng	dragon dance
农历 nóng lì	lunar calendar; the traditional Chinese calendar
端午节 duān wǔ jié	Dragon Boat Festival
粽子 zòng zi	sticky rice dumpling
中秋节 zhōng qiū jié	Mid Autumn Festival
月饼 yuè bing	moon cake
作为 zuò wéi	as

GRAMMAR: The use of verb + 好/完

The structure *verb* + 好/完 (hǎo/wán) shows the result of an action and it very often has 了 at the end.
For example:
我看完了。I've finished (watching).
新做好的饺子　freshly made/finished dumplings

5
Writing

Write to your pen pal in China telling them about Christmas or another festival.

圣诞节是英国...的节日。

圣诞节在每年的...

圣诞节我们送...给...

在圣诞节我们一般吃...

我喜欢 / 不喜欢圣诞节，因为...

EXAM TIP

Being familiar with cultural knowledge will help you with your reading comprehension when it comes to texts about Chinese customs and traditions.

LISTENING

Warm-up! Identify the topic of the listening activity from the English instructions and questions in 2 below. Think about the Chinese words that frequently come up in this context.

Listen to Mrs Zhang complaining about her food in a restaurant. Choose the four correct statements.

1 Mrs Zhang ordered a bowl of hot soup.
2 The soup is spicy.
3 Mrs Zhang doesn't like spicy food at all.
4 Mrs Zhang thinks the dish is greasy.
5 The waiter offers to bring some different soup for Mrs Zhang.
6 Mrs Zhang asked the waiter to change the dish for her.
7 The restaurant offers Sichuan and Shanghai food.
8 The waiter is going to give Mrs Zhang a pot of tea for free.

TIP

Using questions to make predictions for listening exams
- Go over the questions before listening.
- Where there is a question that gives you information about the topic, think about related Chinese words and phrases which you may hear in the passage.
- For each statement, think about other possibilities, including the opposite situation. For example, for the statement 'The soup is spicy', other possibilities may be that the soup is 'tasty', 'thick' or 'not spicy'.

GRAMMAR: 一点儿都不 and 一下

一点儿都不 (or 一点儿也不) means 'not… at all'. It is used before adjectives and with some verbal adjectives. For example:
我一点儿都不累。 I'm not tired at all.
我一点儿也不喜欢这个电影。 I don't like the film at all.
一下 is used after a verb, showing that an action happens briefly and does not last. It is used in spoken Chinese. For example:
等一下 wait for a moment
看一下 have a (quick) look
休息一下 have a (quick) rest

READING

Choose a picture that best matches each description below.

What do I eat in the morning?

1 我早晨只吃水果, 听说这样对身体好。
2 年龄大了容易缺钙, 我每天早晨和晚上都喝一杯牛奶。
3 我不爱吃菜, 爱吃肉。早晨没有肉是不行的。
4 我不太喜欢吃鸡蛋。不过我听妈妈的话, 每天早晨还是要吃一个。
5 我以前早饭常常吃面包, 现在我吃面条。

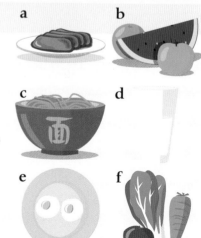

a
b
c
d
e
f

TIP

Finding the right information to answer a question.
- Pay attention to the words indicating change, such as 但是 and 不过 . Usually the phrase following these words is emphasised and is where the opinion lies.
- Look carefully at contrasting or comparative situations. Make sure that you choose the correct 'side'. For example, for a statement talking about change from the past to the present, a question can be asked either about the past or about the present. Identify and choose.
- For a sentence starting with 因为, there is usually a question asking for a reason.
- Double negation such as 没有... 不行 is a strong positive statement.

Reading

Read the passage below and choose the correct answer for each question.

A letter to the manager of a supermarket

经理先生：
上个周末，我和我丈夫去你们的超市购物。我发现那里的东西比原来多了，也便宜了。不过，因为指示牌不清楚，我找不到饼干和酸奶。幸好有一位顾客非常热心，帮了我的忙。选完东西后去结帐，我们排队排了二十多分钟。希望你们多增加几个收款台，要不然我们等的时间太长了！

谢谢！
刘小丽
八月二十六日

1　Who did Xiaoli go to the supermarket with?
　　a　her father
　　b　her grandmother
　　c　her husband

2　How have the goods in the supermarket changed?
　　a　cheaper
　　b　less variety
　　c　less well displayed

3　She couldn't find some food items because
　　a　the supermarket was too big
　　b　the staff were not helpful
　　c　the signs were not clear

4　Who helped her find the things she wanted?
　　a　the staff
　　b　a customer
　　c　a friend

5　What does she think the manager should do?
　　a　extend trading hours
　　b　have more check-out counters
　　c　put up more signs

GRAMMAR: Words indicating a turning point

可是, 但是, 不过, 却, 只是, 然而, 要不然 are all words that indicate a turning point in a sentence, similar to 'but' or 'otherwise' in English.

For example:
我想给他打电话, 可是忘了他的电话号码。 = I wanted to ring him, but I've forgotten his phone number.
他的新学校很不错, 不过离家有点儿远。 = His new school is good, but it is a bit far from home.

口语 kǒu yǔ Speaking
Preparing for a speaking task (open interaction)

TASK AND PREPARATION

You are taking a visitor from Beijing to a local English restaurant.

Your Chinese visitor needs your help to order food from the menu.

Use the menu below to help you answer the questions. You will need to:

- Recommend some food to your visitor.
- Ask questions to find out what food your visitor likes.
- Talk about your food preferences.
- Talk about your experience of eating out.
- Give opinions about some dishes you have eaten.
- Talk about differences in restaurant etiquette.

FARMHOUSE CAFÉ

Soups	Chef's Speciality	Main courses	Desserts	Drinks
Vegetable Soup	Lamb (with mixed vegetables)	Roast Chicken with Salad	Chocolate Cake	Cola
Chicken Soup		Salmon with Rice	Ice Cream	Fruit Juice
		Beef Sirloin with Yorkshire Pudding		Tea

---

1 Writing Make a list of questions in Chinese you will need to ask to complete the task, plus two extra questions you could ask.

2 Listening You will hear a model conversation between Amy and her teacher. Her teacher is playing the role of the Chinese visitor. Listen to the first part of their conversation and note how to ask the following questions in Chinese:

1 What would you like to eat?

2 What do you like to eat?

3 What are we going to eat today?

3 Listening Listen to the second part of the conversation and answer the questions in English.

1 What does Amy say about how to use a knife and fork?

2 Amy is asked if she prefers healthy food, fast food or tasty food. How does Amy expand her answer?

3 How does Amy compare vegetables in Chinese restaurants and English restaurants?

4
Listening

Listen to the second part of the conversation again
and fill in the gaps.

1　在英国，我们 ____a____ 喝汤， ____b____ 吃主食。
2　你 ____c____ 左手拿筷子， ____d____ 右手拿筷子？
3　____e____ 你右手拿筷子，你 ____f____ 左手拿叉，右手拿刀。
4　我 ____g____ 喜欢去中国餐馆。
5　中国餐馆的青菜 ____h____ 英国餐馆的青菜 ____i____ 。

5
Listening

Listen to the third part of the conversation and note down in
English the four questions Amy asks her Chinese visitor.

6
Listening

Listen to the third part of the conversation again and note down in
pinyin Amy's comments about the following.

1　Chinese desserts
2　Chinese food in China compared to Chinese food in England

YOUR TURN NOW

Prepare your answers to the task, and then have a conversation with your teacher or partner.
- Use the ideas in the ResultsPlus to enhance what you say.
- Take the initiative by asking some questions yourself. This helps to keep the flow of conversation natural.

 ResultsPlus
Maximise your marks

To aim for a **Grade C** you need to:
Use simple sentences that you are confident about saying, and link them together with a joining word or phrase that you know how to use. In this way you can convey some complex ideas and impress the examiner. (我爸爸不喜欢做饭，所以他喜欢简单的食物。)
Express an opinion where appropriate. For example: 我觉得食品店里的甜点太甜。and "有的中国餐太辣。

To aim higher than a **Grade C** you need to:
- Use a variety of verb phrases (想吃、喜欢吃 ；会选择 ；不能放、可以放)
- Use 吧 to give advice (remember 吧 can also be used to make requests). For example, look at how Amy advises her visitor to order fish and rice.
- Take the initiative in the conversation. Notice how Amy asks questions whenever possible

To produce your best spoken Chinese and to aim for an **A or A* grade** try to:
- Use the structure with 如果...，就... （如果你右手拿筷子，你就右手拿刀，)
- Show how you can use more complex structures to make comparisons, for example: 我觉得中国餐馆的青菜比英国餐馆的青菜好吃。

写作 xiě zuò Writing

Preparing for an extended writing task about healthy living

PREPARATION

1
Speaking

Warm-up! Tell a partner three things in Chinese about your own eating habits and preferences.

Read the article about healthy eating and complete Activities 2–5.

> ### 饮食与健康
>
> 　　今年是我和家人的"健康年", 也就是说, 我们今年要多吃青菜, 水果和鱼, 少吃肉, 油炸食品和甜食。
>
> 　　小时候, 我很喜欢吃薯条和巧克力。医生说, 我必须少吃油炸食品和糖果, 要不然我就会成为一个"小胖子"。
>
> 　　在家里, 妈妈很会做饭, 她经常给我们做好吃的东西。有时我们也会全家人去饭馆吃北京烤鸭。
>
> 　　现在我们住的城市里有很多超市和快餐店, 比如说, 麦当劳、肯德基。麦当劳和肯德基的东西又好吃又方便, 可是它们容易让人发胖。有时候, 如果我和我的朋友出去吃饭, 我就选择吃素。我爸爸妈妈的朋友中有人抽烟、 有人喝酒, 可是我觉得这些习惯不健康。我将来不会抽烟, 我只会在一些庆祝活动上喝些酒, 但是我不会多喝。
>
> 　　小王

2
Reading

- Write down all the names of food and find the meaning of each.
- Find all the characters with the fire 火 radical on the left and copy them out, noting down their meaning and looking them up in a dictionary where necessary.

3
Reading

Find the characters in the text which mean:

1 health/healthy
2 must
3 otherwise
4 supermarket
5 convenient
6 eat vegetarian food
7 in the future
8 celebrate

4
Reading

Look at the sentences talking about the future. What are the key words and structures used? Try writing two sentences referring to a future event using these words and structures.

5

Speaking

Answer the questions.

1 What does Xiao Wang's family plan to do in the Year of Good Health?

2 What did Xiao Wang like to eat when he was little?

3 Name three things about food at McDonald's and KFC, according to the passage.

4 What does Xiao Wang eat when he goes out nowadays?

5 On what occasions does Xiao Wang think he might drink alcohol in the future?

6 What is he not going to do?

YOUR TURN NOW

A Chinese friend has asked you to write a short article for the school magazine about healthy living. Write between 100 and 150 characters, about half the length of the article opposite. You should include information about the following:

- Your own eating habits – now, in the past and in the future
- Exercise
- Relaxation – including drinking and smoking

TIP	CHECK
Use the vocabulary in this chapter to help you. There is no need to include specialist vocabulary, but you might like to look up one or two words to describe the particular food or sport you like. Use a dictionary or the Internet to help you with your research. The article here concentrates on food, but you should also look at exercise.	Check the characters and word order. Make sure that you have not accidentally missed out components of characters that you know well. Don't embark on sentence structures you are unsure of and avoid translating from the English.

ResultsPlus
Maximise your marks

To aim for a **Grade C** you need to:

Show you can write about past, present and future events and give your opinions about them.

Xiao Wang talks about:

- present events when referring to his current eating habits
- past events when talking about what he used to eat
- future events when he talks about what he will do when he grows up

To aim higher than a **Grade C** you need to:

- vary sentence structure to ensure that an article like this does not just become a list
- use subordinate clauses such as 'when I was young'; and connecting words such as 'if', 'and', 'but', 'or', 'both…and'.

To produce your best written Chinese and to aim for an **A* grade** you need to:

- use 的 clauses as a substitute for the noun, as in 我是吃素的。
- try to write the Chinese characters very accurately
- state your opinions clearly

食品和饮料 shí pǐn hé yǐn liào Food and drinks

早饭/餐	zǎo fàn/cān	breakfast	蛋糕	dàn gāo	cake
午饭/餐	wǔ fàn/cān	lunch	蔬菜	shū cài	vegetable
晚饭/餐	wǎn fàn/cān	supper	豆腐	dòu fu	bean curd
饭菜	fàn cài	meal; food	中餐	zhōng cān	Chinese food
汤	tāng	soup	西餐	xī cān	Western food
面条	miàn tiáo	noodles	口味	kǒu wèi	flavour
水果	shuǐ guǒ	fruit	爱	ài	to like; to love
素菜	sù cài	vegetarian dishes	我更爱吃…	wǒ gèng ài chī	I like to eat…more
北京烤鸭	běi jīng kǎo yā	Beijing roast duck	…和…一样好吃	…hé…yí yàng hǎochī	…is as tasty as…
火锅	huǒ guō	hot pot	我和家人都爱…	wǒ hé jiā rén dōu ài…	I and my family all like…
炒菜	chǎo cài	fried dishes			
炒面	chǎo miàn	fried noodles	我早饭常常吃…	wǒ zǎo fàn cháng cháng chī…	I often eat…for my breakfast
稀饭	xī fàn	porridge			
烤肉	kǎo ròu	roast meat	妈妈做的鱼好吃	mā ma zuò de yú hǎo chī	The fish mum cooks is delicious
鸡蛋	jī dàn	egg			

描述食物的形容词 miáo shù shí wù de xíng róng cí Adjectives to describe Food

咸	xián	salty	好吃	hǎo chī	tasty; delicious (food)
甜	tián	sweet	好喝	hǎo hē	tasty; delicious (drink)
辣	là	spicy	香	xiāng	(smell/taste) delicious; fragrant
酸	suān	sour			

生活方式 shēng huó fāng shì Lifestyle

一日三餐	yí rì sān cān	three meals a day	…对身体好	…duì shēn tǐ hǎo	…is good for one's health
快餐	kuài cān	fast food			
抽烟	chōu yān	to smoke; smoking	我不做饭	wǒ bú zuò fàn	I don't cook
戒烟	jiè yān	to quit smoking	他不会做饭	tā bú huì zuò fàn	He doesn't know how to cook
喝酒	hē jiǔ	to drink alcohol	我自己带中饭	wǒ zì jǐ dài zhōng fàn	I bring my own lunch
瘦	shòu	thin	常常出去吃饭	cháng cháng chū qù chī fàn	often eat out
胖	pàng	fat; plump			
肥胖症	féi pàng zhèng	obesity	饭前	fàn qián	before the meal
…让人得…	ràng rén dé	…make people get…	饭后	fàn hòu	after the meal
健康	jiàn kāng	health; healthy	活动	huó dòng	(do) physical activity
我吃素	wǒ chī sù	I eat vegetarian food/I am a vegetarian			

节日饮食 jié rì yǐn shí Food and festivals

春节	chūn jié	Spring Festival (Chinese New Year)	汤圆	tāng yuán	stuffed dumplings made of glutinous rice flour served in soup
中秋节	zhōng qiū jié	Mid Autumn Festival (The Moon Festival)	粽子	zòng zi	a pyramid-shaped mass of glutinous rice wrapped in leaves
端午节	duān wǔ jié	Dragon Boat Festival			
圣诞节	shèng dàn jié	Christmas	火鸡	huǒ jī	turkey
包饺子	bāo jiǎo zi	to make/wrap dumplings	看月亮	kàn yuè liang	to watch the moon
月饼	yuè bing	moon cake	龙舟	lóng zhōu	dragon boat

在外面吃饭 zài wài miàn chī fàn Eating out

餐馆	cān guǎn	restaurant	安静	ān jìng	quiet
餐厅	cān tīng	restaurant; canteen	我要一个…	wǒ yào yí gè	I'd like to have a…
夜市	yè shì	night market	我们点…吧	wǒ men diǎn…ba	Shall we order…
烤鸭店	kǎo yā diàn	roast duck restaurant	请给我…	qǐng gěi wǒ…	Please can I have…
快餐店	kuài cān diàn	fast food restaurant	你要…还是…	nǐ yào…hái shì…	Would you like to have…or…
热闹	rè nao	lively; bustling; noisy			

复习 Review – Describing clothes

1 **Reading**

Read the statements and decide which are true according to the pictures.

红色的头发

白色的运动鞋

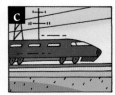
绿色的火车

咖啡色的篮球

一只黑白两色的猫

EXAM TIP

Always check that you have used a measure word, particularly when an object is described with some detail. But remember that the number and the measure word should always go together. If you can get them right, you will impress the examiner.

For example:
一只很大的狗。A big dog.
一个红黑两色的球。
A black and red ball.

2 **Listening**

Listen to three teenagers talking about themselves.
Copy out the chart and complete it. (1–3).

	Age	Hobbies	Item(s) they bought/got	Colour	Price
1					
2					
3					

3 **Speaking**

Describe the pictures, as in the example.

这是 Serena Williams
她是网球运动员。　　　她穿白色的运动服。
我（不）会打/喜欢 网球。　　我（不）想做一个网球运动员。

Serena Williams

Tiger Woods

Beyoncé

Nicole Kidman

Yang Yang

书法 shū fǎ	calligraphy
山水画 shān shuǐ huà	Chinese landscape painting
印章 yìn zhāng	stamp; seal

4
Reading

Read the passage and answer the questions in English.

我叫Mike，我十五岁，我家在英国北方。我上中学，我有中文课，我很喜欢中国书法。 我也喜欢美术课，因为我喜欢画画 儿，我的美术老师也很好。我去年学了中国山水画，中国山水画也叫国画。国画常常只有两种颜色，黑色和白色，但是很漂亮。画上常常有一个红色的印章：印章上一般是画家的名字。
画中国山水画很有意思，也不太难。

1 Where does Mike live?
2 What is Mike's favourite subject and why does he like it?
3 What did Mike learn last year?
4 What colours can you usually find on Chinese ink and wash painting?
5 What is the red stamp for?
6 What does Mike think of his own Chinese landscape painting?

5
Reading and Writing

Read the passage above again and complete the sentences.

Mike住在 ___1___ 。
Mike最喜欢上 ___2___ 课。
去年Mike学了 ___3___ 。
中国山水画也叫 ___4___ 。
中国山水画的颜色常常是 ___5___ 和 ___6___ 。
印章的颜色是 ___7___ ，它上面是 ___8___ 的名字。
Mike觉得 ___9___ 有意思，也 ___10___ 。

6
Writing

Look at the pictures in Activity 3 and choose one of the famous people to write about. Use the framework below to help you.

这是…
他/她是…
他/她会/喜欢
他/她在…很有名
他/她穿…色的…
他/她的衣服…

CULTURE: CHINESE PAINTING

Also known as 水墨画 (shuǐ mò huà – ink and wash painting), Chinese landscape painting was developed in the Song Dynasty (960–1279). Artists usually grind their own ink stick on an ink stone to obtain ink. Brushes are traditionally made from bamboo with hair from goat, ox, horse, etc. The painting may be done either on Chinese paper (rice paper) or silk.

1 服饰 fú shì Clothing and accessories

Describing what people wear

① Listening

Listen and match the colours with the clothes. For example, 1c. (Some items have more than one colour.)

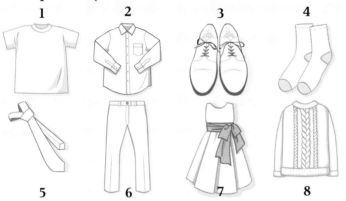

1 2 3 4

5 6 7 8

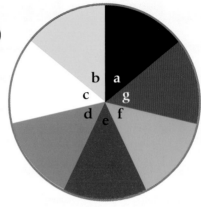

② Listening

Listen and choose the correct answers.

1 Menswear at the exhibition included:
   a suits **b** shirts **c** shorts

2 Womenswear included:
   a trousers **b** skirts **c** swimsuits

3 The accessories Xiaohong saw were:
   a wallets **b** scarves **c** hats

4 The accessories Xiaohong didn't see were:
   a necklaces **b** ties **c** belts

5 They wanted to go to the exhibition by:
   a bus **b** taxi **c** bicycle

时装 shí zhuāng	fashion (referring to clothes)
展 zhǎn (short for 展览 zhǎn lǎn)	exhibition
首饰 shǒu shì	jewellery
项链 xiàng liàn	necklace
手镯 shǒu zhuó	bracelet
耳环 ěr huán	earring
路 lù	route (bus, etc.)

③ Speaking

Describe the people in the pictures.

他 / 她看起来 .... 多岁。

他 / 她个子 ....

他的头发 .... (长/短)，是 .... 色的。

他 / 她穿/戴 .... 。

他 / 她的 .... 是 .... 色的。

我觉得他 / 她的 .... 。

我(不)喜欢他/她的 .... ，因为 .... 。

| 戴 dài | to wear (see grammar box) |

1

2

3

4

Reading

Read the passages and copy and complete the chart.

1 我叫王丽, 我今年十六岁, 我住在北京西城区。我周末
常常和朋友一起去看电影, 有时候我也和我妈妈去
买东西, 我们两个人都喜欢买衣服。我喜欢红色,
我妈妈喜欢黑色, 她的毛衣、裤子、鞋都是黑色的。
我觉得黑色很难看。

2 我叫Peter, 我今年十五岁, 我家在英国南部。我有
一个妹妹, 我妹妹比我小五岁, 她的房间是粉红色的,
因为她喜欢粉红色。她有很多粉红色的裙子。我喜欢
绿色, 所以我的房间是绿色的。周末爸爸妈妈带我们
去买衣服, 我喜欢一件咖啡色的大衣, 可是那件大衣
太贵了, 我最后买了一件不太贵的大衣。爸爸妈妈给
妹妹买了一条围巾。

3 我叫Francois, 我家在法国北部, 我今年十五岁。
我每个周末都去我的中国朋友家学中文, 我很喜欢
汉字, 因为汉字的笔画很有意思。有时候, 我和朋友
一起去买衣服, 我最喜欢蓝色和白色的衣服, 黑色的鞋。
上个星期六, 我去给爸爸买了一条领带, 因为星期天
是他的生日。领带是深蓝色的, 我爸爸很喜欢。

GRAMMAR: Use of 穿/戴

穿(chuān) and 戴 (dài) both mean
'wear', but 穿 generally goes
with clothes, e.g. 穿裙子 =
to wear skirt/dress, 穿裤子 =
to wear trousers,
穿鞋 = to wear shoes.

戴 is usually used with
accessories, e.g.
戴眼镜 = to wear glasses,
戴手套 = to wear gloves,
戴耳环 = to wear earrings.

Now look around in the class
and use 穿 and 戴 to describe
a classmate and let the class
guess who the person is.

城 chéng	city; (originally) a walled city
粉红色 fěn hóng sè	pink
围巾 wéi jīn	scarf
笔画 bǐ huà	Chinese character stroke
深 shēn	dark; deep

	Age	Where they live	Favourite colours	What they do/ did during the weekend	What they bought if they went shopping
王丽					
Peter					
Francois					

Writing

**Imagine you are going to meet your penpal for the first time.
Describe what you look like and what you will be wearing,
so that your friend can identify you at the airport.**

我个子 ___1___ 。
我的头发很 ___2___ , 是 ___3___ 色的。
我穿 ___4___ 色的 ___5___ , ___6___ 色的
___7___ 和 ___8___ 色的 ___9___ 。
我戴 ___10___ 和 ___11___ 。

2 买东西 mǎi dōng xi Shopping

Buying and returning goods

1 **Writing**

Write out the missing floor number for the gaps 1–6.

去几层？ *cén*

1 买中文书去 ……
2 买碗和杯子去 ……
3 买游泳衣去 ……
4 吃饭去 ……
5 买手机去 ……
6 买乒乓球拍去 ……

一层　化妆品、餐具，
二层　男装、女装、运动衣裤
三层　电器、家具、玩具、皮包
四层　床上用品、书籍、运动用品
五层　中餐、西餐、小吃、冷热饮

饮料
xǐn liào
drinks

化妆品 huà zhuāng pǐn	cosmetics
具 jù	utensil/tool
装 zhuāng (short for 服装 fú zhuāng)	clothes
包 bāo	bag
用品 yòng pǐn	appliances/ articles for use
球拍 qiú pāi	racquet; bat

2 **Listening**

Listen to the conversation between a customer and a shop assistant and answer the questions.

1　What item did the customer want to return to the shop?
2　When did he buy them?
3　Why did he want to return them?
4　What was the shop assistant's initial response?
5　Was he allowed to return the goods?
6　What did she recommend to him?
7　Why didn't the customer want them after he tried them?
8　What did the customer decide to buy finally?

退货 tuì huò	to return goods
名牌 míng pái	famous brand
问题 wèn tí	problem; questions
另外 ling wài	other

3 **Speaking**

Buying clothes. Pair work. One student plays the part of the customer and the other of the shop assistant. Swap roles at the end. Use the framework to help you.

Customer	Shop assistant
请问你们有…吗？	我们有/没有…
你们有…色的吗？	对不起….卖完了/没有了，可是我们有…
好,我很喜欢这件…多少钱？	…元/块, 角/毛, 分
太大/小/贵了,不好看	我们也有…
我去…再看看。	好的。

Reading Read the e-mail from Kate to her Chinese penpal and choose the four correct statements.

互相 hù xiāng (to) each other

TO: 小花   转送

圣诞节是我们国家最大的节日。 我们**互相**送礼物。
今年圣诞节，我从网上给我的家人买了礼物。我给妈妈买
了一条红色的项链，因为我妈妈有一条红色的长裙，她穿
红色的裙子，戴这条红色的项链，很漂亮。 我给爸爸买了
一条咖啡色的皮带，他很喜欢。我还给弟弟送了一个网
球拍，因为他爱打网球，他很高兴有一个新球拍。我爸爸
妈妈给了我一个MP3，因为听音乐是我的爱好。

我不喜欢圣诞节前去市中心买东西，因为商店里的
人太多了，所以我常常在网上买东西。网上的东西比
商店里便宜，用信用卡付钱也很方便，但是如果东西不好，
退货要花很多时间。中国最大的节日是春节，春节的时候，
你们也要买很多礼物吗？

再见! Kate

1 I bought some presents from shops and some on the Internet for my family.
2 I bought Mum a red dress.
3 I bought Dad a brown belt.
4 I bought my little brother a tennis racket.
5 I often buy things on the Internet.
6 I do Internet shopping because I enjoy using the computer.
7 It is cheaper to buy things on the Internet.
8 It is convenient to return goods which you've bought on the Internet

GRAMMAR: Use of 互相

互相 (hù xiāng) means '(to) each other'. In English, the structure is *verb phrase + each other*, for example 'We give presents to each other'. In Chinese, the structure is 互相 (hù xiāng) + *verb phrase*, for example:
我们互相送礼物。 = We give presents to each other.
我们互相打电话。 = We phone each other.

Writing It will be your friend's 15th birthday next month. You went out with another friend to buy a present for him/her. Write about your shopping experience. You can use these phrases to help you.

...是...的生日。   我们先看了...

我想...礼物。   然后....
                last
我和...一起去了...   最后...

下个月
Next

上个月
last

Describing famous people

Read the passage and answer the questions about David Beckham (贝克汉姆 bèi kè hàn mǔ).

Reading

贝克汉姆是世界著名的足球运动员。他一九七五年五月二日出生在英国伦敦。他身高一米八多。贝克汉姆从很小的时候就踢足球,他去过很多国家参加足球赛。贝克汉姆每年收入很高,因为他是一个球星。 他也做很多广告,做广告让他的收入更高。贝克汉姆的妻子跟他一样有名,不过,她不是球星,她是一个歌星。他们有三个孩子,都是男孩。

著名 zhù míng	famous
收入 shōu rù	income
球星 qiú xīng	(football/basketball) star
广告 guǎng gào	advertisement
更 gèng	even; more
妻子 qī zi	wife

1　贝克汉姆的生日是几月几号?
2　贝克汉姆多高?
3　为什么他的收入很高?
4　他的妻子做什么工作?
5　他们有几个孩子?

GRAMMAR: Comparison

To say 'A is as... as B', use the structure: A跟(gēn) /和(hé) B一样(yī yàng) ... which literally means 'A and B the same...'. For example:

他的妻子跟他一样有名。His wife is as famous as he is.
她和弟弟一样喜欢看电视。She and her little brother both like to watch TV.
丽丽和小海一样从中国来。Lili and Xiaohai are both from China.

Look at the profile of Li Ning, the former world champion gymnast, and then introduce him verbally in full sentences.

Speaking

姓名	李宁
职业 (现在)	商人
职业 (过去)	体操运动员
国籍	中国
出生日期	一九六三年九月八日
出生地	广西
身高	1.64米
婚姻状况	已婚
现居地	香港

广西 guǎng xī	Guangxi (province)
婚姻状况 hūn yīn zhuàng kuàng	marital status
现居地 xiàn jū dì	place of residence

Listening

3 Listen to the dialogue and answer the questions in English.

1 What has Zhang Lan been busy doing?
2 Where does she go to play badminton?
3 With whom does she play badminton?
4 Does she take part in badminton matches? Why/why not?
5 Does she want to become a professional athlete? Why/why not?
6 How does she think one can become a professional athlete?

日子 rì zi	days
天资 tiān zī	talent; a natural gift
训练 xùn liàn	training; to train
健身 jiàn shēn	keep fit

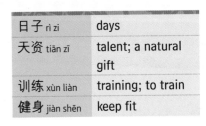

 Reading and Writing

4 Read the text, then copy and complete the form.

她是中国也是世界著名的乒乓球运动员。邓亚萍一九七三年二月六日出生在河南省。邓亚萍从五岁就跟着爸爸学习打乒乓球。她虽然身高只有一米五0, 可是打球打得很好。她在国际比赛中得过很多块金牌。后来邓亚萍去大学读书, 她先去了清华大学, 然后又到英国的大学学习, 几年后, 她获得了剑桥大学的博士学位。邓亚萍现在和丈夫、儿子住在北京。

河南 hé nán	Henan (province)
国际 guó jì	international
清华大学 qīng huá dà xué	Qinghua University
获得 huò dé	to gain; to obtain
剑桥 jiàn qiáo	Cambridge
博士 bó shì	doctorate
学位 xué wèi	academic degree
丈夫 zhàng fu	husband

姓名		出生地	
国籍		婚姻状况	
年龄		现居地	
身高		学历	
出生日期			

 Speaking

5 Interview your classmate to find out about each other's favourite sports personality.

1 你最喜欢的运动员是谁？
2 他/她长得什么样？
3 说说他/她的一些 基本情况, 比如, 国籍、出生日期、出生地、身高等等。
4 他/她的爱好是什么？
5 你为什么喜欢他/她？

| 基本情况 jī běn qíng kuàng | basic information |
| 比如 bǐ rú | such as |

6 **Writing**

Write a short paragraph about your favourite sports personality. You could start your paragraph like this:

(name of sportsman/woman) 是中国/世界有名的 (name of sport) 运动员。

Conducting an interview

1
Listening

Listen to a journalist interviewing an actor and answer the questions in English.

1 According to the man being interviewed, what's the best thing about being an actor?
2 Where has his film-making taken him?
3 Why does he like going to different places?
4 What did he want to be when he was young? And what did his parents want him to be?
5 Has he regretted becoming an actor?

采访 cǎi fǎng	to interview
做 zuò	to be; to do
观众 guān zhòng	audience
拍电影 pāi diàn yǐng	making a film

2
Listening

Listen to a scientist being interviewed and decide which four statements are correct.

1 赵女士是世界著名的科学家。
2 赵女士没有来过英国。
3 赵女士来过英国旅游。
4 赵女士喜欢英国, 因为英国有很多漂亮的地方。
5 赵女士觉得自然历史博物馆很好, 因为它很大。
6 自然历史博物馆里有很多人, 赵女士觉得不好, 因为人太多了。
7 赵女士小时候就很想做科学家, 因为她的爸爸妈妈想让她做科学家。
8 赵女士小时候喜欢上科学课。

自然 zì rán	nature; natural
一定 yí dìng	surely; certainly
一直 yì zhí	always; all the time

3
Listening and Writing

Listen to the dialogue in Activity 1 again and complete the sentences.

Note down the missing words in pinyin while listening and write the characters later.

1 陈先生是一个…
2 陈先生觉得做演员最好的方面是观众…他。
3 做演员让陈先生去过…
4 做演员让陈先生认识…
5 陈先生小时候想…
6 陈先生的爸爸妈妈想让他…

4

Speaking

Pair work. Take turns imagining you are celebrities and journalists. Interview each other. Use the structures below to help you ask and answer the questions.

1　你喜欢做…吗？

2　你为什么觉得做…好 / 不好？

3　你的工作让你去很多地方吗？

4　你去过哪些地方？

5　你喜欢这些地方吗？为什么？

6　你小时候想做…吗？

5

Reading

Read the passage and answer the questions.

我最佩服的一个名人

我最佩服马可•波罗。马可•波罗是一个大旅行家，十三世纪从欧洲来到中国。他在中国住了十几年，去了很多地方，还写了一本书叫《马可•波罗游记》。这是欧洲人写的第一本描述中国历史、文化和艺术的游记。我很喜欢旅游，我希望我有一天也能去一个很远的国家，写一本有用的书。

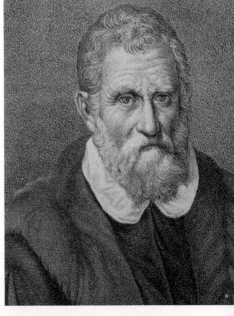

1　马可•波罗是做什么的？

2　他什么时候来到中国？

3　他从哪里来中国？

4　他在中国住了多长时间？

5　他的书叫什么名字？好在哪里？

6　我的希望是什么？

佩服 pèi fú	to admire
马可•波罗 mǎ kě bō luó	Marco Polo
世纪 shì jì	century
游记 yóu jì	travel notes
描述 miáo shù	to describe
有用 yǒu yòng	useful

EXAM TIP

It is useful to memorize the question words ('what?', 'when?', 'who?', 'how long?', etc.) in Chinese and practise them constantly when you revise. You will then find it easier to identify quickly the type of question you are being asked and gain valuable time in examinations.

6

Writing

Imagine you are in your twenties with a job you like. Write a short paragraph about yourself. You could talk about:

• how you like your job

• what the best part of your job is

• what you wanted to be when you were young

• what your parents wanted you to be when you were young

我是一个…　　　　小时候我想…

我喜欢我的工作，因为…　我爸爸妈妈想让我…

我的工作可以让我…

5 历史人物 lì shǐ rén wù Historical figures

Talking about figures from the past

Listening

1 Listen to the dialogue and answer the questions.

人物 rén wù	figure; character
三国演义 sān guó yǎn yì	'Three Kingdoms' *(historical Chinese novel)*
兵 bīng	army; soldier
文学 wén xué	literature
文章 wén zhāng	writings; article

Zhuge Liang

1 What type of books does Long Long like to read?

2 Which historical figure does Long Long like?

3 Why does Long Long like him?

4 Apart from making excellent use of his army, what else was Zhuge Liang good at?

5 What did Xiaohong know about Zhuge Liang? Where did she find out this information?

Reading and Writing

2 Read the passage and note down the Chinese for the English words listed.

孔子是中国历史上著名的思想家、教育家。他出生在春秋时期的鲁国 (今天的山东省)。孔子一生中, 教过很多学生, 最有名的 学生有七十二人。他们记下了孔子说的很多话, 比如：三人行, 必有我师。孔子的思想对中国文化有很深的影响。中国很多地方有孔庙, 用来纪念孔子。

孔子 kǒng zǐ	Confucius
思想家 sī xiǎng jiā	thinker
时期 shí qī	a particular period
鲁国 lǔ guó	*one of the Warring States into which China was divided during the Eastern Zhou period (770–256 B.C.)*
一生 yì shēng	throughout one's life
记下 jì xià	to write/jot/take down
行 xíng	to go; walk; travel *(formal)*
必 bì	certainly; surely
对…有影响 duì…yǒu yǐng xiǎng	have/has an effect/influence on
纪念 jì niàn	to commemorate; mark

1 history
2 educator
3 province
4 students
5 deep
6 Confucius temple

Confucius

Reading

3 Read the passage in Activity 2 again and match the two halves of the sentences.

1	孔子是中国历史上	a	是在今天的山东省。
2	孔子教过很多学生,	b	对中国文化影响很深
3	孔子出生的地方	c	有名的教育家和思想家。
4	孔子说过	d	最有名的学生有七十二人。
5	孔子的思想	e	三人行, 必有我师

4 Reading

Read the statements and match them to the pictures.

1 孙悟空见了他的师傅。
2 一路上有很多妖怪。
3 孙悟空是《西游记》里的人物,在中国谁都知道孙悟空。
4 孙悟空也叫孙猴子, 他最早是一个石猴。
5 他们最后到了西天。

孙悟空 sūn wù kōng	Monkey King
师傅 shī fu	master
西游记 xī yóu jì	Journey to the West (title of book)
妖怪 yāo guài	monster
石 shí	stone; rock
西天 xī tiān	Western Heaven (Ancient Buddhist name for India)

a   b   c   d   e

 5 Speaking

Use one to two full sentences to describe each of the pictures. Use the structures to help you.

《西游记》是一本…的书。
这本书的人物有…
孙悟空最早是一个…

一路上有很多…
这些妖怪都…
最后…

6 Listening

Listen to the dialogue and choose the correct answers.

1 Mulan is a character
   a in a Chinese novel
   b in a Chinese poem
   c on TV
2 What is Mulan's full Chinese name?
   a Fa Mulan   b Hua Mulan   c Mulan Hua
3 Mulan
   a is the only girl in the family
   b has a little sister
   c has no brother or sister
4 Most Chinese people know about Mulan through
   a the film   b the poem   c the TV

首 shǒu	measure word for songs and poems
古诗 gǔ shī	ancient poetry
差不多 chà bu duō	about the same; similar
唯一 wéi yī	only; sole
勇敢 yǒng gǎn	brave

 7 Writing

Choose a famous person from history and write a paragraph about him or her. Use the framework to help you.

…是我最喜欢的一个历史人物。
他/她是一个…
他/她对…很有影响。
我 喜欢/佩服他/她, 因为…

TASK AND PREPARATION

Your Chinese friend is staying with you. She wants to buy some typical British products before she returns home. You take her to a department store and find her a leaflet in the store. Use the leaflet to help answer your friend's questions. Remember to ask your friend at least one question.

WELCOME TO OAK TREE HOUSE!
Monday–Saturday 9.30am–5.30pm Sunday 11.00am–4.00pm
Or buy online at www.oaktree.co.uk   All credit cards accepted

Billabong bag
(red, green)
£15
Ground Floor

Manchester United scarf
(red)
£20
Ground Floor

Clarks shoes
(black)
£35
1st Floor

Christy's bowler hat
(green, brown)
£38
1st Floor

中国货 zhōng guó huò	Chinese goods
英国货 yīng guó huò	British goods
质量 zhì liàng	quality

① Speaking **Warm up! Work with a partner. Answer the questions in Chinese.**

1 When was the last time you bought clothes?
2 What did you buy? How do you like it?
3 When shopping for clothes, what's important to you? Looking nice, quality, or low price?

② Listening **You will hear a model conversation between Zoë and her teacher. The teacher is playing the role of Zoë's Chinese friend. Listen to the first part of their conversation and make notes in English on the following:**

1 Zoë's comments on British goods
2 Zoë's comments on the jeans she bought

③ Listening **Listen to the first part of the conversation again and fill in the gaps.**

1 我觉得在英国买礼物 ___a___ 买英国货。
2 我会买 ___b___ 便宜、___c___ 好看的衣服。
3 ___d___ 我爷爷、爸爸、妈妈 ___e___ 礼物
4 一 ___f___ 帽子、一 ___g___ 皮包、一 ___h___ 围巾、一 ___i___ 皮鞋

Listening Listen to the second part of the conversation and find Zoë's answer in Chinese for the following questions.

1 What do you think of this kind of leather bag?

2 Why is the scarf so expensive?

Listening Listen to the second part of the conversation again and find how Zoë says the following in Chinese.

1 We can pay for everything together after we have chosen the shoes and the hat.

2 I take a size 7.

3 Try this pair on.

6 Listening Listen to the third part of the conversation and note down in English what Zoë thinks of buying things online.

YOUR TURN NOW

Prepare to do this task with your partner.
- Give detailed answers and take the initiative by asking some questions yourself.
- Record the conversation. Ask a partner to listen to it and say how well you performed.

Award each other one star, two stars or three stars for each of the following categories:
- pronunciation
- confidence and fluency
- range of time frames
- variety of vocabulary
- using sentences with more complex structures
- taking the initiative

Also note down what you need to do next time to improve your performance.

ResultsPlus
Maximise your marks

To aim for a **Grade C** you need to:
- use pronouns where necessary to avoid repetition. Listen for where 这、这儿、这些、and 这双 are used.
- respond naturally to questions and keep answers coherent. Note how Zoë answers the question 'Have you bought Chinese goods before?' Give opinions wherever possible.

To aim higher than a **Grade C** you need to:
- use some more complex structures. Zoë shows she can use the 的 structure as in 英国戴帽子的人 and 我要买的东西.
- show that you can make use of conjunctions, for example 除了一些老年人以外, 英国人都不喜欢戴帽子。
- give advice where appropriate. 最好 is useful, as in 在英国买礼物最好买英国货。

To produce your best spoken Chinese and aim for an **A or A*** try some of these ideas:
- show that you can use a variety of measure words. Look at the different measure words Zoë uses for hat, bag, scarf and shoes.
- show that you can use the 给 structure properly as in 给你妈妈买一个皮包.
- show that you can express sophisticated ideas. Look at how Zoë talks about what she looks for regarding style, quality and price.
- Show that you can explain a range of viewpoints. Look at how Zoë explains what she thinks of shopping online.

写作 xiě zuò Writing

Preparing for an extended writing task about a family makeover

PREPARATION

Speaking

1 Warm up. Tell a partner in Chinese about what you like to wear at the weekend.

Read the article about Xiaohong's family fashions and complete Activities 2–5.

> ### 我的衣服
>
> 我今年十六岁。我喜欢粉红色的衣服。我十六岁生日的那天, 妈妈和爸爸给我一件粉红色的毛衣和一条棕色的短裙。小时候, 我不喜欢红色, 只喜欢绿色, 所以我的衣柜里有很多深绿、浅绿的衣服。可是, 现在我觉得它们不好看了。长大以后, 我想穿各种各样颜色的衣服。
>
> ### 妈妈的衣服
>
> 妈妈今年42岁。因为她经常穿颜色鲜艳的套装, 所以看起来像是32岁。她最喜欢的一套衣服是紫色的丝绸上衣和紫色的西式裙子。她还喜欢穿高跟鞋。
>
> ### 爸爸的衣服
>
> 爸爸对衣服不在乎。只要衣服舒服, 他就喜欢。他常常穿棉质的衬衣和长裤。他每年只在过新年时买一次衣服。
>
> ### 奶奶的衣服
>
> 奶奶总是穿得整齐、简单。她常常穿棉质衣服, 有灰色的, 也有蓝色的。她穿的衣服是自己做的。她不喜欢去商店买衣服。
>
> 如果我能在写作比赛中获奖, 我会给家人买各种各样的新衣服!
>
> 小红

Reading

1 Go through the passage and copy out all the characters for items of clothing, then memorise how to write them.

2 In the same way, copy down as many colours as you can and learn them.

3 Find the characters in the text which mean:

Reading

1 when I was small
2 dark green/light green
3 high heels
4 cotton
5 tidy
6 he only buys clothes once a year at the Spring Festival
7 simple, plain
8 if I win this competition

Reading

4 Look at how Xiaohong uses 的 in this article to link adjectives or phrases to the noun. Find each instance of 的 in the article. Try to work out the meaning of each phrase where 的 occurs and check you understand why it has been used.

5 Reading

Find the four correct statements.

1 Xiaohong likes pink clothes.
2 When she was little, she liked blue clothes.
3 She has a wardrobe full of green clothes.
4 Xiaohong's mother is 32.
5 Xiaohong's father thinks more about comfort than fashion.
6 Xiaohong's grandmother makes her own clothes.
7 Xiaohong's grandmother also likes going shopping for clothes.

YOUR TURN NOW

You are going to enter a competition to win money for a fashion makeover for you and one other member of your family. You need to write an article about your fashion preferences and what kind of clothes you will buy with the money if you win. Write between 100 and 150 characters, less than half the length of Xiaohong's article. You should include information about the following:

- What you and another member of the family used to wear and your opinions.
- What you and another member of the family wear now and your opinions.
- What clothes you would buy for both of you with the money and how this would improve your 'look'.

TIP

Use the vocabulary in this chapter and in Xiaohong's article to help you. Xiaohong's article focuses on what she used to wear and what she and her family wear now. You need to include more about what you would buy in the future with the prize money. You can use a dictionary or the Internet to help you find a few additional words for this section. Structure your text; organise what you write into paragraphs.

CHECK

Check the characters and word order. Make sure that you have not accidentally missed out components of characters that you know well. Check that you have some linking words and that you have used 的 correctly. Check you have added measure words where necessary.

ResultsPlus
Maximise your marks

To aim for a **Grade C** you need to.
- plan the task and structure it carefully, showing that you can write about past, present and future events and give opinions

Xiaohong talks about:
- present events when referring to the clothes her family wears
- past events when referring to what she used to wear
- future events in the final sentence summing up what she will do with the money; your article will need to cover more in the future time frame.

To aim higher than a **Grade C** you need to:
- use a variety of adjectives and verb-adjectives
- use linking words. For example, Xiaohong uses 因为…所以 (because) and 虽然… 但是 (although).

To produce your best written Chinese and to aim for an **A* grade** you need to :
- try using some Chinese idiomatic phrases, for example 爸爸对服装不在乎.
- try introducing some more unusual colours or items of clothing.
- make sure that characters show a high level of accuracy.

衣物和饰品 yī wù hé shì pǐn Clothing and accessories

穿	chuān	to wear	帽子	mào zi	hat/cap
戴	dài	to wear (accessories)	游泳衣	yóu yǒng yī	swimming suit
大衣	dà yī	coat	皮鞋	pí xié	leather shoes
衬衣	chèn yī	shirt	袜子	wà zi	socks
毛衣	máo yī	woolen sweater/ cardigan	领带	lǐng dài	tie
			手镯	shǒu zhuó	bracelet
T恤衫	T xù shān	T shirt	耳环	ěr huán	earring
裤子	kù zi	trousers	项链	xiàng liàn	necklace
裙子	qún zi	skirt/dress	眼镜	yǎn jìng	glasses
围巾	wéi jīn	scarf			

描述衣服 miáo shù yī fu Describing clothes

白色	bái sè	white	深绿色	shēn lǜ sè	dark green
黑色	hēi sè	black	浅蓝色	qiǎn lán sè	light blue
红色	hóng sè	red	舒服	shū fu	comfortable
绿色	lǜ sè	green	漂亮	piào liang	beautiful; pretty
黄色	huáng sè	yellow	好看	hǎo kàn	pretty; nice to look at
蓝色	lán sè	blue	太大/ 小/ 长/ 短	tài dà/xiǎo/cháng/duǎn	too big/small/long/short
红白两色	hóng bái liǎng sè	red and white			

购物 gòu wù Shopping

贵	guì	expensive	卖完了	mài wán le	sold out
便宜	pián yi	cheap	名牌	míng pái	famous brand
多少钱?	duō shǎo qián	how much is it?	试	shì	to try
买	mǎi	to buy	问题	wèn tí	problem; question
在网上买东西	zài wǎng shàng mǎi dōng xi	online shopping	退货	tuì huò	to return goods
卖	mài	to sell			

名人 míng rén Celebrities

科学家	kē xué jiā	scientist	有名	yǒu míng	famous
歌星	gē xīng	singer	著名	zhù míng	famous; well known
球星	qiú xīng	football/basketball etc. star	国际	guó jì	international; internationally
演员	yǎn yuán	actor;actress	对… 有影响	duì… yǒu yīng xiǎng	has influence on…
运动员	yùn dòng yuán	athlete	想做	xiǎng zuò	want to be
旅行家	lǚ xíng jiā	traveller	我做 / 教 / 写 过	wǒ zuò/jiāo/xiě guò	I have done/taught/written…
教育家	jiào yù jiā	educator			
历史人物	lì shǐ rén wù	historical figure	做广告	zuò guǎng gào	to make an advertisement
出生在…	chū shēng zài…	was born in…	拍电影	pāi diàn yǐng	to make a film

9 工作 gōng zuò THE WORLD OF WORK

复习 Review – Talking about jobs

1

Reading

Match the characters to the English words.

1	工人	5	记者
2	教师	6	护士
3	牙医	7	校长
4	医生	8	科学家

a doctor	e worker
b headteacher	f dentist
c teacher	g scientist
d nurse	h journalist

2

Reading

Match the sentences with the pictures to show which jobs Ming Ming's parents and siblings do.

1 明明的妈妈在中学教汉语。

2 明明的姐姐在医院工作。

3 明明的哥哥是记者。

4 明明的爸爸每天早上八点坐车去工厂上班。

3

Reading

Read the text about Zhou Wei's family and answer the questions in English.

我叫周伟, 我家有六口人。我爸爸是一家大医院的医生, 他的工作很忙, 每天早上七点半就去上班。我妈妈是教书的, 她在一个男校教数学。虽然她经常说做教师很累, 可是她还是很喜欢她的工作, 因为她的学生都很可爱。哥哥和姐姐也都工作了, 哥哥是工程师, 姐姐是记者。我和弟弟都在妈妈工作的学校上学, 所以我们每天早上坐妈妈的车去学校。

家 jiā	measure word for hospital, company etc
男校 nán xiào	boys school

1 How many people are there in Zhou Wei's family and who are they?

2 Where does Zhou Wei's dad work?

3 What time does Zhou Wei's dad leave for work in the morning?

4 What does Zhou Wei's mum do?

5 Does Zhou Wei's mum like her job? Why?

6 What do Zhou Wei's older brother and sister do?

7 How does Zhou Wei go to school every day? Why?

4
Listening

Listen to the dialogue. Copy out the grid and tick the correct boxes.

	校长	科学家	演员	学生	护士	教师
爸爸						
妈妈						
哥哥						
姐姐						
妹妹						
我						

GRAMMAR: Verb-adjective/adverb 得不得了

Use the structure of verb-adjective/adverb 得不得了 (liǎo) to express the idea of 'extremely', for example:
好得不得了 extremely good
累得不得了 extremely tired

5
Listening

Listen again to the dialogue in Activity 4.
Copy out the words and number them 1–10
in the order you hear them in the dialogue.

每天　　科学　　教师　　在哪儿　　演员　　大学　　中学生　　校长　　工人　　科学家

6
Speaking

Interview your classmates. Find out about what they want or don't want to do in the future and why.
Use the questions to help you. Record your results in a chart like the one below.

Q: 你想做什么工作？
A: 我想做…, 因为我觉得…。
Q: 你想做…吗？
A: 我不想做…, 因为…。

同学的名字	What job would they like to do?	Why?	What job wouldn't they like to do?	Why?
1				
2				
3				

Report back to the class in Chinese about what you have recorded, using 'he/she…'.

7
Writing

Complete the sentences stating what you want or don't want to do in the future and say why.

我想做…
我很想做…
我最想做…
我不太想做…
我不想做…
因为…

1 工作经验 gōng zuò jīng yàn Work experience

Talking about work experience

经验 jīng yàn		experience
社会实践 shè huì shí jiàn		school work experience

Reading

Match the sentences with the pictures.

a   b   c   d   e   f

1　我在学校社会实践。

2　他去超市社会实践。

3　明明喜欢在博物馆社会实践。

4　丽丽不想去商店社会实践。

5　我哥哥说他在快餐店社会实践很累。

6　陈兰的姐姐很喜欢在办公室社会实践。

Reading

Read the text about Li Xi's work experience and answer the questions in English.

帮助 bāng zhù	to help
哭 kū	to cry

李希在十年级的时候，去一个小学参加了一个星期的社会实践。因为她家离那个小学很远，她每天坐公共汽车去学校要坐三刻钟。虽然她每天都感到很累，可是她觉得在那儿工作非常快乐。每天上午她除了帮助学生们学习，还跟他们一起做游戏。孩子们太可爱了！李希在最后一天跟他们说再见的时候哭了。

1　When and where did Li Xi go for her work experience?

2　How did she travel to her workplace and how long did it take her to get there?

3　Did she enjoy her work experience? Why?

4　How did she assist the teacher in the lesson?

5　What happened on her last day of work experience?

Listening

Listen to the dialogue and choose the four correct statements from the list.

努力 nǔ lì	to make great efforts
药店 yào diàn	chemist; pharmacy
兼职 jiān zhí	part time job; to work part-time
送报纸 sòng bào zhǐ	to deliver newspapers

1　Xiaohai worked as a chef in McDonald's for his work experience.

2　Xiaohai does not live far from the McDonald's.

3　Xiaohai enjoyed working in McDonald's because the job kept him busy.

4　Xiaohai always knows how many people work in McDonald's.

5　Xiaohai appreciated the hard working staff in McDonald's.

6　Zhang Hong completed her work experience last year.

7　Zhang Hong delivers newspapers for an hour before going to school.

GRAMMAR: The use of 到

到 (dào) is known as a 'resultative ending'. It comes after the verb and shows that the action of the verb has been completed with the expected result, for example: 学到 = have learned (as a result of 学习), 看到 = have seen, 听到 = have heard, 得到 = have gained, etc.

GRAMMAR: The use of 是…的

You can use 是…的
a) to highlight the circumstances of a past action;
b) for emphasis.
For example: 我是坐火车来的。= I came by train./It was by train that I came.
我是去年去社会实践的。= I did work experience last year./It was last year when I did work experience.

4 Speaking Ask your classmates about their work experience. Record their name, when and where they did work experience, what they did and whether they enjoyed it.

你叫什么名字？	（我叫…）
你去社会实践过吗？	（我去过/没去过。）
你是什么时候去社会实践的？	（我是在…前/的时候去的。）
你去哪儿社会实践了？	（我去…社会实践了。）
你在社会实践的时候都做了些什么？	（我除了…、…也/还…）
你喜欢这个社会实践吗？为什么？	（我喜欢/不喜欢…，因为…）

Then report back to the class.

这是…
他/她去 / 没去社会实践过。
他/她在…年级的时候去…社会实践的。

他/她在社会实践的时候，做…、…、还…。
他/她喜欢/不喜欢这个社会实践，因为…。

5 Writing Write a short paragraph (about 100 characters) about your own work experience or part-time job. Remember to include when, where and what you did, whether you liked it or not, and why.

For example:
我去/没去社会实践过
我在…年级的时候去…社会实践的。
我在社会实践的时候，除了…、…，也/还…。
我喜欢/不喜欢这个社会实践，因为…。

EXAM TIP

Remember to try to include your opinion 我觉得… and conjunctions such as 除了…、…也/还…。Use the correct word order *time + place + verb*, for example 我在十年级的时候去了一个小学社会实践。

2 未来计划 wèi lái jì huà Future plans

Talking about future plans

1 Listening

Listen to the sentences and write down the letter of the correct picture. (1–6)

2 Listening

Listen again to Activity 1 and fill in the blanks with the missing words.

1　我想做 ___a___ ，我很喜欢写书，我要写很多 ___b___ 。
2　我想学习 ___c___ ，我最喜欢看李小龙演的功夫 ___d___ 。
3　我很喜欢 ___e___ ，我明年暑假想去学习中国的 ___f___ 。
4　我希望去中国 ___g___ ，一边工作一边学习 ___h___ 。
5　我想做 ___i___ ，我打算先上大学，然后自己 ___j___ 。
6　我打算去很多国家 ___k___ ，我想去看中国的 ___l___ 。

3 Reading

Read the following passage about Xiao Hong's dreams and answer the questions in English.

每个人都有自己的 理想 ，我也一样。我从很小的时候开始，就想当一个女 警察 。后来，我上小学了，特别喜欢画画儿，老师说我画得非常好，我又想当画家了。上中学的时候，我除了想做音乐教师，还对学习外语特别有兴趣，我又想当 翻译 又想当作家。从小到大我有过很多理想，我觉得没有理想就没有 目标 。虽然我现在还不知道我毕业后做什么工作，可是我知道我想做一个有用的人。

1　What was Xiao Hong's first dream?
2　Why did Xiao Hong want to be an artist?
3　Who influenced Xiao Hong when she was in primary school? In what ways?
4　What was Xiao Hong favourite subject in secondary school?
5　What is her opinion about having dreams?

GRAMMAR: Reporting what someone said

Someone + 说... = 'someone said that...', for example:
老师说我跳舞跳得非常好。 = The teacher said that I dance very well. The same structure works for indirect questions also. For example, 他问我去哪儿？ = he asked me where I was going.

理想 lǐ xiǎng	dream, ideal
警察 jǐng chá	police
翻译 fān yì	translator, interpreter, to translate
目标 mù biāo	aim, target

4

Listening

Listen to some students talking about going to university.

Answer the questions in English. (1–4)

1 What does Lili want to study at university? Why?

2 What does Lili think about the subject?

3 What is Wenwen's dream job?

4 What are Xiaohong's future plans?

5 Does Xiaohai want to go to university? Why?

6 What does Xiaohai want to do?

将来 jiāng lái	future, in the future
文学 wén xué	literature

5

Listening

Listen again to the students in Activity 4. Copy out and complete the chart.

名字	Wants to go to university?	Why?	Wants to do what job?	Why?
Lili				
Wenwen				
Xiaohong				
Xiaohai				

6

Speaking

Interview your classmates about their future plans.

Compare their plans with yours.

Questions:

你想上大学吗？/ 你想不想上大学？

为什么？

你想上 / 去 哪个大学？

你将来想做什么工作？/ 你喜欢做什么
工作？为什么？

Answers:

我想/不想…, 因为…

我想上/去… (name of university) 大学 or
我想去… (city/place) 上大学。

我将来想做…。我喜欢做…, 因为…

7

Writing

Write a report using your findings in Activity 6.

For example:

Mike 说他想上大学, 因为他对电脑科学很有兴趣。

他将来想做电脑工程师, 因为他想设计很多电脑游戏。

EXAM TIP

Make comparisons to improve
your marks, for example: A比B
+ *adjective*/A跟B一样/不一样.

设计 shè jì	design, to design

3 理想的工作 lǐ xiǎng de gōng zuò Ideal jobs

Talking about your ideal job

Reading

Read the text and answer the questions in English.

刘小伟的爸爸是医生,他常说:"医生是最好的职业,因为每个人生病了都得来看医生。"当教师的妈妈说:"教师是最好的职业,我教过的学生中有几个人已经是名人了。"在商店当售货员的姐姐说:"我觉得售货员是最好的职业,因为比较容易。"小伟听了爸爸、妈妈和姐姐的话后,说:"我毕业以后要当厨师,我认为厨师是最重要的职业,要是一个人三天不吃饭的话,你们说的这些工作就都不用做了。"

1   What does Xiaowei's dad do? What does he think of his job?

2   What does Xiaowei's mum do?

3   Do you think Xiaowei's mum is proud of her job? Why?

4   What does Xiaowei's elder sister think of her job?

5   What will Xiaowei do after he leaves school? Why?

生病 shēng bìng	to be ill
得 děi	must, have to
厨师 chú shī	chef
重要 zhòng yào	important
要是…的话 yào shi…de huà	if…

GRAMMAR: 得 + *verb* 'must, have to'

得 (děi) + *verb* indicates something you have to do. For example: 我得走了。= I have to go now. 你得先吃晚饭,然后看电视。= You must eat your dinner first, then watch TV.

GRAMMAR: 要是…的话 'If…'

To make a conditional sentence you can use 要是…的话 (yào shi…de huà) meaning 'If…', for example: 要是有时间的话,她想去公园散步。= If she has time, she wants to go for a walk in the park.

Reading

Complete the half sentences found in Column A by matching them up with an appropriate ending from Column B.

Column A

1   我认为最理想的工作是做教师,

2   我觉得当售货员最舒服,一点儿也不累,

3   我最理想的工作是开一个小吃店,卖各种各样的点心和蛋糕,

4   我最想做的工作是当电脑工程师,设计很多好玩儿的电脑游戏,

5   因为我喜欢学外语,也喜欢文学,我除了会英文、德文,还会法文和中文,

Column B

a   虽然自己做生意会很忙,每天上班的时间很长,可是我会赚很多的钱。

b   因为每天早上八点上班,下午五点下班,卖东西挺容易的。

c   所以我的理想是做翻译,我要翻译很多有名的小说。

d   除了孩子们可以玩儿,大人也可以玩儿得很高兴。

e   学校每年都放几次假,他们的假期很多。

点心 diǎn xin	snacks, refreshments
赚…钱 zhuàn qián	to earn money
大人 dà ren	adult

3 Reading

Read the job advert below and answer the questions in English.

1 What is the job advertised?
2 How many children are involved? Who are they? How old are they?
3 When is the job for?
4 What are the working hours and pay?
5 How do you apply for the job if you are interested in it?

请家庭教师
我家有两个孩子, 女孩8岁半, 男孩6岁, 想请一个大学生在暑假期间来家里教英语。每周五天, 每天两个小时, 每小时十八元。
联系电话：13551562348 陈女士。

请 qǐng	to employ *(but more commonly used to mean 'to ask/invite')*
期间 qī jiān	during a period of
周 zhōu	week
联系 lián xì	to make contact

4 Listening

Listen to the four job adverts and match the job with the picture, e.g a2. (1–4)

a   b   c   d

1 翻译   2 社会实践   3 服务员   4 厨师

必须 bì xū	must
工资 gōng zī	salary, wages
面谈 miàn tán	to discuss face to face
至 zhì	to, until

5 Listening

Listen to the job adverts in Activity 4 again.
Copy out and complete the chart with details.

Job	Work place	Working days	Full/part time	Salary	Contact phone number
1					
2					
3					
4					

6 Speaking

Work in pairs or in small groups and discuss your ideal jobs.
What do you want to do? Where do you want to work?
Part time or full time? How much do you want to earn? etc.

我的理想是… / 我想做…
我想/ 喜欢去…工作。
我想/不想/喜欢/不喜欢/打算做全职/兼职, 因为…
我想赚…钱。

EXAM TIP
You will gain more marks if you can add your reason and/or opinion for what you want to do.

4 申请工作 shēn qǐng gōng zuò Applying for a job

Writing a CV and letter of application

Reading

Read Xiao Dong's CV and answer the questions in English.

个人简历

姓名： 陈小东	性别：男
出生日期： 1986年3月26日	年龄：18岁
住址： 北京东城区方家胡同十五号	出生地点：中国北京
联系电话： 0100263859	邮编： 123456
电子邮件： xdc@sina.mecom	

教育背景： 1998年9月–2004年7月 南海中学
1992年9月–1998年7月 阳光小学

技能： 会说流利的中、英文。会用电脑。

工作经验： 2003年6月–2003年8月 在肯德基快餐店当兼职服务员

1 What is Xiao Dong's surname?
2 When and where was he born?
3 Where does he live?
4 How can he be contacted?
5 What are his qualifications?
6 What skills does he have?
7 What did he do in KFC (肯德基)?
8 How long did he work there?

个人简历 gè rén jiǎn lì	CV
邮编 yóu biān	post code
背景 bèi jǐng	background
技能 jì néng	skills
流利 liú lì	fluent

Speaking

Interview your classmates to find out information required for a CV. You may find the following prompts useful. Record your results. You can make up the information if you prefer.

你叫什么？姓什么？
你多大了？
你是什么时候出生的？
你是在哪儿出生的？
你的住址是什么？
你的邮编是什么？

你的电话是多少？
你的电子邮件是什么？
你在哪儿上的学？
你会做什么？
你做过什么工作？

Writing

Prepare a CV in Chinese either for yourself or for a classmate you interviewed in Activity 2.

4
Listening

Listen to the dialogue at a job fair. Make notes in English under the following headings:

- what does the woman looking for a job say first
- her experience
- her interest in the job on offer

申请 shēn qǐng	application, to apply
公司 gōng sī	company
试 shì	to try
没关系 méi guān xi	it doesn't matter
面试 miàn shì	(job) interview
名片 míng piàn	business card

5
Reading

Read the following application letter and decide which statements are true.

尊敬的先生/女士：

　　您好！我在网上看到贵公司的招工广告, 我对中、英文兼职翻译的工作很感兴趣。

　　我会说流利的中、英文, 还会用电脑打中文和英文, 我各个科目的考试成绩都是A。

　　随信附上我的简历, 如有机会参加面试, 我将十分感谢。

此致

敬礼

赵丽丽　2006年8月12日

尊敬的 zūn jìng de	respectful; esteemed
贵 guì	your *(respectful)*
招工 zhāo gōng	to recruit
广告 guǎng gào	advertising
考试 kǎo shì	exam
随信附上… suí xìn fù shàng	Enclosed is …
如…, 我将十分感谢 rú… wǒ jiāng shí fēn gǎn xiè	I would be grateful if …
此致/敬礼 cǐ zhì/ jìng lǐ	*equivalent to* 'with best wishes'

1　Lili saw the job advert on the Internet.
2　She is interested in the full time job.
3　She wants to work as a typist.
4　She can speak and write two languages.
5　She will take her CV with her to the interview.

CULTURE

Chinese letter format is different from English. A Chinese letter or message opens with just the name, for example 小丽/伟伟/爸爸/李老师, or in a formal letter尊敬的赵先生/尊敬的张校长, or in a close relationship, 亲爱的 (qīn ài de) 'dear' 妈妈/亲爱的爷爷, 奶奶. To close a Chinese letter, 此致/敬礼 jìng lǐ 'greetings' is equivalent to 'with best wishes', or 祝身体健康/学习进步/生日快乐/新年快乐 ('wishing you good health/progress in your studies/happy birthday/happy new year'), etc. A Chinese letter ends with a signature, followed by the date.

GRAMMAR: 贵

贵 (guì) is used in a respectful way to say 'your', for example 贵国 'your country', 贵校 'your school', 贵姓 'your surname', etc.

EXAM TIP

You will gain marks by using the correct format for writing a letter. Learn the phrases used for opening and closing a letter by heart.

6
Writing

Write an application letter for a job you are interested in. Use the letter in Activity 5 as a model.

5 博客 bó kè Blogs

Talking about the Internet

Reading

Read the text and answer the questions in English.

什么是博客？博客的英文是Blog, 全名应该是Weblog, 就跟在网上写日记一样。博客也叫博客网站，一个博客就是一个网页。博客的内容有很多，比如有日记、照片、小说，还有记者博客、新闻博客等，什么博客都有。就跟用电子邮件一样，谁都可以有自己的博客网页。

博客的历史不长，最早的博客是在1997年12月。1998年互联网上的博客网站还非常少，但现在博客已经越来越多了，各种各样的博客多得不得了。网民们除了用博客写东西，还可以在网上认识很多人，交新朋友。

1　What is the Chinese for blog?
2　What can you read in a blog?
3　Who can have a blog?
4　How long is the history of blogging?
5　What do people do with blogs?

博客 bó kè	blog
全名 quán míng	full name
网页 wǎng yè	web page
内容 nèi róng	content
网民 wǎng mín	people using Internet

GRAMMAR: Question words used for emphasis

什么 whatever/everything, 谁 whoever/everybody, 哪儿 wherever/everywhere, 怎么 whichever way.
For example: 他什么都喜欢。= He likes everything (whatever it is).
谁都可以有自己的博客。= Everyone (whoever it is) can have his own blog.

Reading

Write down the missing words for the gaps a–j.
The missing words can be found in the text in Activity 1.

1　博客的 ___a___ 是Blog。
2　博客的内容很多，比如有 ___b___ 、照片、 ___c___ ，还有 ___d___ 博客等。
3　博客的历史 ___e___ ，最早的博客是在 ___f___ 。
4　现在博客 ___g___ 多，各种各样的博客多得 ___h___ 。
5　网民们 ___i___ 用博客写东西， ___j___ 可以在网上交朋友。

Listening

Listen to the dialogue and put Mrs Li's lines in the order in which she says them.

打字 dǎ zì	to type
聊天 liáo tiān	to chat

a　我去上电脑课，每个星期一晚上有课。
b　我们除了学习打字，还学习怎样上网。
c　我们在一个很大的电脑教室里上课，一人用一个电脑。
d　我从夏天开始学，到现在已经学了五个月了。
e　我可以在网上写日记、写小说，还可以跟人聊天、交朋友。
f　现在我觉得不难了，我还学了怎样做博客，我有自己的博客了。

Reading

4 Read about what these people like doing. Copy and complete the chart with the correct information.

A: 我是马小伟。我的爱好是在家玩儿电脑游戏, 什么电脑游戏我都喜欢。我觉得每天不要玩儿得太多就不会有什么坏处。

B: 我叫张小丽。我喜欢写博客, 我每天在我的房间里写我的博客。我觉得我的博客网页就跟我的房间一样, 是我自己的地方, 我的朋友们也可以进来看看。

C: 我叫李海兰。我喜欢在网上聊天, 我和朋友在一起什么都说。我觉得上网聊天的好处是大人看不见也听不见, 因为我们不想让他们知道我们在做什么。

D: 我是毛大龙。我也很喜欢上网玩儿电脑游戏, 可是我们家不能上网, 所以我只能去网吧上网。我爸爸、妈妈说上网吧又贵又浪费时间, 可是我觉得不错。

	马小伟	张小丽	李海兰	毛大龙
有什么爱好？				
在什么地方？				
有什么感想？				

坏处 huài chu	harm, disadvantage
网吧 wǎng bā	Internet café
感想 gǎn xiǎng	thoughts, impressions

GRAMMAR:
看得见、看不见

The ability or inability to do something is often expressed by placing 得 or 不 between the two parts of the verb. For example, 老师, 我看不见 = teacher, I can't see; 我听得懂 = I can understand; 我听不懂 = I can't understand.

Speaking

5 Work in pairs or in groups to discuss the advantages and disadvantages of the Internet. You may find the following prompts useful.

你的爱好是什么？
你喜欢上网吗？
你在家能上网吗？
你上网做什么？
你有没有自己的博客网页？
你用博客做什么？
你对上网有什么感想？
你觉得上网有什么好处和/或坏处？

我的爱好是…。
我喜欢/不喜欢…。
我在…上网。
我上网写博客/玩儿电脑游戏/聊天, etc.
我/我们家有/没有…。
我觉得/认为…。

6 **Writing**
Write an article of 100 characters for the school magazine about the advantages and disadvantages of the Internet.

EXAM TIP

Remember to make your points clear, then support them with more detailed information to cover the points such as what/when/where/how etc. Use a variety of vocabulary and sentence structures to make your writing more interesting and more effective, e.g. 因为…/所以…, 虽然…/可是…, 除了…以外 or 也, as well as comparisons.

Describing people

Reading **1** Read the text and answer the questions in English.

你属什么?

中国人在问年龄的时候, 常常会问 "你属什么", 每个中国人都有自己的"属相", 比如有的人属猪, 有的人属狗。属相也叫生肖, 是用十二个动物来代表每一个人的出生年份, 所以十二生肖又叫十二属相。

中国属相的历史很长, 五千多年前中国就有属相了。中国人几乎没有人不知道自己的生肖属相的, 他们还认为, 出生在不同年份的人--属相不同的人, 性格也会不同。

人们常说:

老鼠代表聪明, 牛代表努力。老虎代表勇敢, 兔子代表小心。龙代表高贵, 蛇代表吉祥。马代表勇往直前, 羊代表顺从。猴子代表灵活, 鸡代表信用。狗代表诚实, 猪代表友好。

属相/生肖 shǔ xiàng/ shēng xiào	zodiac
代表 dài biǎo	representative, to represent
年份 nián fèn	particular year
几乎 jī hū	almost
性格 xìng gé	personality
勇敢 yǒng gǎn	brave, courageous
高贵 gāo guì	noble
吉祥 jí xiáng	lucky
勇往直前 yǒng wǎng zhí qián	march forward bravely
顺从 shùn cóng	meek
灵活 líng huó	flexible, quick-witted
信用 xìn yòng	keep one's promise
诚实 chéng shí	loyal

1 What is the common way for Chinese people to ask someone's age?

2 How does the Chinese zodiac work?

3 How long is the history of the Chinese zodiac?

4 How popular is the Chinese zodiac in China?

5 What do Chinese people think about the influence the Chinese zodiac has on people's personalities?

Reading **2** Re-read the last paragraph of the text in Activity 1 and match the adjectives with the correct animal sign.

1 聪明   2 小心   3 高贵   4 努力   5 吉祥   6 勇敢
7 信用   8 灵活   9 诚实   10 顺从   11 友好   12 勇往直前

3
Listening

Listen to the dialogue between Wang Hai and Zhang Lan. Answer the questions in English.

文化 wén huà	culture
排位 pái wèi	to put in order
壮 zhuàng	strong, sturdy
肥 féi	fat

1   What is Wang Hai busy doing?
2   What are the first and last animal signs in the Chinese zodiac?
3   Why do the animals decide to walk in the street one by one?
4   Try to retell briefly the story about the mouse becoming the first symbol in the Chinese zodiac.

GRAMMAR: Measure Words (MW)

Although 'measure words' for counting things also exist in English, they are used only with collective or plural nouns, for example 'three *cups* of coffee' and 'a *school* of fish'. In Chinese, however, the use of a measure word between a number and a noun is *obligatory* to indicate the unit of measurement of an object: number (e.g. 一, 两, 九, etc.) + *MW* + *noun*, or
这 / 那 / 哪 + *MW* + *noun*
For example, 他买了两本书。= He bought two books.

4
Speaking

Work in pairs or in small groups. Ask each other questions using the prompts to find out your classmates' year of birth, animal sign and personality.

你/你哥哥/兰兰/Mark, etc. 是哪一年出生的？	– 我/他/她是…年出生的。
你/他/她属什么？	– 我/他/她属…。
你 /他/她是一个什么样的人？	– 我/他/她是一个很/非常… (adj.) 的人。
你的/他的/她的性格怎么样？	– 我的/他的/她的性格很好/不太好, 又…(adj.) 又…(adj.)。

5
Writing

Write about yourself including your year of birth, animal sign and personality. You can refer to the prompts in Activity 4. You can also add more points such as which zodiac sign you like/dislike and why, or if you had a choice, which year and zodiac sign you would like to have been born in (如果…).

EXAM TIP

Remember to use a variety of adjectives to describe the appearance and personality of someone. Avoid using the same vocabulary repeatedly in the same piece of writing. It will be helpful to use some conjunctions appropriately in order to raise the level of your writing. eg. in addition to using 因为…所以/虽然…可是, you can use 如果…。

LISTENING

1 **Warm-up!** Think about what questions might be asked at a job interview? How might the interviewee answer?

2 Listen to Wang Xiaojing at a job interview. Answer the following questions in English.

1 How does Wang Xiaojing introduce herself?
2 Why does she want to have a job?
3 What is her response when the manager says it is hard work?
4 What is she able to do in the kitchen?
5 What's she like in her friends' eyes?
6 When does the manager expect her to start?
7 When will her holiday begin?

TIP

- Predict what you will hear and what words will appear in the passage by looking at the title or introduction.
- When you come across a new word, don't worry. Usually you can work out the meaning from the context. Make a guess.
- Questions are usually asked in the order in which information appears in the passage. By reading through the questions, you will be prepared for what information will appear first and what will appear last.
- Make notes, especially if the passage is long. If you are sure of your answer, write it immediately. If you are uncertain, make notes and answer after you listen the second time.

GRAMMAR: 什么的

什么的 is used in spoken Chinese after one or more phrases of the same category to mean 'and so on', 'etc.'.
他不喜欢打球什么的，就爱下棋。
她从超市买了苹果、香蕉、桔子什么的。

READING

Reading

Read the webpage below. Then answer the questions in English.

www.yourworksearch.cn　　　　　　　　　　　　　　搜索

王强找工作

　　听说深圳工作机会多，大学毕业生王强来到深圳找工作。一个月过去了，父母的钱差不多花光了，还是没有找到工作。

　　后来，有一个朋友介绍王强到一家工厂当了工人。他性格开朗，工作能力强，不久，就当了经理助理。但是，因为这家工厂人们之间的关系太复杂，半年后他辞了这份工作。

　　为了找工作，王强在网上发了很多简历，但没有收到什么回音。到了7月，全球经济危机开始了，找工作更难了。

　　最后，王强终于在一家电子公司找到了一个工作，因为他们看上了他的专业和工作，经验。王强高兴地说：“我又可以赚钱养活自己了。”

1　Why did Wang Qiang go to Shenzhen to look for a job?
2　Did he find any jobs in the first month?
3　What personal attributes did he have that made him valued in the factory?
4　Why did he resign from his post in the factory?
5　How did he publicise his CV?
6　Why did the electronics company offer him a job?

TIP

Reading strategies for different types of question:

- Skimming. This strategy is used when you read for general meaning or 'the big picture'. For this purpose, do not read word by word. Read quickly to gain a rough idea of what the text is about.
- Scanning. This strategy is used when you read for specific information such as 'who', 'what', 'when', 'where', 'why' or 'how''. For this purpose, you need to locate the sentence first and then find the information you want.
- Inference. This strategy is used when you read 'between the lines' to work out what the author really means. Sometimes opinions are expressed in an implicit way rather than stated clearly.

GRAMMAR: 越来越

越来越 (yuè lái yuè) is used with adjectives and has similar meaning to 'more and more'. Sentences including 越来越 can only have one subject.
天气越来越热。 = The weather is becoming hotter and hotter.
北京越来越漂亮。 = Beijing is becoming more and more beautiful.

口语 kǒu yǔ Speaking

Preparing for a speaking task (presentation)

TASK AND PREPARATION

You did your work experience in China. Prepare a presentation.
You could include:

- When do students in your school go on work experience and for how long?
- When did you do your work experience?
- Where did you do it? What did you do? And for how long?
- How did you travel to work everyday?
- What was a typical day like during your work experience?
- How did you like your work experience?
- Has the work experience had any impact on your future career plans?
- Are you still in touch with the people you met during your work experience?
- Do you know if students in China participate in any work experience?

1
Speaking
Work with a partner. In Chinese make a list of work places that students might consider for their work experience.

2
Listening
You will hear a model presentation by Dan. Work with a partner and work out how to say the sentences below in Chinese. Then listen to Part 1 of the presentation and compare your answers to what you hear.

1 Some did work experience for one week. Some did work experience for two weeks.
2 He did his work experience in Beijing. I did my work experience in my hometown.
3 Some went to a post office. Some went to a bookshop.
4 He did his work experience in a travel agency. I did my work experience in a library.

3
Listening
Read the sentences, and then listen to the beginning of Part 1 and the beginning of Part 2 and work out exactly what the underlined nouns refer to.

1 中学生都很喜欢这个活动。
2 这个学校很大, 有小学生, 也有中学生。

4
Listening
Listen to Part 2 again and copy down the sentence which uses the structure 除了…, 还… Then rewrite the following sentences, using the same structure.

1 我们学习中文, 也学习怎样教英文。
2 在北京的时候, 我们又教英文, 又教体育。
3 他们上体育课的时候, 又学篮球, 又学英文。

5
Listening

Listen to the end of Part 2 and answer the following questions in Chinese.

1 Which three adjectives does Dan use when describing his two-week stay in Beijing?

2 What does he think of working as an English teacher in China? And why?

3 What is the impact of his work experience on his future career plans?

6
Listening

Listen to the follow-up discussion. Answer the following questions in English.

1 What does Dan say about the hotel he lived in when he was in Beijing?

2 What does he say about the teacher who delivered the training in Beijing University?

3 What is the comparison he makes between teaching English and teaching PE?

4 What does he say about why English students like to do work experience?

5 What does he say about why the Chinese students enjoyed his PE lessons in Beijing?

YOUR TURN NOW

Prepare a presentation.

- Make yourself a prompt sheet (A5 size, containing up to 30 English words or 50 Chinese characters which can be written in pinyin) and practise your presentation until you are fluent.

- Record your presentation and play it to your partner. Discuss with your partner what questions the teacher could ask you about your presentation.

ResultsPlus
Maximise your marks

To aim for a **Grade C** you need to:

- give an opinion when appropriate. Notice how Dan gives an opinion about the hotel he stayed at in Beijing.

- include different time frames. Dan mainly uses a past time frame in the presentation. He also uses the present when giving opinions, and the future when describing his career plans.

- use a variety of verbs. Note how many different verbs Dan uses in this task.

If you are aiming higher than a **Grade C** you need to:

- produce full answers and communicate detailed information. Dan gives full details when talking about where his schoolmates went for their work experience.

- show that you can avoid the influence of English and use Chinese structures correctly. In Chinese, the 在 phrase goes before the main verb, not after. How many examples can you find of Dan using 在 phrases?

To produce your best spoken Chinese and to aim for an **A* grade** you need to :

- use 除了…, 还… and 又…, 又… to add complexity to sentence structures and to convey comprehensive ideas.

- demonstrate competent use of different time references. Note that the structure of …以后 is used three times in Dan's presentation. Also notice where Dan uses the structure …的时候 in the questions and answers.

写作 xiě zuò Writing

Preparing for an extended writing task applying for a holiday job

PREPARATION

Reading

1 Warm-up! Tell a partner three things in Chinese about your work experience or part-time job.

Read the application letter and complete Activities 2–5.

尊敬的王先生,

　　您好! 我最近在报纸上看到了您的小学需要暑期英语老师的广告。我对这份工作很感兴趣。

　　我今年十六岁,住在英国。因为我喜欢中国的语言和文化,所以我从十一岁就开始学习汉语。我刚刚参加完英国的中文中学会考。今年暑假,我希望能在北京找一份教英语的工作,同时我还可以练习说中文。

　　在英国,我有过一些教书的工作经验。去年夏天,我去了我们家附近的小学教三年级的学生认字和读英文课文。那里的老师和学生都认为我对他们帮助很大。将来,我想上大学学习中文和中国文化,而且以后想当老师。如果我能得到这份暑期的工作,我会非常高兴,因为这会对我的将来有帮助。

　　最后,请问这份工作每月的工资是多少,还有,学校是不是会付英国到中国的机票钱呢?我期待您的回信。

　　　　　　此致,

敬礼!

　　　　　　　　　　　　石红梅　二零零九年二月九日

2 Reading
- Use the dictionary to work out the meaning of the opening phrase of the letter.
- What is the difference in the sign-off when compared to the layout of an English letter?

3 Reading Find the characters in the text which mean:

1 recently
2 advertisement
3 I am interested in this job
4 hope

5 at the same time
6 obtain
7 monthly salary
8 I look forward to your reply

4 Reading Look at how Shi Hongmei uses 想, 希望, 期待 in the letter and write down a sentence of your own using each verb. Work with a partner to discuss the use of 会 to show the future in the second to last paragraph. Make up some sentences orally using 会 and check them with your teacher.

5 Find the four correct statements.

Reading
1 Shi Hongmei saw the job on the Internet.
2 Shi Hongmei is applying to teach English.
3 She wants to work in Beijing.
4 She has just completed GCSE Chinese.
5 She has never taught in a primary school.
6 She wants to become a teacher in the future.
7 She says she'll pay for her own flight.

YOUR TURN NOW

Write a letter applying for a holiday job in China. There are two jobs on offer in Shanghai: one as a child-minder and one as a waiter/waitress in a Chinese restaurant.
Choose which job you prefer and write between 100 and 150 characters, about half the length of Shi Hongmei's letter. You should include the following:

- formal beginning and ending to the letter
- which job you are applying for
- who you are and why you want the job
- what relevant experience you have had
- how this job will help your future plans
- some practical questions about the job

TIP

For a formal letter, use the opening 尊敬的 + name, as in the example. Use 您, as in the first line of the letter above. You can end with 此致 敬礼！ or just with 此致, but keep the layout as above with the date under the sender's name.

CHECK

Check that you have started and ended the letter appropriately and used 您 when referring to the employer or 您的 when referring to the organisation. Make sure you have the date at the end of the letter (under the sender's name) and that you write it in the correct order – year, month, date. Then go through all the character and grammar checks as normal.

ResultsPlus
Maximise your marks

To aim for a **Grade C** you need to:
- start and end the letter appropriately, making use of the guidance on these pages
- talk about past, present and future events. Shi Hongmei talks about:
    present events when giving her background
    past events when referring to her relevant experience
    future events when talking about how this holiday job will help her in future

To aim higher than a **Grade C** you need to:
- make sure word order is correct, for example the importance of having time 'when' near the beginning of the sentence, before the main verb, as when Shi Hongmei talks about 'this summer', 'last summer', etc.
- use linking words. For example, Shi Hongmei uses 'because' 因为….所以, 并且 'furthermore' and 同时 'at the same time'.

To produce your best written Chinese and to aim for an **A* grade** you need to :
- demonstrate awareness of how to use 了 to show a completed action and 过 to show experience. The negative of both are formed with 没.
- show you know how to use 会 in the context of a future event.

工作经验 gōng zuò jīng yàn Work experience

家	jiā	measure word for hospital, company etc	帮助	bāng zhù	to help
男校	nán xiào	boys school	哭	kū	to cry
经验	jīng yàn	experience	努力	nǔ lì	make great efforts
社会实践	shè huì shí jiàn	work experience arranged for students as part of school curriculum	药店	yào diàn	chemist's shop
			兼职	jiān zhí	part time job; to work part-time
			送报纸	sòng bào zhǐ	to deliver newspapers

计划将来 jì huà jiāng lái Future plans

理想	lǐ xiǎng	dream, ideal	将来	jiāng lái	future, in the future
警察	jǐng chá	police	文学	wén xué	literature
翻译	fān yì	translator, interpreter; to translate	名胜古迹	míng shèng gǔ jì	famous spots and historic sites
目标	mù biāo	aim, target	蛋糕	dàn gāo	cake

理想的工作 lǐ xiǎng de gōng zuò Ideal jobs

生病	shēng bìng	to be ill	各种各样的	gè zhǒng gè yàng de	various types of
得	děi	ought to	点心	diǎn xin	snacks, refreshments
厨师	chú shī	chef	设计	shè jì	design, to design
重要	zhòng yào	important	赚…钱	zhuàn qián	to earn money
要是…的话	yào shi…de huà	if…	大人	dà ren	adult

工作广告 gōng zuò guǎng gào Job adverts

广告	guǎng gào	advertising	联系	lián xì	to make contact
请	qǐng	to employ (more commonly meaning 'to ask/invite')	必须	bì xū	must
期间	qī jiān	during a period of	工资	gōng zī	salary, wages
			面谈	miàn tán	to discuss face to face
周	zhōu	week	至	zhì	to, till

申请工作 shēn qǐng gōng zuò Job application

个人简历	gè rén jiǎn lì	CV	公司	gōng sī	company
邮编	yóu biān	post code	试	shì	to try
背景	bèi jǐng	background	没关系	méi guān xi	it doesn't matter
技能	jì néng	skills	面试	miàn shì	(job) interview
流利	liú lì	fluent	名片	míng piàn	business card
申请	shēn qǐng	application, to apply			

写中文信 xiě zhōng wén xìn Chinese letter format

尊敬的	zūn jìng de	respectful, esteemed	随信附上…	suí xìn fù shàng	Enclosed is …
贵	guì	(respectful) your	如…, 我将十分感谢	rú…, wǒ jiāng shí fēn gǎn xiè	I would be grateful if…
招工	zhāo gōng	to recruit employee			
考试	kǎo shì	examination	此致	cǐ zhì	(with) best wishes

互联网与博客 hù lián wǎng yǔ bó kè Internet and blogs

博客	bó kè	blog	打字	dǎ zì	to type
全名	quán míng	full name	聊天	liáo tiān	to chat
网站	wǎng zhàn	website	坏处	huài chu	harm, disadvantage
网页	wǎng yè	web page	网吧	wǎng bā	Internet café
内容	nèi róng	content	感想	gǎn xiǎng	thoughts, impressions
网民	wǎng mín	people using Internet			

十二生肖 shí èr shēng xiào Chinese zodiac

性格	xìng gé	personality	几乎	jī hū	almost
属相	shǔ xiàng	zodiac	文化	wén huà	culture
生肖	shēng xiào	zodiac	排位	pái wèi	to put in order
代表	dài biǎo	representative, to represent	壮	zhuàng	strong, sturdy
年份	nián fèn	particular year	肥	féi	fat

性格 xìng gé Describing personality

勇敢	yǒng gǎn	brave	顺从	shùn cóng	meek
高贵	gāo guì	noble	灵活	líng huó	flexible, quick-witted
吉祥	jí xiáng	lucky	信用	xìn yòng	keep one's promise
勇往直前	yǒng wǎng zhí qián	march forward bravely	诚实	chéng shí	loyal

读和写 dú hé xiě Reading and Writing 1
Extra Reading and Writing practice

1
Reading

Find each person's place of work.

a 医院   b 电影院   c 学校   d 公共汽车站   e 饭店
f 工厂   h 家   i 商店   j 公园   k 动物园

试验 shì yàn	experiment
照顾 zhào gù	to look after
顾客 gù kè	customer
价格 jià gé	price

1   张丽喜欢做试验, 所以她教科学。

2   毛红每天都要照顾病人, 虽然很累, 但她喜欢这样的工作。

3   赵海是汽车司机, 他工作的地方很大, 有很多工人在那里上班。

4   大明是服务员, 他的工作是给顾客送上咖啡、茶、汽水和蛋糕。

5   李东工作的地方没有狗、猫、鱼什么的, 但是有很多别的
   动物。孩子们都喜欢去参观。

6   小兰知道包, 衣服, 电视等东西的价格。她是售货员。

7   陈希没有电视和电脑, 可是她每天都可以看电影。

2
Reading

Find the characters in the text in Activity 1 for the following.

a patient   b bag   c computer   d cake   e fish

3
Writing

Describe Zhang Hai's friends.

For example: 她是日本人。她喜欢看书。
            她有一头黑色的长发, 眼睛是棕色的, 耳朵不大。

1      2      3   4

4

Reading

Read the text and put the pictures in the correct order.

星期六我不用上学，所以有时间玩儿。

早饭以后，我从九点到十点上跳舞课。下课以后，因为我们家没有电脑，所以我常常去图书馆看书、玩儿电脑。午饭以后我去朋友的家。因为我的朋友很喜欢听音乐，所以他有许多国家的音乐光盘。他最喜欢听印度音乐，也爱看印度电影。他觉得印度人跳舞跳得非常好。每星期六我都跟他在一起看最新的印度电影。看电影以后，我们去游泳池。因为我很喜欢游泳，所以星期六、星期天都去游泳。我很想去海边游泳，但是我们家住在北京市中心，离海边太远了。

回家以后，我总是一边看电视，一边做饭。星期六爸爸妈妈都工作，所以我得做饭。我有时候做牛肉面，有时候做鸡蛋炒饭。爸爸最喜欢吃牛肉，妈妈喜欢鸡蛋和蔬菜，他们都爱喝葡萄酒。晚上我们常常去奶奶家。

5

Reading

Match the halves of the sentences.

A	B
1 爸爸每天都七点起床，	a 可是他现在住在英国。
2 你常常看电影吗？	b 她天天从天安门广场开车到北京大学。
3 李兰是司机，	c 六点三刻。
4 姐姐什么时候回家？	d 然后吃面包和奶酪。
5 老师来自台湾，	e 有的时候看。

6

Writing

What do you do on Sundays? 你星期天做什么？

Use all of these phrases and connectives in your paragraph.

常常 (often)   有的时候 (sometimes)
然后 (and then)   或者 (or)
可是 (but)

Reading

Read the adverts for two schools, then choose the correct statements.

A: 欢迎大家来我们的学校读书! 我们的学校有六百个学生,五十多个老师。学校里有一个大图书馆、一个大操场、两个体育馆,也有一个游泳池。学校没有食堂。学生们每天早上六点三刻上课,最后一节课是一点半下课。我们学校的第一节课是体育课,上课时,大家都去操场或者体育馆一起做运动。因为下午没有课,所以学生可以回家、在图书馆看书、做作业或者玩儿电脑。下午我们也可以去体育馆和游泳池锻炼身体。不过,学生们星期六也必须上课!

B: 我们的学校是最好的! 我们的学生比较多(一千五百名),所以会交很多朋友。我们每天早上都上科学课和数学课,午饭以后,学习音乐、戏剧或者美术。三点到五点,我们有历史课、地理课或者英语课。五点以后学生们可以学习经济、电脑或者手工。我们都很喜欢上课,因为老师们都很亲切!

必须 bì xū	must

1 If you attend school A you will have to go to school on Saturdays.
2 Schools A and B both have swimming pools on site.
3 School A is much bigger than school B.
4 The first period in school B is always either science or maths.
5 Students in school A can go home earlier than those in school B.
6 Students in school B can do what they want in the afternoons.

Reading

Read the texts in Activity 1 again. Choose the correct answer for each statement.

1 学校A的学生
   a 六点三刻上课,一点下课。
   b 六点半上课,一点半下课。
   c 六点三刻上课,一点半下课。

2 学校A
   a 有图书馆、操场、体育馆和食堂。
   b 没有食堂,可是有体育馆和操场。
   c 没有体育馆和食堂,可是有很大的操场。

3 学校B的学生
   a 早上上数学课和戏剧课。
   b 吃午饭以后上戏剧课。
   c 五点以后上戏剧课。

4 学校B的学生
   a 从三点到五点会学习英语。
   b 从三点到五点会学习经济。
   c 从三点到五点会学习科学。

Writing

欢迎来我们的学校!

Write a paragraph advertising the type of school you would like to attend. Write about 科目、学校的建筑、学生、老师 and 食堂.

4
Reading

Read the text and answer the questions in English.

我们的学校在加拿大, 老师们都会说英语和法语, 有的老师也会说汉语。我觉得他们都很聪明！在我们住的地方, 天气常常很冷, 所以我们的校服都比英国学生的校服暖和。在学校里, 我们都穿黑裤子、红衬衫、黑毛衣和黑色的长夹克, 也戴红黑两色的帽子、红色的手套和红色的围巾。上学的路上我们穿皮鞋,但是在学校里面, 我们都得穿白色的运动鞋。我觉得白色的运动鞋和校服很不好看！上体育课的时候, 我们必须穿黄色的T恤和红色的短裤！太不好看了！

我们的老师都很有意思。我觉得经济老师比手工老师有趣,可是她也很严格。化学老师比较厉害, 所以我不太喜欢上化学课。我最喜欢生物老师, 因为他非常好玩儿。

加拿大 jiā ná dà	Canada
暖和 nuǎn huo	warm
戴 dài	to wear *(for accessories)*
手套 shǒu tào	gloves
围巾 wéi jīn	scarf

1 In which country can you find this school?
2 How many languages can some of the teachers speak and what are they?
3 What comparison does the student make between his school uniform and that worn by British students? Why does it need to be so different?
4 Describe the student's school uniform in detail.
5 What is interesting about the footwear these students have to wear?
6 What does the student think about the PE uniform? Why?
7 Which teacher does he describe as being strict?
8 Which subject does the student not particularly like?

5
Writing

Look at the adjectives below. Find the opposite or near opposite for each one in the text in Activity 4.

1 冷
2 漂亮
3 有意思
4 亲切

6
Writing

Write a detailed description of your school. Describe your uniform, teachers, lessons, school buildings, canteen food and give your opinions of them.

读和写 dú hé xiě Reading and Writing 3

Extra Reading and Writing practice

卫视 wèi shì	satellite TV	
橄榄球 gǎn lǎn qiú	rugby	
聚餐 jù cān	to have a dinner party	

1 Reading

Below are six statements about three different activities. Decide what the three activities are and find the two texts that relate to each activity.

1 明天晚上天空卫视有英格兰队和苏格兰队的橄榄球比赛。我们家没有天空卫视，我想上你们家去看，方便吗？

2 星期六朋友生日聚餐，我是第一个到的。有人说：住最远的，通常是第一个到。以前也去过羊大爷餐馆，味道不错。

3 刘欢演唱会在北京工人体育馆举行。演唱会日期：星期六。演唱会时间：晚上七点到九点。票价：50元。

4 下个星期六我过生日，你有空吗？来参加我的生日聚餐吧！我订了桌子，晚上七点，在香港路的羊大爷。

5 没问题，你来吧！比赛六点半开始，我妈妈说，放学后，你跟我一起回家，你可以在我们家吃晚饭。

6 明晚工体有演唱会，我有两张票，一起去吧？请在家等我，我六点坐出租车到你们家接你。别忘了带上照相机。

2 Writing

Copy and fill in the grid for the other activities, using the texts in Activity 1.

Parts of the message	Activity A	Activity B	Activity C
Activity	橄榄球比赛		
Invitation	一起吃晚饭 一起看比赛		
Time	放学后		
Place	我们家		

3 Writing

You have read the following notice at a leisure centre. Write an email inviting your friend to join you. Use the bullet points 1–4 to help you.

1 when to go mountain climbing　(明天)
2 what time to meet up　(早上八点半)
3 where to meet up　(运动中心门口)
4 what to take　(钱、水、雨衣)

这个星期六去郊区爬山，车去车回。

报名费　　：3英镑。
开车时间　：上午九点。
上车地点　：运动中心门口。

4
Reading

Your new friend from China, Bai Xue, is writing to you about her hobby. Read her letter below and answer the questions in English.

我叫白雪，我最大的爱好是听音乐。妈妈告诉我，
在我很小的时候，每次她放音乐，我都会很安静。
上次过生日，爸爸妈妈送了我一个很贵的手机。
手机上有MP3，有很多我喜欢听的流行音乐。早上上学和
下午放学回家，我喜欢一边走路，一边听手机里的
音乐。你呢？除了打电话以外，你还用手机做什么？
做作业的时候，我也喜欢听音乐。我很少看电视，
但是电视上有好的音乐节目的时候，我都会看。
我会弹吉他，晚上在家里，没有作业的时候，我喜欢
一边弹吉他，一边唱歌。在我们中学里，很多女生都
喜欢听音乐。我觉得喜欢音乐的人都是快乐的人。

1 What was her reaction to music when she was very little?
2 What present did she get for her last birthday from her parents?
3 What is her favourite kind of TV programme?
4 What does she like to do at home in the evening?
5 What type of school does Bai Xue attend?

5
Writing

Fill in the gaps to match the English in brackets.

1 我 __a__ 喜欢听音乐。 (most)
2 我经常听 __b__ 的音乐。 (on a mobile phone)
3 我喜欢 __c__ ，一边听音乐。 (while doing homework)
4 我觉得 __d__ 都是快乐的人。 (people who love music)

6
Writing

A Chinese friend has asked you to write a short article about what you think of sport as a British secondary school student. Use a variety of sentence structures in your writing.

1
Reading

In the dialogue below Shaun and Tom are talking about what Gordon Brown and David Beckham were doing in the photo. What do you think they were doing? Have a guess, and then read the text below and answer Shaun's question in English.

Shaun: 你认识照片上的这两个人吗？

Tom: 认识。左边是英国首相 Brown, 右边是足球明星Beckham.

Shaun: 你知不知道, 他们两人在一起做什么？

Tom: 不知道。

Beckham希望能够帮助年轻人，所以他在伦敦开办了一所足球学校。足球学校有很多有名的教练, 每天都有很多有趣的活动，足球踢得好的和踢得不好的年轻人都可以去学校训练。在学校里，教练告诉他们，要想成功，就必须努力。每天晚上要早一点儿睡觉，每天都要锻炼身体。教练还告诉他们，吃东西的时候，青菜、水果、鱼、肉、鸡蛋，面包、奶酪，什么都要吃，不能只吃这个，不吃那个。

2008年1月10号英国首相Brown参观了这所足球学校，他感谢Beckham为英国年轻人做了一件好事。

首相	shǒu xiàng	prime minister
教练	jiào liàn	coach
奶酪	nǎi lào	cheese

2
Reading

Match up the two halves of the sentences according to the text in Activity 1.

1 我不知道 …   a … 都吃。

2 Beckham 希望能够 …   b … 都可以去学校训练。

3 足球学校的教练 …   c … 他们在一起做什么。

4 喜欢踢足球的年轻人 …   d … 一所足球学校。

5 他什么 …   e … 帮助年轻人。

6 照片上他在参观 …   f … 都很有名。

3

Reading

Read the following text about Dashan, a Canadian working in China. Identify the four correct statements.

相声 xiàng sheng	crosstalk
多伦多 duō lún duō	Toronto
话剧 huà jù	modern drama

大山来自加拿大, 他的中文很棒。他是中国最有名的外国人, 乡下的老奶奶都知道这个外国人相声说得好。

大山的英文名字叫 Mark Rowswell, 19岁上多伦多大学的时候, 就开始学中文, 他的中文名字叫路士伟, 可是他不太喜欢这个名字。23岁来北京大学学习。不久, 他在电视上表演了一个节目, 节目里他演的那个人物叫大山。中国人看了这个节目以后, 都认识了他。大山很忙, 他去过中国很多地方说相声。现在他也演电视剧和话剧。他还在电视上教英文, 也给在中国的外国人教中文。

大山结婚了, 他太太是北京人, 他们有两个孩子, 孩子们在多伦多读书。大山每年一半的时间在北京, 一半的时间在多伦多, 他说: "我们工作在北京, 生活在多伦多。" 在北京他是名人, 在多伦多他不是名人, 他觉得这两种生活都很有意思。

1 Young people in Chinese cities don't know about Dashan.
2 Dashan is famous in China because of his work on TV.
3 Dashan had a Chinese name before he went to Beijing.
4 Dashan started to learn Chinese at the age of 23.
5 Dashan teaches English in Beijing University.
6 Dashan works in Beijing and has his family home in Toronto.
7 Many people in Toronto don't know who Dashan is.
8 Dashan thinks life in Beijing is more interesting than in Toronto.

4

Reading

Find the Chinese for the following from the text in Activity 3.

1 two countries
2 two cities
3 three types of performance
4 two educational TV programmes

5

Writing

You are a celebrity for one day. Describe what you are going to do and what kind of life style you would like to have for that day.

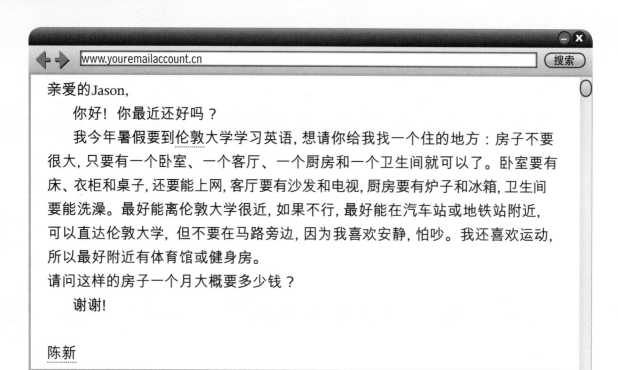

亲爱的Jason,

　　你好！你最近还好吗？

　　我今年暑假要到伦敦大学学习英语, 想请你给我找一个住的地方：房子不要很大, 只要有一个卧室、一个客厅、一个厨房和一个卫生间就可以了。卧室要有床、衣柜和桌子, 还要能上网, 客厅要有沙发和电视, 厨房要有炉子和冰箱, 卫生间要能洗澡。最好能离伦敦大学很近, 如果不行, 最好能在汽车站或地铁站附近, 可以直达伦敦大学, 但不要在马路旁边, 因为我喜欢安静, 怕吵。我还喜欢运动, 所以最好附近有体育馆或健身房。

　　请问这样的房子一个月大概要多少钱？

　　　　谢谢！

陈新

Read the email and answer the following questions in English.

1　Where is Chen Xin going this summer holiday?

2　Why is he going there?

3　What kind of house does he want?

4　What facility does he need in the bedroom?

5　Where does he want to stay?

6　Why doesn't he want to live near the road?

7　What is his hobby according to the text?

8　What does he want Jason to do for him?

Decide if these sentences about the email are true or false.

1　陈新想要一个大房子。

2　陈新喜欢热闹的地方。

3　陈新想住在大学旁边。

4　陈新希望他住的地方附近有体育馆。

5　陈新想要Jason帮他买房子。

3

Writing

Imagine you are Jason and you have found a place for Chen Xin. It is a single room in a shared house with all the facilities he wants: a ten-minute walk from the tube station (to get to the University of London), in a quiet area, not far from a gym. Write a letter in Chinese to Chen Xin to tell him about the house. Use the vocabulary in the box to help you.

single room
单人房 dān rén fáng
share...with others
和别人共用... hé bié rén gòng yòng

4

Writing

Look at the email invitation below. Draw a map for Ming Ming to show how to get to Mike's house by tube. Show all the landmarks mentioned in the email.

www.youremailaccount.cn   搜索

亲爱的明明：

　　这个周末是我的生日，我想请你到我家参加我的生日会。我家在 6 Roman Road, Beckton.

　　你可以坐 262 路公共汽车来，在 Kingsford Way 站下车，下车后往右拐，走一会儿就到我家了。

　　你也可以坐地铁，在 Beckton 站下车。我家附近有一个大超市，叫 ASDA，我家对面有一个中学，叫 Kingsford Community School。你如果坐地铁，下了地铁，地铁对面就是大超市，穿过大超市，顺着一条小路往前走，小路右边有一个银行，左边有一个酒吧。走到 Kingsford 学校往右拐，过了马路再走两分钟就到了。

　　希望你能来参加我的生日会！

你的朋友
迈克

5

Writing

Imagine you are going to invite a Chinese friend to your birthday party. Write an email to her/him and describe how she/he can get to your house, mentioning different means of transport and landmarks near your house.

读和写 dú hé xiě Reading and Writing 6

Extra Reading and Writing practice

1 **Reading**

Read the text about Wang Yue, Zhao Ming, Chen Hua and Zhang Xin. Copy and fill in the table below.

我是王月，我家在西安。西安有很多名胜古迹，但自然风景不是很美，我没去过南方，我很想去南方玩，去山清水秀的地方。谁想和我一起去？

我是赵明。我家在昆明。今年暑假我想去北方旅游。我想去西安和北京，因为它们都是中国的历史名城，有很多名胜古迹，也是很现代化的大城市。我想先去西安，参观西安的兵马俑，然后去北京，去看故宫、爬长城。谁想跟我一起去？

我是陈花，从小生长在西部的农村，没去过很多地方。农村很安静，但是不热闹，我很想去热闹的地方玩。我的爸爸在广州工作，今年暑假我要先去广州看他，然后再去广州附近的城市看看。我打算坐火车去，这样还可以看铁路两边的风景。

我是张新，我是南方人，我生在桂林，长在桂林，桂林虽然很美，但不很大，也不是很现代化。我没去过北方，也没去过大城市，我很想去北方的大城市看看。

山清水秀 shān qīng shuǐ xiù	beautiful mountains and waters
兵马俑 bīng mǎ yǒng	terracotta warriors
从小 cóng xiǎo	since childhood
生长 shēng zhǎng	to grow up
铁路 tiě lù	railway

姓名	哪里人？	想去哪儿？	旅行计划？
王月			
赵明			
陈花			
张新			

2 **Reading**

Decide if these sentences about the text are true or false.

1 Wang Yue likes places with beautiful natural scenery.
2 Zhao Ming likes historical sites as well as modern cities.
3 Chen Hua is going to Guangzhou by train because it is cheaper.
4 Zhang Xin is growing up in a big modern city in southern China.

3
Writing

Write about where you are from, where you would like to go for the summer holiday and why. Use the text in Activity 1 as an example.

我从小生长在… (I grew up in…)
我生在…/长在… (I was born in…/grew up in…)
我没去过…/我很想去… (I have never been to…/ I really want to go to…)

中国西北旅行社：上海、苏州、杭州四日游

999 元

第一天： 西安—上海
早上乘飞机到上海。下午参观上海博物馆。晚上住新上海大酒店。

第二天： 上海—苏州
上午参观外滩，下午购物。晚上乘火车到苏州, 住苏州花园饭店。

第三天： 苏州—杭州
上午参观苏州园林。下午乘空调大巴到杭州。晚上住西湖酒店。

第四天： 杭州—西安
游览西湖。晚上乘火车回西安。

出发日期：每星期一、五。
电话：0293 3576328

 4
Reading

Read the travel advertisement and answer the questions in English.

1 What will the tour include in Shanghai?
2 How do they get to Suzhou?
3 Where do they go by coach?
4 Which day does the travel group leave for Shanghai?

旅行社 lǚ xíng shè	travel agency
外滩 wài tān	The Bund (a famous area in Shanghai)
园林 yuán lín	gardens
游览 yóu lǎn	tour, visit

 5
Writing

Imagine you are writing an itinerary for a group of Chinese visitors who are touring London and Scotland for four days.

For each day include activities, means of transport and accommodation details. (You can use English hotel names.)

British Museum	大英博物馆 dà yīng bó wù guǎn
Houses of Parliament	国会大厦 guó huì dà shà
Buckingham Palace	白金汉宫 bái jīn hàn gōng
London Eye	伦敦眼 lún dūn yǎn
Edinburgh	爱丁堡 ài dīng bǎo
Scottish Highlands	苏格兰高地 sū gé lán gāo dì

读和写 dú hé xiě Reading and Writing 7

Extra Reading and Writing practice

Reading

1 This interview is part of a survey on local people's eating habits in Shanghai and appeared in the magazine *Everyday Food* (天天饮食). Read and answer the questions in English.

记者：刘东, 你是上海人吗？

刘东：我出生在山东, 我十四岁的时候和爸爸妈妈从山东来上海。

记者：那你现在是上海口味了吧。

刘东：虽然我在上海生活了十几年了, 可是我的饮食习惯还是北方人的。

记者：那你们家一定吃面食多？

刘东：对, 我们家是吃很多面食, 因为我们觉得面食更好吃。

记者：那你们都吃什么呢？

刘东：我们经常吃馒头、面条, 还吃饺子、包子等等。

记者：你们自己做这些东西吗？

刘东：不, 做这些东西花太多时间, 我和妻子都很忙, 所以我们一般去超市买。上海的超市里有各种各样的现成的东西, 很方便, 而且吃的东西也不贵。

现成 xiàn chéng	ready made

1 When did Liu Dong move to Shanghai?

2 Which region's cuisine does Liu Dong like best?

3 List two food items that Liu Dong likes.

4 Why don't Liu Dong and his wife cook their own food?

5 Why does Liu Dong often buy food from the supermarket? Give two reasons.

Reading and Writing

2 Choose a word to fill in each gap, according to the information given in Activity 1.

1 刘东出生在 ___a___ 。

2 刘东十四岁的时候, 他和爸爸妈妈来 ___b___ 。

3 刘东喜欢吃 ___c___ 。

4 刘东常常吃的东西有 ___d___ , ___e___ 。

5 刘东和妻子都很忙, 所以他们常常去 ___f___ 买现成的东西吃。

> 包子　饺子
> 超市　面食
> 上海　山东

Writing

3 Write about your eating habits. Use these words and phrases to help you.

经常 often	做 to make	因为 because
一般 generally	买 to buy	

4
Reading

Read the two texts in which teenagers talk about their lunch. Choose the four correct statements.

A 小文

我们学校早上八点上课，十二点到两点半是中饭时间。我一般在我们学校的餐厅吃中饭。我们学校有一个教师餐厅和两个学生餐厅。两个学生餐厅都很大，因为我们学校有很多学生。餐厅的饭菜很好，每天中午都有米饭、面条、包子，还有很多各种各样的菜，有肉菜、素菜，还有海鲜等等。除了去餐厅，我有时候也和好朋友去学校外面的餐馆吃中饭。我们学校外面有好几个小餐馆，那里有饺子，还有火锅，都很好吃，价钱只比学校餐厅的贵一点。

价钱 jià qian	price

B Marie

我们学校中饭时间是从一点到一点五十分，我们的中饭时间不长。我一般自己带饭。我的中饭常常是两个三明治、一个苹果、一个酸奶、一瓶果汁和一包薯片，有时候也有巧克力。我也去学校的餐厅吃过一两次中饭，我不喜欢去学校餐厅吃饭，因为那里人很多，而且没有我喜欢吃的东西。我喜欢每天的午饭时间，因为除了吃东西以外，我还可以和朋友聊天，很高兴。

三明治 sān míng zhì	sandwich
酸奶 suān nǎi	yoghurt
薯片 shǔ piàn	crisps

1 The lunch break in the Chinese school is longer than that in the British school.

2 There are three student canteens in the Chinese school.

3 Marie's lunch normally consists of two sandwiches, an apple, a yoghurt, a bottle of water and a packet of crisps.

4 Xiao Wen thinks the food in his school canteen is good.

5 Marie doesn't like her school canteen because the food there is too expensive.

6 Xiao Wen sometimes goes to have lunch in a restaurant outside his school.

7 Marie enjoys the lunch break because it is the time for her to be with her friends.

8 The food in the restaurants near to Xiao Wen's school is much more expensive than their canteen food.

5
Reading

Find characters in the text of Activity 4 to match the pictures.

a  b c d

e  f  g  h

6
Writing

Write about your lunch time.

- What do you have for lunch?
- What types of food and drink does the school canteen offer?
- Do you prefer the school canteen or packed lunch? Why?
- What else do you do in the lunch break?

1

Reading

Read the article and choose the four correct statements.

"超级女声"这几年在中国是一个很流行的电视节目，很多女孩子在电视上参加唱歌比赛，希望自己成为有名的歌星，它有点儿像英国的X Factor 和美国的Pop Idol。不过，参加"超级女声"节目的都是女生，她们来自全国不同的地方，她们唱完后，观众投票。这个电视节目已经让好几个女孩子成为了有名的歌星。

流行 liú xíng	popular
像 xiàng	be like
投票 tóu piào	to vote

GRAMMAR: 好

As well as meaning 'good/nice', 好 can also be used to mean 'quite'. For example:

好几个女孩子 quite a few girls
今天好冷。 Today is quite cold.

1 Super Girl ("Super Voice Girls") is a popular television programme in East Asia.

2 This programme has been popular for a few years.

3 Many contestants go on the programme to show their talent in singing and dancing.

4 The programme is similar to X Factor in Britain and Pop Idol in America.

5 The singing contest is for female singers only, regardless of their age.

6 The contestants come from many different areas of China.

7 The television audience vote for their favourite contestants before and after the performances.

8 This programme has created quite a few famous singers.

EXAM TIP

It is not uncommon for one character to have more than one meaning, so it is important to look at the context in which the character is used. Looking at the characters before and after will help you to decide on the right meaning.

2

Reading

Match the two halves of the sentences.

A	B
1 超级女声是一个电视节目，	a 她们来自全国不同的地方。
2 这个节目和外国的几个节目很像，	b 这几年在中国很流行。
3 来参加比赛的女孩子很多，	c 观众投票。
4 很多女孩子来参加比赛，	d 比如，英国的X Factor 和美国的Pop Idol
5 她们表演完后，	e 因为她们都想成为有名的歌星。

3
Reading

Look up the single characters and then try to work out the meaning of their combinations appearing in the text.

> 我有一个好朋友叫陈东明,他今年十七岁。他个子很高,
> 短头发,大眼睛,高鼻子,很多人都说他长得像电影明星。他很
> 喜欢运动,他羽毛球打得很好,跑步也很快。每次运动会,他都
> 得短跑第一名。他学习也很好,他去年参加了全市数学比赛,
> 得了第三名。所以陈东明在我们学校是一个名人。这个名人
> 除了要刻苦学习然后参加高考以外,他还要参加很多课外活动,
> 比如羽毛球比赛。他在学校有很多朋友,他也要花时间和朋友
> 们在一起。这个校园名人真是太忙了!

e.g. 电 (diàn electronic) + 脑 (nǎo brain) = 电脑 (computer)

1 短 (...) + 跑 (...) = 短跑 (...)

2 运动 (...) + 会 (...) = 运动会 (...)

3 高 (...) + 考 (...) = 高考 (...)

4 课 (...) + 外 (...) = 课外 (...)

4
Reading

Read the previous text again and answer the questions.

1 Describe what Chen Dongming looks like.

2 How does he do in sports? Give an example.

3 How does he do with his schoolwork? Give an example.

4 Why is Chen Dongming always busy?

5
Writing

Write a paragraph about a celebrity you like, including:

• his/her physical appearance

• what he/she likes to wear.

• what kind of person he/she is

• his/her hobbies

• why you like him/her

• whether you want to be a celebrity (why or why not)

Reading

Read the text and answer the questions in English.

张丽在北京上大学，她学习中国历史，她说学习中国历史很有意思，她非常喜欢。快放暑假了，她今年夏天不打算回英国度假，她想在中国做家教，赚钱以后就去旅游。她来中国快一年了，她只去过北京的长城，还没有去过别的地方。除了北京的名胜古迹，她还想去上海、杭州和西安等地方玩儿，看看那儿美丽的风景。放假要放两个月，她打算先做兼职做六个星期，再去旅游。她准备去教中学生或小学生学习英语。在中国，父母都希望孩子学习学得好，如果父母自己不会英语的话，都愿意请家教来帮助他们的孩子学习英语。张丽是英国人，她应该是他们最理想的家教。

家教 jiā jiào	home tuition, private tutor
希望 xī wàng	hope, to hope
愿意 yuàn yì	to be willing

GRAMMAR: 再

You can use 再 to indicate sequence, for example:
我先做作业，再看电视 = I do homework first, then I watch TV.

1 Which university does Zhang Li go to? What does she study?
2 Why does she decide not to go back to the UK in the summer?
3 What does she want to do in the summer?
4 Where has she been for sightseeing since she came to China?
5 How long is the summer holiday? How long does she intend to work?
6 Will it be easy for her to find the job of her choice? Why?

Reading

Read the text in Activity 1 again and find the Chinese equivalent of the following phrases:

1 Chinese history is very interesting
2 the summer holiday will start soon
3 go back to the UK for a holiday
4 have been in China for almost one year
5 have only been to…, not been to…
6 famous places and historical sites
7 work part time for… then go travelling
8 be willing to employ a home tutor

Writing

Write a passage of about 100 characters about Zhang Li's friend Liu Lin (刘林). You can refer to Activity 1 and use the following information about Liu Lin to help you:

- She came to Shanghai two years ago.
- She works in a company and enjoys her job.
- She likes travelling and has been to many places in China.
- She wants to go to different places with Zhang Li in the summer.
- She hasn't been back to see her parents for two years.
- She wants to do some teaching in the evenings to earn more money for travelling.

You may find these expressions useful:

刘林来中国快…了。

她在…工作, 她…喜欢…。

她的爱好是…, 她去过…。

她打算… (time)跟… (people)一起去…
　　(place)。

她… (length of time)没有回英国看…了。

她想先…再…。

4
Reading

Read the extract from the reader's column of a magazine and decide whether the statements are true or false.

我的一个好朋友, 大学毕业三年了, 换了五次工作, 可是每次都觉得很不理想。你认为什么工作才是理想的工作呢？

我们很多人常常不知道自己要些什么。你有没有问过自己这些问题：你想做什么？你的理想是什么？你会做什么？你做什么做得好？等等。

有的人认为理想的工作就是自己喜欢的工作, 有的人认为是赚钱多的工作, 有的人认为是能做出成绩的工作, 也有的人认为是容易的工作, 还有的人觉得好玩儿的工作就是理想的工作, 等等。

什么是最理想的工作？当教师, 当运动员, 当工人, 还是当经理？你能不能告诉我什么是最理想的工作呢？

1   The writer of the query has a friend who changes jobs frequently because he likes new things.

2   The advisor says that people always know what they want.

3   The advisor suggests that you can find out what you want to do by asking yourself questions.

4   Different people have different opinions about what an ideal job is.

5   The advisor is sure what his ideal job is.

换 huàn	to change
成绩 chéng jì	achievement
经理 jīng lǐ	manager

5
Reading

Read the text above again and complete the sentences using the words in the box:

1 认为   2 当   3 每次   4 问过   5 换了   6 理想   7 成绩   8 赚钱   9 常常   10 还是

1   我好朋友 ___a___ 五次工作, 可是 ___b___ 都觉得很不理想。

2   我们很多人 ___c___ 不知道自己要些什么。你有没有 ___d___ 自己这些问题：…。

3   有的人 ___e___ 理想的工作就是自己喜欢的工作, 有的人认为是 ___f___ 多的工作, 有的人认为是能做出 ___g___ 的工作, ……等等。

4   什么是最 ___h___ 的工作？ ___i___ 教师, 当运动员, 当工人, ___j___ 当经理？

6
Writing

Write 100 characters about your family or friends and their jobs.

You can include the following points:

•   who you are writing about

•   what jobs they do

•   whether they like their jobs? why?

•   what do you want to do? why?

Here are some useful phrases:

我有一个…, 叫…。

他/她是…, 他/她在…工作。

他/她很喜欢/不喜欢做……,
因为…。

我想/不想做…, 因为…。

语法 GRAMMAR

This section of the book does not aim to repeat all the grammar you will have covered; we have picked out some of the tricky bits to do with **the use of 的** and **nouns**, **verbs** and **word order**. The section ends with a useful list of **conjunctions** and **question words**. Each grammar point has a clear description of how it works and when to use it, why it is important and things to watch out for. This is followed, where appropriate, by exercises for you to try out to brush up your ability to use the grammar correctly. This section covers:

- **Nouns** the use of measure words for nouns

  using 的 to link pronouns, adjectives and noun phrases to nouns

- **Verbs** the use of 过 after a verb

  the use of 了 after a verb

  the use of 在 to express an action in progress

  talking about the future

  the use of 得 after a verb

  expressing coming and going

  using a suffix after the main verb to show the result of an action

  using 得 or 不 between the two parts of a verb

- **Use of 了 at the end of a sentence**
- **Word order**
- **Conjunctions**
- **Question words**

名词 NOUNS

1 The use of measure words for nouns

When a number is used with a noun, then there must be a measure word between the number and the noun. (A small number of nouns are measure words in their own right and so do not take another measure word, e.g. 四天, 三年.) You will by now have learnt all about this. If in doubt, use 个, but if you want to try to use the correct measure word for the noun you are using, here is a list below to help you.

Measure word	Nouns
个 ge	**the most frequently used measure word** **people**: 人, 中国人, 哥哥, 朋友, 老师, 学生, etc. **places**: 学校, 中学, 工厂, 教室, 运动场, 房间, etc.
本 běn	**books**: 书, 英文书, 作业本, 日记, 杂志, etc.
匹 pǐ	**horses**: 马
头 tóu	**cattle**: 牛, 奶牛, etc.
只 zhī	**some animals**: 动物, 狗, 猫, 羊, etc.
双 shuāng	**a pair of**: 鞋子, 皮鞋, 运动鞋, 袜子, 眼睛, 手, 筷子, etc.
件 jiàn	**clothes**: 衣服, 夹克, 毛衣, 衬衣, T恤, etc.
条 tiáo	**long, winding, flexible things**: 领带, 裙子, 裤子, also: 鱼, 金鱼, etc.
张 zhāng	**flat objects**: 照片, 画儿, 地图, 纸, 报纸, 桌子, etc.
瓶 píng	**bottles of**: 牛奶, 汽水, 可乐, 酒, 水, 果汁, etc.
杯 bēi	**a cup/glass of**: 茶, 咖啡, 牛奶, 酒, etc.
家 jiā	**restaurant/hospital/company/factory etc.**: 饭馆, 医院, 公司, 工厂, etc.

2 Using 的 to link pronouns, adjectives and phrases to nouns

HOW DOES IT WORK AND WHEN DO I USE IT?

1 的 is used to link pronouns to nouns to make possessive adjectives. For example:

我的书在哪儿？ = Where is my book?

的 is often omitted where the relationship between the nouns and possessive is close. For example:

我爸爸　　　= my father

我姐姐　　　= my older sister

2 的 also links adjectives to nouns where the adjective is not just a single syllable. For example:

很无聊的课　= boring lessons

新鲜的草莓　= fresh strawberries

的 is often not used if the adjective is a single syllable or a place name. For example:

中国地图　　= map of China

一条黄裙子　= a yellow skirt

3 的 links noun phrases to nouns. For example:

我喜欢的电影　= the film that I like

的 is used to join the two parts: 'I like' and 'film'.

Moreover, in Chinese 'that I like' goes before 'the film', following the structure of 'I like' + 的 + 'film'.
It is often useful to think of the 的 as 'that (or which)' and then to remember that the 'that (or which)' clause must come before the noun.

4 的 + pronoun = possessive pronoun. For example:

那只狗是谁的？　　=　(literally) That dog is whose?

这只狗是我的。　　=　That dog is mine.

5 的 with no following noun. This can happen if the context is clear. For example :

我喜欢这件新的。　=　I like this new one (probably clothing in this case).

WHY IS IT IMPORTANT?

的 is a key particle in Chinese and is one of the aspects of grammar that makes the language structurally very different from English. To be able to express yourself in Chinese and to be able to understand it, you need to understand 的。

THINGS TO WATCH OUT FOR

我妈妈做的饭很好吃 = The food (that) my mother makes is really tasty.

Notice the difference in word order between the two languages. You need to think of 'my mother makes' as describing the noun 'food', and then you won't end up with the 的 in the wrong place!

Make sure you don't get 的 muddled up with measure words. In a standard noun phrase with an adjective, the word order is as follows:

一个很聪明的学生 = a very intelligent student = number + measure + adjective + 的 + noun.

TRY IT OUT

1 Sort out the word order for the following sentences and translate them into English.

1 那是我书的。

2 弟弟房间的很小。

3 他写字的真漂亮。

4 她是一个的可爱女孩子。

5 英国人的很多会说汉语。

6 今天天气好极了的。

7 这儿有两个苹果，你的吃红，我的吃绿。

8 要是的你不喜欢话，就别买了。

2 Decide whether or not 的 is needed in the gaps (a, b, etc.) in the following sentences.

1 这是我 ___a___ 书包。

2 哥哥拿了一个大 ___b___ 箱子。

3 饭是谁做 ___c___ ？

4 我吃了两个 ___d___ 鸡蛋。

5 那是一个美丽 ___e___ 地方。

6 我 ___f___ 妈妈是医生。

7 他住在一个很小 ___g___ 房子里。

8 她去过美国 ___h___ 。

9 公园里 ___i___ 人不少。

10 那只小 ___j___ 狗真可爱。

动词 VERBS

1 The use of 过 after a verb to express having experienced an action

HOW DOES IT WORK AND WHEN DO I USE IT?

To say you have had the experience of doing something, place 过 after the verb. For example:

> 我去过马来西亚。 = I have been to Malaysia.
>
> 我吃过中国饭。　 = I have eaten Chinese food.

To turn this into a negative statement, place 没 (not) in front of the verb and follow the verb with 过。
For example:

> 哥哥没去过日本。 = My brother hasn't been to Japan.

WHY IS IT IMPORTANT?

Although there are no tenses in Chinese, it is important that you know how to use different timeframes so that you can make yourself understood, and understand what other people are saying to you. 过 is used to express past experience.

THINGS TO WATCH OUT FOR

Remember that 过 is used for past experience, whereas 了 after a verb is used for a completed action.

TRY IT OUT

Now is the chance for you to get some practice. Have a go at translating the sentences below and then decide whether it is grammatically correct if you change the 过 to 了. See if you can work out the difference in meaning between the 过 sentence and the 了 sentence. This is tricky, but it will help you when you come to reading Chinese.

1 姐姐当过医生。　　　　4 这本书我读过三遍。

2 他弹过钢琴。　　　　　5 她说过那样的话吗？

3 我从来没坐过飞机。

2 The use of 了 after a verb to express completed action

HOW DOES IT WORK AND WHEN DO I USE IT?

1 When an event has happened/an action has been completed and the object of the sentence is specified or defined (that is, it has a number before it), then put 了 after the verb and before the number. For example:

> 今天早上我吃了三碗米饭和一条鱼。 = I ate three bowls of rice and
> 　　　　　　　　　　　　　　　　　　 a fish for breakfast today.
>
> 我昨天买了六本书。　　　　　 = I bought six books yesterday.

2 To turn this into a negative statement, use 没有 without 了. For example:

> 他没买书。　　　　　　　　 = He didn't buy (any) books.

WHY IS IT IMPORTANT?

No one is expected to have perfected the use of 了 at GCSE, but you do need to be able to show that you are aware of its use in this way to express completed action.

THINGS TO WATCH OUT FOR

Remember that 了 does not express tense.

In Chinese, time expressions show the time of the action of the verb.

TRY IT OUT

1 Translate the following sentences into Chinese:

1 He bought three bottles of beer.

2 Xiao Li learnt Chinese for five years.

3 She made a big cake.

4 Uncle lost a bike.

5 He drank two cups of coffee.

6 I went to the Great Wall yesterday.

7 The child slept for two hours.

8 How long did she work as a teacher?

2 Put 了 in the correct place (indicated by the letters a, b, c) and translate the sentences.

1 他休息 ___ a ___ 好 ___ b ___ 几天。

2 弟弟吃 ___ a ___ 二十个 ___ b ___ 饺子。

3 小鸭跑 ___ a ___ 一会儿, 就累 ___ b ___ 。

4 他赚 ___ a ___ 很多 ___ b ___ 钱。

5 学校来 ___ a ___ 几个新学生 ___ b ___ 。

6 上星期他爬 ___ a ___ 两座高山 ___ b ___ 。

3 The use of 在 to express an action in progress

HOW DOES IT WORK AND WHEN DO I USE IT?

1 在 or 正在 is used before a verb to show that something is/was going on at a particular time. Sometimes you will also find 呢 at the end of a sentence. For example:

marked by 在: 她在睡觉。	= She is asleep.
marked by 正在 and 呢: 她正在睡觉呢。	= She is asleep.

2 在 before a verb in this way can also refer to a past timeframe. For example:

那是 1998 年, 她在上大学。That was 1998. She was studying at university.

WHY IS IT IMPORTANT?

If you want to express that someone is in the process of doing something, then you need to be able to use 在 in this way before the verb.

THINGS TO WATCH OUT FOR

在 is used in this way now much more often than it was 20 years ago. However, you don't need to use it all the time. Remember that it is the time expressions that indicate the time of the action. In sentences like 你今天穿什么？ (= What are you wearing today?), there is no need for 在, but in the sentence 你在穿什么？ (= What are you wearing?), it needs to be there.

TRY IT OUT

Translate the following sentences into Chinese.

1 She is on the phone.

2 Dad is having supper.

3 At that time, he was studying at a secondary school.

4 The teachers are having a meeting.

5 The children are playing table tennis in the gym.

4 Talking about the future

HOW DOES IT WORK AND WHEN DO I USE IT?

1 If you want to talk about the future, simply put in a time phrase indicating future, such as next year, next week etc., and use verbs such as 想 , 打算 , 计划, 要. For example:

下个星期六我打算去博物馆。 = I am planning to go to a museum next Saturday.

2 会 is often used to indicate possibility/probability, that is, something may/is likely to happen. For example:

明天会下雪。　　　　　　　= It looks like it'll snow tomorrow.

3 Imminent future indicated by:

要…了　　要下雨了。　　= It's about to rain.

快要…了　快要下雪了。　= It's about to snow.

快…了　　快到了。　　　= It's about to arrive.

WHY IS IT IMPORTANT?

To use the Chinese language properly, you need to be able to demonstrate good use of different timeframes. In reading, if you don't know how these timeframes work, then you are likely to struggle when decoding reading passages.

THINGS TO WATCH OUT FOR

Don't overuse these verbs to indicate the future. Often just one in a paragraph is enough to set the context You certainly don't need 会 in every sentence.

TRY IT OUT

Complete the following sentences with 要 or 会 where the gaps are (a, b, etc.)。

1 你　a　去哪儿？

2 明天　b　冷吗？

3 我们　c　开学了。

4 我　d　好好学习。

5 你　e　参加我的生日聚会吗？

6 　f　下雪了。

7 她就　g　大学毕业了。

8 快　h　到家了。

9 别担心, 她的身体　i　好起来的。

10 不用等了, 他不　j　来了。

5 The use of 得 after a verb

HOW DOES IT WORK AND WHEN DO I USE IT?

1 得 is used to express the manner in which an activity is usually carried out. The main verb of the sentence must be repeated and the repeated verb is directly followed by 得.

The structure goes as follows: verb + object + verb + 得 + adverb. For example:

他弹钢琴弹得非常棒。 = He plays the piano very well.

她说英文说得不太好。 = She doesn't speak English very well.

2 Sometimes you will see the object of the verb placed before the verb, so as to avoid the repetition of the verb. For example:

他钢琴弹得很好。

You need to be able to recognise both ways, even if you stick to just one way of doing it when writing yourself.

WHY IS IT IMPORTANT?

You need to be able to express how an action is done; it will make your written work more interesting for you and for the reader.

THINGS TO WATCH OUT FOR

Don't be tempted to miss out the 得.

TRY IT OUT

Work through the following exercise, but beware: it involves 的 too! Fill in the gaps with 的 or 得 and translate into English. You might need to work with a friend to puzzle out the ones near the end.

1 他跑 __a__ 真快！

2 她的中文说 __b__ 很好。

3 弟弟玩儿 __c__ 很高兴。

4 同学们做 __d__ 认真。

5 他 __e__ 字太漂亮了！

6 去上海 __f__ 票没有了。

7 昨天晚上下雨下 __g__ 很厉害。

8 她跳舞跳 __h__ 忘了时间。

9 她气 __i__ 脸都红了。

10 这个小商店 __j__ 东西都卖完了。

6 Expressing coming and going

HOW DOES IT WORK AND WHEN DO I USE IT?

1 从…来 Normally a place is inserted between the two parts of this structure to show where you come from. For example:

她从美国来。	= She comes from America.
你从什么地方来？我从山东来。	= Where are you from? I am from Shandong.

2 去 and 来 are verbs of movement. When stating the purpose of going or coming, we can use the structure subject + 去 or 来 + (somewhere) + action. For example:

我去公园玩儿滑板。	= I go to the park to skateboard.
你们明天来我家看电视吧？	= Why don't you come round to my house tomorrow to watch TV?

WHY IS IT IMPORTANT?

Chinese is slightly stricter about the use of 去 (movement away from the speaker) and 来 (movement towards the speaker) than we are in English with 'going' and 'coming'. It is important to differentiate clearly.

THINGS TO WATCH OUT FOR

Consider the position of the speaker when working out whether to use 去 or 来.

7 Using a suffix after the main verb to show the result of an action

HOW DOES IT WORK AND WHEN DO I USE IT?

The structure verb + e.g. 好 or 完 shows the result of the completion of an action and it very often has 了 at the end. For example:

我看完了。	= I've finished (watching).
新做好的饺子	= newly made/finished dumplings

WHY IS IT IMPORTANT?

These endings on a verb are commonly used to show the result of a completion of an action. For instance, 找 is to 'look for' and 找到 is 'to find' (that is, to look for with the result of finding). There is not a completely separate verb for 'find', so it is important to know how these endings work.

THINGS TO WATCH OUT FOR

You need to learn the meanings of these resultative endings, otherwise you may come to the wrong conclusion. Only a few will be used at GCSE.

TRY IT OUT

Choose an appropriate character from the box below for each sentence. Use each character once. 完, 饱 (full, replete); 好, 醉 (drunk, intoxicated); 见 (after 听, i.e. 听见, or 看, i.e. 看见, means hear or see respectively); 错 (incorrect); 到 (arrival, attainment).

1 作业写 __a__ 了。   6 衣服穿 __f__ 了。

2 饭做 __b__ 了。   7 我吃 __g__ 了。

3 他喝 __c__ 了。   8 你准备 __h__ 了吗？

4 他踢 __d__ 了足球。   9 你的钱包找 __i__ 了吗？

5 这个字写 __e__ 了。   10 我说的话，你听 __j__ 了没有？

8 Using 得 or 不 between the two parts of a verb

HOW DOES IT WORK AND WHEN DO I USE IT?

Ability to do something or inability to do something is often expressed by a 得 or a 不 between the two parts of the verb. For example:

老师，我看不见.	= Teacher, I can't see.
我听得懂.	= I understand.
我听不懂.	= I don't understand.

WHY IS IT IMPORTANT?

The structure of a 得 or a 不 between the parts of a verb is widely used in Chinese, but at this stage it is just important that you recognise it. It is quite distinctive.

9 了 at the end of the sentence

HOW DOES IT WORK AND WHEN DO I USE IT?

1 了 can be used at the end of a sentence to indicate a new situation, progression or a change of state. The speaker is updating the listener:

我不去。	= I am not going. (statement of fact)
我不去了。	= I was going, but now have changed my mind and am <u>not</u> going. (changed situation)
他去北京了。	= He has gone to Beijing. (He was here until recently.)

Negation by 没有 and without 了 = 他没(有)去北京。 = He didn't go to Beijing.

2 A further use of 了 at the end of a sentence is to express 'too' (meaning excessive).

To express 'too ...', use the structure 太 (adjective) 了！ For example:

T恤太小了!	= The T-shirt is too small!
我们的校服太不好看了!	= Our school uniform looks really bad! (Literally: It's too bad-looking.)

WHY IS IT IMPORTANT?

Although Chinese has no tenses, you need to be able to demonstrate that you know how to recognise or express a change of state, a progression or a new situation.

THINGS TO WATCH OUT FOR

了 is quite tricky to get to grips with and many native speakers of Chinese differ a little in how they use it. The updating 了 is used far more in spoken than in written Chinese. Avoid having a 了 at the end of every sentence in your written work and keep checking your usage with your teacher.

TRY IT OUT

The following exercises will ensure you get the idea and know when to try to include a 了 in your written or spoken Chinese.

1 Make changes, where necessary, to the Chinese sentences below to make them into correct translations of the English.

1 天很冷。 It is getting cold.

2 不要生气。 Don't be angry any more.

3 我明白了。 I understand now!

4 他去游泳。 He's gone swimming.

5 这本书我不想看。 I don't want to read this book anymore.

6 我喜欢学中文了。 I like learning Chinese.

7 她太好! She is very nice.

8 他生病。 He is ill.

9 我不等他。 I won't wait for him any longer.

10 春天到了。 Spring has arrived.

2 Translate the following sentences into English showing the change of state/updating function of 了.

1 他不抽烟。— 他不抽烟了。

2 我看书呢! — 我看完书了。

3 我不想去电影院。 — 我不想去电影院了。

4 爷爷的头发是白的。 — 爷爷的头发白了。

5 我在北京工作。 — 我在北京工作三年了。

6 我很饿。 — 我太饿了。

7 关门! — 门关上了。

8 我在吃早饭。 — 我吃过早饭了。

9 我会唱歌。 — 我会唱歌了。

10 她上过大学。 — 她上大学了。

词序 SOME ASPECTS OF WORD ORDER

Word order is important in Chinese. In particular, you should make sure that you remember that 'time when' comes at the beginning of a sentence, whereas 'time how long' comes after the verb. You should also ensure that you are completely confident in the use of time, manner, place sentences, such as:

他明天坐火车去上海。   = He tomorrow (time) by train (manner) go (verb) Shanghai (place).

It is important that you try to get these aspects of word order correct. Try to improve your word order knowledge by putting the characters in the sentences below into the correct order.

TRY IT OUT

1 明天我去学校骑自行车。

2 哥哥去了北京开车昨天。

3 我打的去了天安门上星期六。

4 你走路吧今天到我家来下午!

5 我们去明天那所大学坐公共汽车。

6 坐飞机你去英国下个月是吗？

7 去莫斯科, 我打算明年暑假做火车。

8 跟丈夫美国一起去了一个月前她。

连词 CONJUNCTIONS

Examiners are very keen on conjunctions. This is a list from the Edexcel exam specification to refresh your memory. Remember they often go in pairs and try to slip them into your written work where possible. Remember 和 only links nouns and pronouns.

和	and	也..., 也	both...and
虽然..., 但是	although	除了..., 以外	apart from
要是..., 就	if	越..., 越...	the more...the more
因为..., 所以	because		

问问题 ASKING QUESTIONS

Forgetting how to ask a question when learning a foreign language is very common. In class, it is more often you who are answering the questions rather than asking them. Below is a quick revision of question types and words as a reference for you. The great thing is that where question words are used, you just take out the question word and put in the answer – no worrying about word order in Chinese. For example:

你是哪国人？ = (literally) You are which country person?

我是英国人。 = (literally) I am England country person.

Using 吗	他来吗？ = Is he coming?
Verb 不 verb	他来不来？ = Is he coming (or not)?
是不是	你是不是北京人？ = Are you from Beijing (or not)?
有没有	你有没有电脑？ = Do you have a computer (or not)?
Verb adjective 不 verb adjective	你累不累？ Are you tired (or not)?
Using question words：	谁 (who) 谁的 (whose) 哪 (which) 哪儿 (where) 几 (how many) 多少 (how many) 为什么 (why) 怎么样 (how) 什么 (what) 什么样的 (what kind of) 什么时候 (when) 几点 (what time)
Using 吧	你是中国人吧？

写汉字 WRITING CHINESE

You have learnt about the evolution of Chinese characters and how to write them in earlier student books. This section is to help you revise writing characters and also gives advice on developing strategies for memorizing them. Learning characters is undoubtedly hard work, but it is also fun and fulfilling.

STROKES IN CHINESE CHARACTERS

The basic strokes in a Chinese character are listed below with their names in English and Chinese. Many of these basic strokes can be found in the character 永 which means 'eternal' – perhaps a good adjective to describe the length of time it takes even native speakers to learn several thousand Chinese characters!

	Stroke	Chinese	English	Examples
1	丶	点 diǎn	the dot	小 六
2	一	横 héng	the horizontal stroke, written left to right	一 有
3	丨	竖 shù	the vertical stroke, written top to bottom	十 中
4	丿	撇 piě	the sweeping left stroke, written top right to bottom left	人 爱
5	乀	捺 nà	the sweeping right stroke, written top left to bottom right	八 欢
6	㇀	提 tí	the rising stroke, written from bottom left to top right	汉 习
7	亅	钩 gōu	The hook can be written in any direction	到 对

TIP

Some people like to learn the names of the strokes and say them as they draw each character – in English or Chinese.
Try it and see if it helps you.

STROKE ORDER FOR WRITING CHINESE CHARACTERS

1 Write from left to right.　　　　　　　　　　北 川
2 Write from top to bottom.　　　　　　　　　三 下
3 Write horizontals before verticals.　　　　十 羊
4 Write left falling before right falling.　　　人 入
5 Write from outside frame to inside strokes.　月 同
6 Write major middle stroke before the two sides.　小 水
7 Finish what is inside the box before you close it.　日 四

川　ノ　川　川

下　一　丁　下

羊　ヽ　ソ　ソ　ソ　兰　羊

入　ノ　入

问　ヽ　亻　门　门　问　问

小　亅　亅　小

四　丨　冂　冂　四　四

TRY IT OUT

Make sure you remember these rules when you have a go at writing the characters below. Copy and complete the grid. Use the correct stroke order and build them up stroke by stroke. Ask your teacher to check you work.

他								
天								
风								
忙								
国								
到								
草								

RADICALS

As you know radicals may give you a clue as to the meaning of a character.
The table below gives you the meaning of some common radicals.

The meaning of radicals

Radical	Meaning			Radical	Meaning	
亠	head, above		文	目	eye	睡
豕	pig		家	竹	bamboo	筷
冫	ice		冰	禾	ear of grain	秋
氵	three-dot water		渴	辶	running	边
冖	cover, roof		写	冂	wilderness	同
宀	roof with chimney		家	艹	grass	花
厂	cliff		厅	扌	hand	打
广	house built on a slope		店	彡	hair, feather	衫
讠	speech		说	夂	follow, slow	冬
刂	knife		到	犭	animal	猫
亻	standing person		住	饣	food	饭
彳	double standing person		得	米	rice	糕
卩	seal, stamp		节	纟	silk	级
阝	double ear		院	牛	ox	物
女	female		妈	攵	knock	放
忄	vertical heart		快	疒	illness	病
心	horizontal heart		忘	礻	ritual	礼
火	fire		灯	衤	clothes	裙
灬	fire		热	覀	west	要
户	house, door		房	钅	metal	钱
口	mouth		吃	皿	plate	盘

TIP

You may like to work out the radical for some characters you learn and
relate it to the meaning; this may help you memorize the character.

TEN IDEAS FOR LEARNING CHINESE CHARACTERS

1 It is impossible to cram Chinese characters at the last minute. You need to practise them a little and often. It can be quite a relaxing break from other school work. Don't try to learn too many in one go.

2 Develop your own method for memorising. Whilst some students chant strokes or learn radicals, others find it helpful to look for pictures in the characters and link an imaginary picture with the real meaning to help jog the memory. Look for patterns or repeated components in groups of characters you are learning.

3 Make sure you are methodical. There will be some characters that you find easy. These don't need to be practised every day, but you still need to revisit them quite often. There will be other characters that you find particularly hard. Make sure you give them special attention.

4 Develop a learning schedule with either flashcards or a computer programme.

5 Look at online Chinese learning programmes (there are many on the Internet) and computer games in order to improve your character recognition. This will make it easier to learn to write them.

6 Stick 'post-it' notes all over your house labelling items with Chinese characters, so that you frequently see the ones you are learning.

7 Remember Chinese calligraphy is an art form. Have a go at writing characters with a brush and ink.

8 Don't get frustrated; it gets easier with time.

9 Have a look at books/websites on the origin of characters.

10 Be positive and enjoy it!

辞典 GLOSSARY

This glossary contains some common characters and their compounds.

商

商人	shāng rén	business person	商场	shāng chǎng	market; bazaar; mall
商店	shāng diàn	shop	商学	shāng xué	business studies

电

电视	diàn shì	TV	电话	diàn huà	telephone
电影	diàn yǐng	film	电子邮件	diàn zǐ yóu jiàn	email
电脑	diàn nǎo	computer	电影院	diàn yǐng yuàn	cinema
电灯	diàn dēng	lamp	电子游戏	diàn zǐ yóu xì	video game

钱

钱包	qián bāo	wallet; purse	花钱	huā qián	to spend money
赚钱	zhuàn qián	to earn money	零花钱	líng huā qián	pocket money
付钱	fù qián	to pay money	(零用钱)	(líng yòng qián)	

物

宠物	chǒng wù	pet	购物	gòu wù	to go shopping
动物	dòng wù	animal	物理	wù lǐ	physics
动物园	dòng wù yuán	zoo	生物	shēng wù	biology
礼物	lǐ wù	present; gift			

路

马路	mǎ lù	road	路灯	lù dēng	street lamp
走路	zǒu lù	to walk	8路公共汽车	bā lù gōng gòng qì chē	No. 8 bus
路上	lù shang	on the road			

年

去年	qù nián	last year	过年	guò nián	to celebrate the New Year
今年	jīn nián	this year	青年	qīng nián	youth; young people
明年	míng nián	next year	老年人	lǎo nián rén	old people; senior citizen
新年	xīn nián	the New Year			

月

月亮	yuè liang	moon	一月	yí yuè	January
月饼	yuè bing	moon cake	二月	èr yuè	February

天

春天	chūn tiān	spring	星期天	xīng qī tiān	Sunday
夏天	xià tiān	summer	天气	tiān qì	weather
秋天	qiū tiān	autumn	晴天	qíng tiān	sunny
冬天	dōng tiān	winter	阴天	yīn tiān	overcast
每天 (天天)	měi tiān (tiān tiān)	every day; everyday	雨天	yǔ tiān	rainy

节

春节	chūn jié	Spring Festival	端午节	duān wǔ jié	Dragon Boat Festival (the 5th day of the 5th lunar month)
圣诞节	shèng dàn jié	Christmas			
			中秋节	zhōng qiū jié	Mid-autumn Festival

花

花园	huā yuán	garden	花钱	huā qián	to spend money
花店	huā diàn	florist's	零花钱	líng huā qián	pocket money
花篮	huā lán	flower basket			

面

面包	miàn bāo	bread	面食	miàn shí	wheat-based food
面条	miàn tiáo	noodles	面试	miàn shì	interview

鱼

金鱼	jīn yú	goldfish	吃鱼	chī yú	to eat fish
钓鱼	diào yú	to go fishing	妈妈做的鱼	mā ma zuò de yú	the fish that mum cooks

鸡

鸡肉	jī ròu	chicken (meat)	火鸡	huǒ jī	turkey
鸡蛋	jī dàn	hen's egg			

肉

鸡肉	jī ròu	chicken (meat)	羊肉	yáng ròu	lamb
猪肉	zhū ròu	pork	牛肉	niú ròu	beef

饭

米饭	mǐ fàn	cooked rice	晚饭	wǎn fàn	supper
做饭	zuò fàn	to cook (rice)	饭店	fàn diàn	hotel
早饭	zǎo fàn	breakfast	饭馆	fàn guǎn	restaurant
午饭	wǔ fàn	lunch	中国饭	zhōng guó fàn	Chinese food

反 餐厅
cān tīng

菜

青菜	qīng cài	greens; green vegetables	法国菜	fǎ guó cài	French cuisine; French food
蔬菜	shū cài	vegetables	意大利菜	yì dà lì cài	Italian cuisine; Italian food
点菜	diǎn cài	to order food	日本菜	rì běn cài	Japanese cuisine; Japanese food
菜单	cài dān	menu			
中国菜	zhōng guó cài	Chinese cuisine; Chinese food	泰国菜	tài guó cài	Thai cuisine; Thai food

水

水果	shuǐ guǒ	fruit	开水	kāi shuǐ	boiled water
汽水	qì shuǐ	soda water			

咖啡

喝咖啡	hē kā fēi	to drink coffee	咖啡色	kā fēi sè	brown colour

人

年轻人	nián qīng rén	young people; youth	大人 (成人)	dà rén (chéng rén)	adult
老年人 (老人)	lǎo nián rén (lǎo rén)	old people; senior citizen	工人	gōng rén	worker
家人	jiā rén	family member	商人	shāng rén	business person

生

学生	xué sheng	student	生意	shēng yì	business
医生	yī shēng	doctor	生活	shēng huó	life
先生	xiān sheng	mister	生病	shēng bìng	to fall ill; to be taken ill
出生	chū shēng	to be born	生气	shēng qì	to get angry
生日	shēng rì	birthday			

友

朋友	péng you	friend	网友	wǎng yǒu	e-pal
笔友	bǐ yǒu	pen pal	友好	yǒu hǎo	friendly

师

老师 (教师)	lǎo shī (jiào shī)	teacher	工程师	gōng chéng shī	engineer
			理发师	lǐ fà shī	hairdresser
厨师	chú shī	chef; cook	大师	dà shī	master; guru

星

明星	míng xīng	star	歌星	gē xīng	singing star
影星	yǐng xīng	film star	星期	xīng qī	week
球星	qiú xīng	sports star			

工

工作	gōng zuò	to work	工厂	gōng chǎng	factory
工人	gōng rén	worker	工资	gōng zī	salary

子

孩子	hái zi	child	裙子	qún zi	skirt; dress
狮子	shī zi	lion	裤子	kù zi	trousers
房子	fáng zi	house	饺子	jiǎo zi	Chinese dumpling (with meat and vegetable stuffing)
桌子	zhuō zi	table; desk			
椅子	yǐ zi	chair	粽子	zòng zi	pyramid-shaped dumpling made of glutinous rice wrapped in bamboo or reed leaves (eaten during the Dragon Boat Festival)
盘子	pán zi	plate			
筷子	kuài zi	chopsticks			
鞋子	xié zi	shoe			
帽子	mào zi	cap; hat			

机

手机	shǒu jī	mobile phone	洗衣机	xǐ yī jī	washing machine
游戏机	yóu xì jī	video game player	司机	sī jī	driver
电视机	diàn shì jī	TV set	飞机	fēi jī	plane
照相机	zhào xiàng jī	camera	飞机场	fēi jī chǎng	airport
收音机	shōu yīn jī	radio			

车

自行车	zì xíng chē	bicycle	火车	huǒ chē	train
校车	xiào chē	school bus	骑车	qí chē	to ride a bicycle
汽车	qì chē	automobile	开车	kāi chē	to drive a car
小汽车	xiǎo qì chē	car	坐车	zuò chē	to travel by (bus, car, coach, train)
公共汽车	gōng gòng qì chē	bus			
长途汽车	cháng tú qì chē	coach	下车	xià chē	to get off (bus, car, coach, train)
出租(汽)车	chū zū (qì) chē	taxi	停车	tíng chē	to stop, to pull up; to park
妈妈的车	mā ma de chē	mum's car	停车场	tíng chē chǎng	car park

网

网球	wǎng qiú	tennis	网民	wǎng mín	one who accesses the Internet
网址 (网站)	wǎng zhǐ (wǎng zhàn)	website	网聊	wǎng liáo	online chat
网页	wǎng yè	webpage	上网	shàng wǎng	to surf the net
			网上购物	wǎng shàng gòu wù	to shop online
网友	wǎng yǒu	e-pal	网络文学	wǎng luò wén xué	net literature

球

篮球	lán qiú	basketball	乒乓球	pīng pāng qiú	table tennis
排球	pái qiú	volleyball	橄榄球	gǎn lǎn qiú	rugby
足球	zú qiú	football	打球	dǎ qiú	to play ball games
网球	wǎng qiú	tennis	踢球	tī qiú	to kick a ball; to play football
羽毛球	yǔ máo qiú	badminton			

服

衣服	yī fu	clothes	服务员	fú wù yuán	waiter; waitress
校服	xiào fú	school uniform	服务台	fú wù tái	information and reception desk

笔

钢笔	gāng bǐ	pen	毛笔	máo bǐ	calligraphy brush
铅笔	qiān bǐ	pencil	笔友	bǐ yǒu	pen pal

运动

运动员	yùn dòng yuán	sportsperson; athlete	运动鞋	yùn dòng xié	trainers
运动衣	yùn dòng yī	track suit	运动场	yùn dòng chǎng	sports ground

照

照相	zhào xiàng	to take a photo (to have a photo taken)	照片	zhào piàn	photo
照相机	zhào xiàng jī	camera	护照	hù zhào	passport

票

球票	qiú piào	football ticket	买票	mǎi piào	to buy a ticket
电影票	diàn yǐng piào	cinema ticket	售票处	shòu piào chù	ticket office
音乐会票	yīn yuè huì piào	concert ticket	售票员	shòu piào yuán	ticket seller; conductor/conductress (of a bus); booking-office clerk (station, airport, cinema, etc.)
车票	chē piào	bus/coach/train ticket			
飞机票	fēi jī piào	plane ticket			
订票	dìng piào	to book a ticket			

手

手机	shǒu jī	mobile phone	手套	shǒu tào	gloves
手表	shǒu biǎo	watch	手工	shǒu gōng	handwork

做

做作业	zuò zuò yè	to do homework	做什么工作	zuò shén me gōng zuò	what job to do
做饭	zuò fàn	to cook	做老师	zuò lǎo shī	to be a teacher; to work as a teacher
做家务	zuò jiā wù	to do housework			
做生意	zuò shēng yi	to do business			

看

看书	kàn shū	to read a book	看杂志	kàn zá zhì	to read a magazine
看电视	kàn diàn shì	to watch TV	看比赛	kàn bǐ sài	to watch a match
看电影	kàn diàn yǐng	to see a film	看病	kàn bìng	to see a doctor
看报纸	kàn bào zhǐ	to read a newspaper			

舞

跳舞	tiào wǔ	to dance	舞龙灯	wǔ lóng dēng	dragon dance
舞蹈	wǔ dǎo	dance	舞狮子	wǔ shī zi	lion dance

滑

滑冰	huá bīng	ice-skating	滑板	huá bǎn	skateboarding
滑雪	huá xuě	skiing			

放

放学	fàng xué	to finish school	放爆竹	fàng bào zhú	to let off firecrackers
放假	fàng jià	to have a holiday	放风筝	fàng fēng zhēng	to fly a kite

打

打篮球	dǎ lán qiú	to play basketball	打羽毛球	dǎ yǔ máo qiú	to play badminton
打排球	dǎ pái qiú	to play volleyball	打太极拳	dǎ tài jí quán	to practise tai ch'i
打网球	dǎ wǎng qiú	to play tennis	打电话	dǎ diàn huà	to make a phone call
打乒乓球	dǎ pīng pāng qiú	to play table tennis	打算	dǎ suàn	to plan; plan

坐

坐公共汽车	zuò gōng gòng qì chē	to travel by bus	坐飞机	zuò fēi jī	to travel by plane
坐火车	zuò huǒ chē	to travel by train	坐船	zuò chuán	to travel by boat/ship

骑

骑自行车	qí zì xíng chē	to ride a bicycle	骑马	qí mǎ	to ride a horse

玩儿

玩儿滑板	wánr huá bǎn	to skateboard	好玩儿	hǎo wánr	interesting; amusing
玩橄榄球	wánr gǎn lǎn qiú	to play rugby	玩儿得很开心	wánr de hěn kāi xīn	to have a good time

赛

比赛	bǐ sài	match; contest; competition	赛马	sài mǎ	horse racing
			赛跑	sài pǎo	race
赛车	sài chē	cycle racing; automobile race; race car	赛龙舟	sài lóng zhōu	dragon boat race

游

游泳	yóu yǒng	to swim	游戏	yóu xì	game
游览	yóu lǎn	to go sightseeing; to visit	旅游	lǚ yóu	tour; tourism

上

上学	shàng xué	to go to school	上周	shàng zhōu	last week
上课	shàng kè	to attend class; to go to class; to give a lesson	上衣	shàng yī	upper outer garment; ~~jacket~~ top wai tao
上班	shàng bān	to go to work	上海	shàng hǎi	Shanghai
上网	shàng wǎng	to surf the net	楼上	lóu shàng	upstairs
上面	shàng mian	above; over			

下

下课	xià kè	to finish class	下雨	xià yǔ	to rain
下班	xià bān	to finish work	下雪	xià xuě	to snow
下岗	xià gǎng	to be made redundant	下午	xià wǔ	afternoon
下棋	xià qí	to play chess	下周	xià zhōu	next week
下车	xià chē	to get off (the bus, coach, train)	下面	xià mian	below; under
下飞机	xià fēi jī	to get off the plane	楼下	lóu xià	downstairs

洗

洗澡	xǐ zǎo	to take a bath	洗衣服	xǐ yī fu	to wash clothes
洗碗	xǐ wǎn	to wash up dishes	洗衣机	xǐ yī jī	washing machine
洗车	xǐ chē	to wash a car	洗衣店	xǐ yī diàn	laundry

见

再见	zài jiàn	goodbye	看得见	kàn de jiàn	able to see
明天见	míng tiān jiàn	see you tomorrow	看不见	kàn bu jiàn	unable to see
看见	kàn jiàn	to see	见面	jiàn miàn	to meet

旅

旅游	lǚ yóu	tour; tourism	旅行社	lǚ xíng shè	travel agency
旅行	lǚ xíng	to travel; journey; tour	旅客	lǚ kè	traveller; passenger; hotel guest

假

假期	jià qī	vacation; holiday	请假	qǐng jià	to ask for leave
暑假	shǔ jià	summer holidays	放假	fàng jià	to have a holiday; to be on holiday
寒假	hán jià	winter holidays			
春假	chūn jià	spring holidays	度假	dù jià	to spend one's holiday; to go on vacation

书

书包	shū bāo	schoolbag	图书馆	tú shū guǎn	library
书房	shū fáng	study	看书	kàn shū	to read a book
书店	shū diàn	bookshop	书法	shū fǎ	calligraphy

文

中文	zhōng wén	Chinese language	西班牙文	xī bān yá wén	Spanish language
英文	yīng wén	English language	文学	wén xué	literature
法文	fǎ wén	French language	文化	wén huà	culture
德文	dé wén	German language			

语

语言	yǔ yán	language	法语	fǎ yǔ	French language
外语	wài yǔ	foreign language	德语	dé yǔ	German language
汉语	hàn yǔ	Chinese language	西班牙语	xī bān yá yǔ	Spanish language
英语	yīng yǔ	English language			

中

中国	zhōng guó	China		中学	zhōng xué	secondary school
中文	zhōng wén	Chinese language		中学生	zhōng xué shēng	secondary school student
中餐	zhōng cān	Chinese food		中午	zhōng wǔ	noon; midday
中医	zhōng yī	traditional Chinese medical science; doctor of traditional Chinese medicine		中饭	zhōng fàn	lunch
				中秋节	zhōng qiū jié	Mid-Autumn Festival
中间	zhōng jiān	middle				

学

学校	xué xiào	school		大学	dà xué	university
学期	xué qī	school term		文学	wén xué	literature
学生	xué sheng	pupil; student		商学	shāng xué	business studies
学习	xué xí	to study		数学	shù xué	maths
上学	shàng xué	to go to school		科学	kē xué	science
小学	xiǎo xué	primary school		科学家	kē xué jiā	scientist
中学	zhōng xué	secondary school				

法

法国	fǎ guó	France		书法	shū fǎ	calligraphy
法文 (法语)	fǎ wén (fǎ yǔ)	French language		办法	bàn fǎ	way; method

目

科目	kē mù	subject		眼睛	yǎn jing	eye
节目	jié mù	programme		眼镜	yǎn jìng	glasses; spectacles
看	kàn	to look; to read; to watch; to see		睡觉	shuì jiào	to sleep

乐

音乐	yīn yuè	music		乐器	yuè qì	musical instrument
乐队	yuè duì	band		快乐	kuài lè	happy

间

时间	shí jiān	time		中间	zhōng jiān	middle
时间表	shí jiān biǎo	timetable		之间	zhī jiān	between
房间	fáng jiān	room				

店

书店	shū diàn	bookshop	洗衣店	xǐ yī diàn	laundry
商店	shāng diàn	shop	眼镜店	yǎn jìng diàn	optician's
酒店 (饭店)	jiǔ diàn (fàn diàn)	hotel	药店	yào diàn	pharmacy
快餐店	kuài cān diàn	fast food restaurant	花店	huā diàn	florist's
外卖店	wài mài diàn	takeaway shop	肉店	ròu diàn	butcher's
手机店	shǒu jī diàn	mobile phone shop			

房

房子	fáng zi	house	健身房	jiàn shēn fáng	gym
楼房	lóu fáng	multi-storey building	房间	fáng jiān	room
平房	píng fáng	single-storey house; bungalow	订房	dìng fáng	to book a room
			单人房	dān rén fáng	single room
厨房	chú fáng	kitchen	双人房	shuāng rén fáng	double-bedded room; twin-bedded room
书房	shū fáng	study			

场

篮球场	lán qiú chǎng	basketball court	商场	shāng chǎng	market; bazaar; mall
排球场	pái qiú chǎng	volleyball court	市场	shì chǎng	market
足球场	zú qiú chǎng	football pitch	超级市场	chāo jí shì chǎng	supermarket
网球场	wǎng qiú chǎng	tennis court	停车场	tíng chē chǎng	car park
运动场	yùn dòng chǎng	sports ground	天安门广场	tiān ān mén guǎng chǎng	Tian'anmen Square
飞机场	fēi jī chǎng	airport			

馆

餐馆 (饭馆)	cān guǎn (fàn guǎn)	restaurant	体育馆	tǐ yù guǎn	gymnasium; gym
			游泳馆	yóu yǒng guǎn	indoor swimming pool
博物馆	bó wù guǎn	museum			
图书馆	tú shū guǎn	library	足球馆	zú qiú guǎn	football stadium

堂

礼堂	lǐ táng	assembly hall	教堂	jiào táng	church
食堂	shí táng	dining hall; canteen			

厅

客厅	kè tīng	sitting room	餐厅	cān tīng	dining room; dining hall; restaurant
饭厅	fàn tīng	dining room			

室

教室	jiào shì	classroom	卧室	wò shì	bedroom
浴室	yù shì	bathroom			

园

花园	huā yuán	garden	动物园	dòng wù yuán	zoo
公园	gōng yuán	park			

院

电影院	diàn yǐng yuàn	cinema	医院	yī yuàn	hospital

局

邮局	yóu jú	post office	警察局	jǐng chá jú	police station

站

火车站	huǒ chē zhàn	railway station	坐3站下车	zuò sān zhàn xià chē	to get off after three stops
公共汽车站	gōng gòng qì chē zhàn	bus stop			
			网站	wǎng zhàn	website
长途汽车站	cháng tú qì chē zhàn	coach station			

社

旅行社	lǚ xíng shè	travel agency	社会实践	shè huì shí jiàn	work experience

国

国家	guó jiā	country	中国	zhōng guó	China
国外	guó wài	overseas; abroad	美国	měi guó	the USA
外国	wài guó	foreign country	法国	fǎ guó	France
英国	yīng guó	the UK	德国	dé guó	Germany

好

你好	nǐ hǎo	hello	好听	hǎo tīng	pleasant to the ear
友好	yǒu hǎo	friendly	好玩儿	hǎo wánr	interesting; amusing
好吃	hǎo chī	delicious	好像	hǎo xiàng	to seem; to be like
好看	hǎo kàn	pretty; beautiful	爱好	ài hào	hobby

有

有意思 (有趣)	yǒu yì si (yǒu qù)	interesting; amusing	有钱	yǒu qián	rich
			有空	yǒu kòng	to have time; to be free
有用	yǒu yòng	useful			
有名	yǒu míng	famous	有时候	yǒu shí hou	sometimes

辞典 GLOSSARY

a	I have a dog.	我有一只狗。	wǒ yǒu yì zhī gǒu.
	Let me have a look	让我看看。	ràng wǒ kàn kan.
able	Will you be able to come?	你能来吗？	nǐ néng lái ma?
about	He is about the same height as me.	他和我差不多高。	tā hé wǒ chà bu duō gāo.
after	after lunch	午饭以后	wǔ fàn yǐ hòu
	the day after tomorrow	后天	hòu tiān
age	I started to learn Chinese at the age of 12.	我12岁开始学中文。	wǒ shí èr suì kāi shǐ xué zhōng wén.
also	She speaks French and German and also a little Chinese.	她会说法语、德语, 还会说一点儿汉语。	tā huì shuō fǎ yǔ, dé yǔ, hái huì shuō yì diǎnr hàn yǔ.
	He is young and good-looking, and also very rich.	他又年轻又漂亮, 而且很有钱。	tā yòu nián qīng yòu piào liang, ér qiě hěn yǒu qián.
	I've read the book and I've also seen the film.	我看过这本书, 也看过这部电影。	wǒ kàn guo zhè běn shū, yě kàn guo zhè bù diàn yǐng.
although	Although she is young, she is famous.	虽然她很年轻, 但是她很有名。	suī rán tā hěn nián qīng, dàn shì tā hěn yǒu míng.
	Although he's famous and rich, he is in poor health.	他虽然又有钱又有名, 但是他身体不好。	tā suī rán yòu yǒu qián yòu yǒu míng, dàn shì tā shēn tǐ bù hǎo.
always	She is always busy.	她总是很忙。	tā zǒng shì hěn máng.
am	at 6 am	早上6点	zǎo shàng liù diǎn
	at 10 am	上午10点	shàng wǔ shí diǎn
and	He is 9, and I'm 15.	他9岁, 我15岁。	tā jiǔ suì, wǒ shí wǔ suì.
	Have dinner first, and then do homework.	先吃饭, 然后做作业。	xiān chī fàn, rán hòu zuò zuò yè.
anything	I'm really hungry – I'll eat anything.	我太饿了, 我什么都吃。	wǒ tài è le, wǒ shén me dōu chī.
	I don't want to buy anything. I just want to have a look.	我不买什么, 我只想看看。	wǒ bù mǎi shén me, wǒ zhǐ xiǎng kàn kan.
to arrive	She has (just) arrived in Beijing now.	她已经到北京了。	tā yǐ jīng dào běi jīng le.
as ... as	He is as tall as his father.	他跟他父亲一样高。	tā gēn tā fù qīn yí yàng gāo.
	Nanjing is not as large as Beijing.	南京没有北京大。	nán jīng méi yǒu běi jīng dà.

to ask	Mum asked me to buy some bread.	妈妈让/要我去买些面包。	mā ma ràng/yào wǒ qù mǎi xiē miàn bāo.
	He asked me to go to the cinema.	他请我去看电影。	tā qǐng wǒ qù kàn diàn yǐng.
at	at home	在家里	zài jiā lǐ
away	The hotel is two miles away from the sea.	酒店离大海两英里。	jiǔ diàn lí dà hǎi liǎng yīng lǐ.
to be	I am 15 years old.	我十五岁。	wǒ shí wǔ suì.
	I am fine. Thanks.	我很好，谢谢!	wǒ hěn hào, xiè xie.
	I am having breakfast.	我正在吃早饭。	wǒ zhèng zài chī zǎo fàn.
	I am (not) interested in video games.	我对电子游戏(没)有兴趣。	wǒ duì diàn zǐ yóu xì (méi) yǒu xìng qù.
	The beach is very clean.	海滩很干净。	hǎi tān hěn gān jìng.
	My school is not big.	我的学校不大。	wǒ de xué xiào bú dà.
	It is quiet in the classroom.	教室里很安静。	jiào shì lǐ hěn ān jìng.
	My elder brother is at university.	我哥哥上大学。	wǒ gē ge shàng dà xué.
	How much is that shirt? It's £50.	那件衬衣多少钱？ 50英镑。	nà jiàn chèn yī duō shǎo qián? wǔ shí yīng bàng.
	My name is Peter.	我叫Peter。	wǒ jiào peter.
	He is a keen footballer in his free time.	他有空的时候很喜欢踢足球。	tā yǒu kòng de shí hou hěn xǐ huan tī zú qiú.
	They are very happy.	他们很快乐。	tā men hěn kuài lè.
	I've been to China. I haven't been to Japan.	我去过中国，我没(有)去过日本。	wǒ qù guo zhōng guó, wǒ méi (yǒu) qù guo rì běn.
	What do you want to be when you're grown up?	你长大了想做什么？	nǐ zhǎng dà le xiǎng zuò shén me?
before	before dinner	晚饭以前	wǎn fàn yǐ qián
	the day before yesterday	前天	qián tiān
behind	The post office is behind the church.	邮局在教堂(的)后面。	yóu jú zài jiào táng (de) hòu mian.
besides	I learn two languages. Besides Chinese, I also learn German.	我学两门外文。除了中文以外，我还学德文。	wǒ xué liǎng mén wài wén. chú le zhōng wén yǐ wài, wǒ hái xué dé wén.
between	The supermarket is between the hospital and the cinema.	超级市场在医院和电影院之间。	chāo jí shì chǎng zài yī yuàn hé diàn yǐng yuàn zhī jiān.
	In the UK children must attend school between 5 and 16.	在英国，5到16岁的孩子必须上学。	zài yīng guó, wǔ dào shí liù suì de hái zi bì xū shàng xué.

both... and...	He is both tall and thin.	他又高又瘦。	tā yòu gāo yòu shòu.
	Both Tom and Jerry are learning Chinese.	Tom和Jerry都在学中文。	tom hé jerry dōu zài xué zhōng wén.
to buy	I bought my mum a present.	我给妈妈买了一个礼物。	wǒ gěi mā ma mǎi le yí gè lǐ wù.
	I didn't buy milk. I bought a bottle of juice.	我没(有)买牛奶, 我买了一瓶果汁。	wǒ méi (yǒu) mǎi niú nǎi, wǒ mǎi le yì píng guǒ zhī.
by	Are you going by train or by plane?	你坐火车去, 还是坐飞机去？	nǐ zuò huǒ chē qù hái shi zuò fēi jī qù?
can	I can run fast.	我能跑得很快。	wǒ néng pǎo de hěn kuài.
	He couldn't answer that question.	他不能回答那个问题。	tā bù néng huí dá nà ge wèn tí.
	He can cook.	他会做饭。	tā huì zuò fàn.
	I can't drive.	我不会开车。	wǒ bú huì kāi chē.
to chat	We chatted over a cup of tea.	我们一边喝茶，一边聊天。	wǒ men yì biān hē chá, yì biān liáo tiān.
check-out	I was at the supermarket the other day, and at the check-out I realised I didn't have my wallet.	有一次去超级市场买东西, 付钱的时候才知道我没带钱包。	yǒu yí cì qù chāo jí shì chǎng mǎi dōng xi, fù qián de shí hou cái zhī dào wǒ méi dài qián bāo.
Chinese food	Chinese food (versus) Western food	中餐 v 西餐	zhōng cān xī cān
	Chinese, French, Italian food/cuisine, etc.	中国菜、法国菜、意大利菜	zhōng guó cài, fǎ guó cài, yì dà lì cài
to clear	I hope it clears up this afternoon.	我希望今天下午天气转晴。	wǒ xī wàng jīn tiān xià wǔ tiān qì zhuǎn qíng.
	It has cleared up now.	天晴了。	tiān qíng le.
close	The school is close to the church.	学校离教堂很近。	xué xiào lí jiào táng hěn jìn.
to close	The shops close at five.	商店5点关门。	shāng diàn wǔ diǎn guān mén.
	The museum is closed on Sundays.	星期天博物馆不开放。	xīng qī tiān bó wù guǎn bù kāi fàng.
(to) cook	I like to cook for my family.	我喜欢给家人做饭。	wǒ xǐ huan gěi jiā rén zuò fàn.
	He works as a cook in a hotel.	他在酒店做厨师。	tā zài jiǔ diàn zuò chú shī.
to come	Would you like to come to dinner tonight?	今晚来吃饭, 好吗？	jīn wǎn lái chī fàn, hǎo ma?
concert	Shall we go to the concert tomorrow?	我们明天去听音乐会吧？	wǒ men míng tiān qù tīng yīn yuè huì ba?
correct	Are you Tom? That's correct.	你是Tom吗？ 是的。	nǐ shì tom ma? shì de.

to cost	The dictionary cost me ¥68.	这本字典花了我68元。	zhè běn zì diǎn huā le wǒ liù shí bā yuán.
(to) do	Do you speak English?	你会说英文吗？	nǐ huì shuō yīng wén ma?
	What do you do (for a living)?	你做什么工作？（你是做什么的？）	nǐ zuò shén me gōng zuò? (nǐ shì zuò shén me de?)
	Where did you do your work experience?	你在哪儿社会实践？	nǐ zài nǎr shè huì shí jiàn?
doctor/GP	to see a doctor/GP	看病	kàn bìng
to draw	You draw beautifully.	你画得很好看。	nǐ huà de hěn hǎo kàn.
to drive	Dad drove me to the railway station.	爸爸开车送我去火车站。	bà ba kāi chē sòng wǒ qù huǒ chē zhàn.
to earn	She earns £50 a week.	她一个星期赚50英镑。	tā yí ge xīng qī zhuàn wǔ shí yīng bàng.
to eat	I've never eaten Italian food.	我没有吃过意大利菜。	wǒ méi (yǒu) chī guò yì dà lì cài.
	Mum was too tired to cook and we ate out.	妈妈太累不想做饭，所以我们去餐馆吃饭。	mā ma tài lèi bù xiǎng zuò fàn, suǒ yǐ wǒ men qù cān guǎn chī fàn.
either	He can't speak Chinese, and he can't speak English either.	他不会说中文，也不会说英文。	tā bú huì shuō zhōng wén, yě bú huì shuō yīng wén.
even	His Maths is very good, but his English is even better.	他的数学很好，他的英语更好。	tā de shù xué hěn hǎo, tā de yīng yǔ gèng hǎo.
every	every day	每天	měi tiān
	every afternoon	每天下午	měi tiān xià wǔ
	every Saturday	每个星期六	měi ge xīng qī liù
	every week/month	每个星期，每个月	měi ge xīng qī, měi ge yuè
	every year	每年	měi nián
	He walks the dog every day.	他天天都遛狗。（他每天都遛狗。）	tā tiān tiān dōu liù gǒu. (tā měi tiān dōu liù gǒu.)
except	The museum is open every day except Sunday.	这家博物馆除了星期天以外，每天都开放。	zhè jiā bó wù guǎn chú le xīng qī tiān yǐ wài, měi tiān dōu kāi fàng.
favourite	These books are great favourites of mine.	这些是我最喜爱的书。	zhè xiē shì wǒ zuì xǐ ài de shū.
	Who is your favourite celebrity?	你最喜欢哪位名人？	nǐ zuì xǐ huan nǎ wèi míng rén?
for	I gave my brother a book for his birthday.	我弟弟生日我送了他一本书。	wǒ dì di shēng rì wǒ sòng le tā yì běn shū.
from	The train station is not far from here.	火车站离这儿不远。	huǒ chē zhàn lí zhèr bù yuǎn.
	It takes ten hours to fly from London to Beijing.	从伦敦到北京坐飞机要10个小时。	cóng lún dūn dào běi jīng zuò fēi jī yào shí gè xiǎo shí.

to give	I'll give you a ring tomorrow.	我明天给你打电话。	wǒ míng tiān gěi nǐ dǎ diàn huà.
to go	He goes to work by bus.	他坐公共汽车上班。	tā zuò gōng gòng qì chē shàng bān.
	At 3.30 I go home.	我三点半回家。	wǒ sān diǎn bàn huí jiā.
	I'll go to hospital tomorrow.	我明天去医院看病。	wǒ míng tiān qù yī yuàn kàn bìng.
	I'll go to the hospital to see a friend.	我要去医院看一个朋友。	wǒ yào qù yī yuàn kàn yí ge péng you.
	How did your weekend go? It went well.	你周末过得好吗？过得很好。	nǐ zhōu mò guò de hǎo ma? guò de hěn hǎo.
good	It's good to eat green vegetables regularly.	常吃青菜对身体有好处。	cháng chī qīng cài duì shēn tǐ yǒu hǎo chu.
hard	He works very hard.	他工作很努力。	tā gōng zuò hěn nǔ lì.
to have	I don't have younger sisters.	我没有妹妹。	wǒ méi yǒu mèi mei.
	We had a good time.	我们玩儿得很开心。	wǒ men wánr de hěn kāi xīn.
	I have dinner at 6.	我6点吃晚饭。	wǒ liù diǎn chī wǎn fàn.
	Did you have a nice holiday?	你假期过得好吗？	nǐ jià qī guò de hǎo ma?
	Let me have a try.	让我试一下。	ràng wǒ shì yí xia.
	I had a photo taken in front of the museum.	我在博物馆前面照相了。	wǒ zài bó wù guǎn qián miàn zhào xiàng le.
health	He has poor health.	他身体不好。	tā shēn tǐ bù hǎo.
	She enjoys the best of health.	她身体非常好。	tā shēn tǐ fēi cháng hǎo.
healthy	healthy lifestyle	健康的生活方式	jiàn kāng de shēng huó fāng shì
holiday	We have six weeks' holiday in summer.	我们夏天有6个星期假期。	wǒ men xià tiān yǒu liù ge
	My school is closed for holiday now.	我们学校放假了。	wǒ men xué xiào fàng jià le.
	I am in Spain on holiday with my parents.	我和爸爸妈妈在西班牙度假。	wǒ hé bà ba mā ma zài xī bān yá dù jià.
if	If the weather is fine, I'll walk to school.	要是天气好，我就走路去学校。	yào shi tiān qì hǎo, wǒ jiù zǒu lù qù xué xiào.

in	in March	三月	sān yuè
	the girl in white	穿白色衣服的女孩	chuān bái sè yī fu de nǚ hái
	Dad is not in.	爸爸不在家。	bà ba bú zài jiā.
	I did work experience in a travel agency.	我在一家旅行社社会实践。	wǒ zài yì jiā lǚ xíng shè shè huì shí jiàn.
	I don't like to read in the library.	我不喜欢在图书馆看书。	wǒ bù xǐ huan zài tú shū guǎn kàn shū.
	I'm going to China in a week.	一个星期以后我去中国。	yí ge xīng qī yǐ hòu wǒ qù zhōng guó.
	The concert will start in a minute.	音乐会马上就要开始了。	yīn yuè huì mǎ shàng jiù yào kāi shǐ le.
	He is interested in calligraphy.	他对书法有兴趣。	tā duì shū fǎ yǒu xìng qù.
	He is in Beijing now. (He was somewhere else yesterday.)	他去北京了。 (indicating a new state)	tā qù běi jīng le.
to invite	He invited me to his home.	他请我去他家玩儿。	tā qǐng wǒ qù tā jiā wánr.
it	It was last October that I went to Beijing.	我是去年10月去的北京。	wǒ shì qù nián shí yuè qù de běi jīng.
	It's me. (on the telephone)	是我。	shì wǒ.
	It's ten past three.	现在三点十分。	xiàn zài sān diǎn shí fēn.
	It's quite warm this spring.	今年春天天气比较暖和。	jīn nián chūn tiān tiān qì bǐ jiào nuǎn huo.
	I find it boring to stay at home.	我觉得呆在家里很无聊。	wǒ jué de dāi zài jiā lǐ hěn wú liáo.
just	You can get there just as cheaply by air as by train.	你坐飞机到那里跟坐火车一样便宜。	nǐ zuò fēi jī dào nà lǐ gēn zuò huǒ chē yí yàng pián yi.
	I was just having lunch when you rang.	你来电话的时候我正在吃午饭。	nǐ lái diàn huà de shí hou wǒ zhèng zài chī wǔ fàn.
to keep	Keep straight on until you get to the church, and then turn right.	一直走就走到教堂了，然后向右转。	yì zhí zǒu jiù zǒu dào jiào táng le, rán hòu xiàng yòu zhuǎn.
to know	Do you know who Yao Ming is?	你知道姚明是谁吗？	nǐ zhī dào yáo míng shì shéi ma?
	I know her.	我认识她。	wǒ rèn shi tā.
last	last time	上次	shàng cì
	last night	昨天晚上	zuó tiān wǎn shang
	last week / month	上个星期，上个月	shàng ge xīng qī, shàng ge yuè
	last winter	去年冬天	qù nián dōng tiān
	last year	去年	qù nián

to learn	I have been learning Chinese for four years.	我学中文学了四年了。	wǒ xué zhōng wén xué le sì nián le.
	He learnt French in secondary school. He didn't learn Chinese.	他上中学的时候学法文,他没学中文。	tā shàng zhōng xué de shí hou xué fǎ wén, tā méi xué zhōng wén.
	I am learning Chinese. I've learnt Japanese before.	我在学中文。我学过日文。	wǒ zài xué zhōng wén. wǒ xué guo rì wén.
to leave	Straight after leaving school, he started work in a factory.	中学毕业以后,他就进了工厂。	zhōng xué bì yè yǐ hòu, tā jiù jìn le gōng chǎng.
long	I haven't phoned him for a long time.	我很久没给他打电话了。	wǒ hěn jiǔ méi gěi tā dǎ diàn huà le.
may	He may have left China already.	他可能已经离开中国了。	tā kě néng yǐ jīng lí kāi zhōng guó le.
more	I think Chinese is more difficult.	我觉得中文更难。	wǒ jué de zhōng wén gèng nán.
must	I must go to bed early tonight.	今晚我得早一点儿睡觉。	jīn wǎn wǒ děi zǎo yī diǎnr shuì jiào.
	They must be twins.	他们一定是双胞胎。	tā men yí dìng shì shuāng bāo tāi.
name	What's your name?	你叫什么名字?	nǐ jiào shén me míng zi?
	My name is Peter.	我叫Peter。	wǒ jiào peter.
near	Where's the nearest bus-stop?	最近的公共汽车站在哪儿?	zuì jìn de gōng gòng qì chē zhàn zài nǎr?
	The supermarket is very near the station.	超级市场离车站很近。	chāo jí shì chǎng lí chē zhàn hěn jìn.
nearly	It's nearly one o'clock.	差不多一点钟了。	chà bu duō yī diǎn zhōng le.
next	next time	下次	xià cì
	next week/next month	下个星期/下个月	xià ge xīng qī/xià ge yuè
	next year	明年	míng nián
nobody	Nobody knows him.	谁都不认识他。	shéi dōu bú rèn shi tā.
or	We could take the bus or go by bicycle.	我们可以坐公共汽车去,也可以骑自行车去。	wǒ men kě yǐ zuò gōng gòng qì chē qù, yě kě yǐ qí zì xíng chē qù.
	Are we eating Chinese or Japanese (food)?	我们是吃中国菜,还是吃日本菜?	wǒ men shì chī zhōng guó cài, hái shi chī rì běn cài?
	Are you writing to him, or emailing him?	你是给他写信,还是给他发邮件?	nǐ shì gěi tā xiě xìn, hái shi gěi tā fā yóu jiàn?
	Do you text in Chinese or in English?	你是用中文发短信,还是用英文发短信?	nǐ shì yòng zhōng wén fā duǎn xìn, hái shi yòng yīng wén fā duǎn xìn?
	Do you eat with chopsticks or with a knife and fork?	你吃饭是用筷子,还是用刀叉?	nǐ chī fàn shì yòng kuài zi, hái shi yòng dāo chā?

old	How old are you? (to a child you presume to be under 10)	你几岁了？	nǐ jǐ suì le?
	How old are you? (to somebody you presume to be over 10)	你多大了？	nǐ duō dà le?
to pay	Dad paid me to wash his car.	爸爸付钱，让我给他洗车。	bà ba fù qián, ràng wǒ gěi tā xǐ chē.
	Dad paid for me to learn the guitar.	我学吉他的钱是爸爸付的。	wǒ xué jí tā de qián shì bà ba fù de.
perhaps	Perhaps he didn't quite understand what I said.	他可能没听懂我的话。	tā kě néng méi tīng dǒng wǒ de huà.
to phone	I didn't phone my parents last week.	上个星期我没给父母打电话。	shàng ge xīng qī wǒ méi gěi fù mǔ dǎ diàn huà.
	I'm going to phone them now.	现在我要给他们打电话。	xiàn zài wǒ yào gěi tā men dǎ diàn huà.
to plan	We plan to visit China this autumn.	我们计划/打算今年秋天去中国旅行。	wǒ men jì huà / dǎ suàn jīn nián qiū tiān qù zhōng guó lǚ xíng.
to play	play tennis	打网球	dǎ wǎng qiú
	play a video game	玩儿电子游戏	wánr diàn zǐ yóu xì
	play on the computer	玩电脑	wán diàn nǎo
	play the guitar	弹吉他	tán jí tā
	play football	踢足球	tī zú qiú
probably	She has probably gone home.	她可能回家了。	tā kě néng huí jiā le.
to read	I like to read novels.	我喜欢看小说。	wǒ xǐ huan kàn xiǎo shuō.
	She read us a story.	她给我们读了一个故事。	tā gěi wǒ men dú le yí ge gù shi.
	He reads English Literature at university.	他在大学学英国文学。	tā zài dà xué xué yīng guó wén xué.
school	There will be no school next week.	下个星期不上课。	xià ge xīng qī bú shàng kè.
	after school	放学以后	fàng xué yǐ hòu
short	He is short and he has short hair.	他个子很矮，头发很短。	tā gè zi hěn ǎi, tóu fà hěn duǎn.
to see	I can see the sea from the room.	从房间里可以看见大海。(从房间里看得见大海。)	cóng fáng jiān lǐ kě yǐ kàn jiàn dà hǎi. (cóng fáng jiān lǐ kàn de jiàn dà hǎi.)
	I can't see the sea from the room.	从房间里看不见大海。	cóng fáng jiān lǐ kàn bu jiàn dà hǎi.
since	They've known each other since childhood.	他们从小就认识。	tā men cóng xiǎo jiù rèn shi.
slowly	I write Chinese very slowly.	我写汉字写得很慢。	wǒ xiě hàn zì xiě de hěn màn.

sometimes	Sometimes we went to the beach and at other times we watched TV in the room.	我们有时候去海滩，有时候呆在房间看电视。	wǒ men yǒu shí hou qù hǎi tān, yǒu shí hou dāi zài fáng jiān kàn diàn shì.
soon	We'll soon be arriving in Beijing. (The train will soon arrive in Beijing.)	我们快到北京了。(北京快到了。)	wǒ men kuài dào běi jīng le. (běi jīng kuài dào le.)
to spend	Last year I spent two weeks in France.	去年我在法国呆了两个星期。	qù nián wǒ zài fǎ guó dāi le liǎng ge xīng qī.
	I spend five hours a week on homework.	我每个星期花5个小时做作业。	wǒ měi ge xīng qī huā wǔ ge xiǎo shí zuò zuò yè.
	How did you spend your pocket money?	你的零花钱是怎么花的？	nǐ de líng huā qián shì zěn me huā de?
to take	I take the bus to school.	我坐公共汽车上学。	wǒ zuò gōng gòng qì chē shàng xué.
	take the coach, plane, train, etc.	坐长途汽车, 坐飞机, 坐火车	zuò cháng tú qì chē, zuò fēi jī, zuò huǒ chē
	The doctor advised her to take more exercise.	医生说她应该多运动。	yī shēng shuō tā yīng gāi duō yùn dòng.
	What size shoes do you take?	你穿多大的鞋？	nǐ chuān duō dà de xié?
	How long will it take us to get to London?	到伦敦要多长时间？	dào lún dūn yào duō cháng shí jiān?
	to take the dog for a walk (or 'to walk the dog')	遛狗	liù gǒu
	to take medicine	吃药	chī yào
	to take a photo (or 'have a photo taken')	照相	zhào xiàng
	to take a holiday	度假	dù jià
to teach	Dad will teach me to drive next year.	明年爸爸要教我开车。	míng nián bà ba yào jiāo wǒ kāi chē.
(more) than	I think football is more interesting than basketball.	我觉得足球比篮球有意思。	wǒ jué de zú qiú bǐ lán qiú yǒu yì si.
	The French classroom is bigger than the Chinese classroom.	法文教室比中文教室大。	fǎ wén jiào shì bǐ zhōng wén jiào shì dà.
	The French classroom is a bit bigger than the Chinese classroom.	法文教室比中文教室大一点儿。	fǎ wén jiào shì bǐ zhōng wén jiào shì dà yì diǎnr.
	The Spanish classroom is even bigger than the French classroom.	西班牙文教室比法文教室更大。	xī bān yá wén jiào shì bǐ fǎ wén jiào shì gèng dà.

that/which	The books that he gave me are all old.	他给我的书都是旧书。	tā gěi wǒ de shū dōu shì jiù shū.
	The fish that mum cooks is very delicious.	妈妈做的鱼很好吃。	mā ma zuò de yú hěn hǎo chī.
	I love all the films that he directed.	他导演的电影我都喜欢。	tā dǎo yǎn de diàn yǐng wǒ dōu xǐ huan.
there is/are	There are 800 students at my school.	我们学校有800个学生。	wǒ men xué xiào yǒu bā bǎi gè xué sheng.
to think/feel	I think jogging is very good exercise.	我觉得慢跑是一种很好的运动。	wǒ jué de màn pǎo shì yì zhǒng hěn hǎo de yùn dòng.
	I feel that the plan is great.	我觉得这个计划很好。	wǒ jué de zhè gè jì huà hěn hǎo.
this	this time	这次	zhè cì
	this morning/afternoon/evening	今天早上(上午)/今天下午/今天晚上	jīn tiān zǎo shang (shàng wǔ)/jīn tiān xià wǔ/jīn tiān wǎn shang
	this week	这个星期	zhè ge xīng qī
	this summer	今年夏天	jīn nián xià tiān
	this year	今年	jīn nián
time(s)	three times a week	每个星期三次	měi ge xīng qī sān cì
	I practise volleyball four times a week.	我每个星期练四次排球。	wǒ měi ge xīng qī liàn sì cì pái qiú.
	I've been to China three times.	我去过中国三次。	wǒ qù guò zhōng guó sān cì.
together	We went for a walk together.	我们一起去散步。	wǒ men yì qǐ qù sàn bù.
too	I've been to Beijing too. (i.e. in addition to other people)	我也去过北京。	wǒ yě qù guo běi jīng.
	I've been to Beijing, too. (i.e. in addition to other places)	我还去过北京。	wǒ hái qù guo běi jing.
	It is too late.	太晚了。	tài wǎn le.
to travel	I love travelling.	我喜欢旅行。	wǒ xǐ huan lǚ xíng.
	She travels to work by bicycle.	她骑自行车去上班。	tā qí zì xíng chē shàng bān.
to treat	Let me treat you to some ice-cream.	我请你吃冰淇淋。	wǒ qǐng nǐ chī bīng qí lín.
to turn	turn right/turn left	向右转/向左转	xiàng yòu zhuǎn/xiàng zuǒ zhuǎn
two	I have two younger brothers.	我有两个弟弟。	wǒ yǒu liǎng ge dì di,
under	The cat is under the table.	猫在桌子下面。	māo zài zhuō zi xià mian.
to visit	to visit a dentist	去看牙医	qù kàn yá yī
	to visit a museum	参观博物馆	cān guān bó wù guǎn
to walk	I usually walk the dog after dinner.	我一般晚饭以后遛狗。	wǒ yì bān wǎn fàn yǐ hòu liù gǒu.

to want	She wants to go to Italy.	她要去意大利。	tā yào qù yì dà lì.
	She wants me to go with her.	她想让我跟她一起去。	tā xiǎng ràng wǒ gēn tā yì qǐ qù.
	I don't want you arriving late.	我希望你不要迟到。	wǒ xī wàng nǐ bú yào chí dào.
	Do you want a boiled egg for breakfast?	你早饭要吃煮鸡蛋吗？	nǐ zǎo fàn yào chī zhǔ jī dàn ma?
to wear	We have to wear uniform at school.	我们上学要穿校服。	wǒ men shàng xué yào chuān xiào fú.
	I like to wear my trainers after school.	放学以后我喜欢穿运动鞋。	fàng xué yǐ hòu wǒ xǐ huan chuān yùn dòng xié.
	I like to wear a cap when going out with friends.	跟朋友出去玩儿的时候我喜欢戴帽子。	gēn péng you chū qù wánr de shí hou wǒ xǐ huan dài mào zi.
	My girlfriend wears glasses.	我的女朋友戴眼镜。	wǒ de nǚ péng you dài yǎn jìng.
	My dad wears a tie to work.	我爸爸上班要戴领带。	wǒ bà ba shàng bān yào dài lǐng dài.
	I don't like to wear a watch.	我不喜欢戴手表。	wǒ bù xǐ huan dài shǒu biǎo.
weight	I have put on weight.	我胖了。	wǒ pàng le.
which	Which library? The library in the city centre.	哪个图书馆？市中心的图书馆。	nǎ gè tú shū guǎn? shì zhōng xīn de tú shū guǎn.
	Which book? This book.	哪本书？这本书。	nǎ běn shū? zhè běn shū.
	Which girl? That girl.	哪个女孩？那个女孩。	nǎ ge nǚ hái? nà ge nǚ hái.
to wish	I'd like to wish you a very happy birthday!	祝你生日快乐！	zhù nǐ shēng rì kuài lè!
year	I'm in Year 10.	我上十年级。	wǒ shàng shí nián jí.
	I've been learning Chinese for three years.	我学中文学了三年了。	wǒ xué zhōng wén xué le sān nián le.
	I'm 16 years old.	我16岁。	wǒ shí liù suì.